The

EAST GERMAN

CHURCH *and*

the END *of*

COMMUNISM

John P. Burgess

New York   Oxford · Oxford University Press   1997

Oxford University Press

Oxford   New York
Athens   Auckland   Bangkok   Bogota   Bombay   Buenos Aires
Calcutta   Cape Town   Dar es Salaam   Delhi   Florence   Hong Kong
Istanbul   Karachi   Kuala Lumpur   Madras   Madrid   Melbourne
Mexico City   Nairobi   Paris   Singapore   Taipei   Tokyo   Toronto   Warsaw

and associated companies in
Berlin   Ibadan

Copyright © 1997 by John P. Burgess

Published by Oxford University Press
198 Madison Avenue, New York, New York 10016

Oxford is a registered trademark of Oxford University Press.

Library of Congress Cataloging-in-Publication Data
Burgess, John P., 1954–
The East German church and the end of communism : / John P. Burgess.
    p.   cm.
Includes bibliographical references and index.
ISBN 0-19-511098-6
1. Church and state—Germany (East)   2. Communism and Christianity—Germany (East)
3. Democracy—Religious aspects—Christianity.   4. Germany (East)—Church history.   I. Title.
BR856.35.B87   1997
261.7'09431'09045—dc20   96-21158

1 3 5 7 9 8 6 4 2

Printed in the United States of America
on acid-free paper

For ———

Matthias and Monika Artzt

Nils and Ulrike Busch-Petersen

Benigna Carstens (née Gill)

Dieter Dietze

Arndt and Elisabeth Farack

Thomas Jeutner and Marianne Subklew

Siegfried and Hanna Kasparick

Jens Michel

Klaus-Henning and Doris Müller

Michael and Ulrike Voigt

Harald and Beate Wagner

Susanne Weichenhan (née Schmidt)

and all those associated with the *Sprachenkonvikt*

Preface and Acknowledgments

In 1984, I had the unusual opportunity to study for a year at the Protestant seminary in East Berlin. It was the first time that the seminary had been allowed to host an American student. Over the course of the year, I was also able to enroll in classes at the state-run Humboldt University. This immersion into East German life put me in regular contact with a variety of Christian and Marxist-Leninist perspectives on the "church in socialism."

I returned to East Germany for two months at the end of 1986, and for shorter visits in 1987 and 1989. In 1991, I lived again in East Berlin for two months, now as a guest of the reorganized theology faculty, a merger of the seminary with the university.

In the essays that follow, the experiences and conversations of this seven-year period have deeply informed my thinking. Written at different times, the essays offer both a chronological overview and a continuing theological assessment of developments in church-state relations.

In particular, the essays describe and assess the role of the East German church in preparing the fall of the communist state, and in consolidating democratic reform. In many cases, I draw on insights from friends and colleagues, several of whom emerged as leaders of die Wende (the turn) in 1989, and who helped to build new political parties and structures.

Few observers have paid adequate attention to the role of religion in these events. While some scholars have noted that the East German church provided a free space in which dissident groups met, they have neither described nor assessed the *theology* that guided the church's political involvement. In these essays, I focus on the church's theological roots in Barth, Bonhoeffer, and Barmen; on the way in which dissident groups drew on Christian symbols and language to develop a popular, alternative theology; and on the way in which the theological commitments of the church and its groups—sometimes in creative tension, sometimes in contradiction—provided impulses for political democratization.

Part I (chapters 1–2) sets the context. In chapter 1, I describe Marxist-Leninist perspectives on religion, as they had evolved in East Germany by the mid-1980s. In chapter 2, I demonstrate the way in which the church developed a language of liberation that challenged the Marxist-Leninist understanding of religion and encouraged public debate of questions that the state sought to keep tabu.

Part II (chapters 3–5) examines the contributions of the church's theology to democratic change, culminating in the peaceful overthrow of the state in the fall of 1989. In chapter 3, I look at the church as both a religious and political force, arguing that the church was constantly tempted to succumb to a political agenda and to lose its religious rooting. In chapter 4, I focus on the theological and political tension between the church and the dissident groups; in chapter 5, on the way in which this tension both shaped and limited the kinds of contributions that religion could make to the process of democratization.

Part III (chapters 6–8) examines the role of the church in consolidating democracy. In chapter 6, I look at two East German theologians who emerged as political leaders in postcommunist East Germany (Wolfgang Ullmann and Richard Schröder), comparing and contrasting their different understandings of democracy and popular participation in government. In chapter 7, I deal with the church's efforts to come to terms with the Marxist-Leninist past, especially with regard to issues of betrayal and forgiveness. In chapter 8, I explore the contributions that the theology of Wolf Krötke, one of East Germany's foremost theologians, can make to current discussions in both the postcommunist East and the West about church and politics in a secular age.

During these years, West German literature on the East German church was extensive. With reunification, it has become a small industry. While I refer to some of this literature, as well as to important articles and books in English, my research approach is distinctive. During my stays in East Germany, I became aware of the variety of sources that I would have to examine if I were to get a full picture of the church in East Germany from the inside: Marxist-Leninist textbooks, underground publications, interviews with church and state officials, party newspapers, and documents "for use within the church only." Though these sources have the disadvantage of not being easily accessible to Western scholars, they have the advantage of illustrating how East Germans themselves came at these issues. All translations are my own unless otherwise noted.

Throughout, I refer to the Evangelische Kirche, in East Germany actually a federation of eight regional Protestant churches. I retain the German name to avoid the confusing connotations of the word *evangelical* in English. The Evangelische Kirche, rooted primarily in Lutheranism, is the dominant Protestant church in Germany, and I often use the term *Protestant* to refer to the Evangelische Kirche in particular.

Because my principal concern has been to explicate the contributions that religion can make to democratization, rather than to provide an overview of the church as a whole, I have focused on those Protestant theologians and church leaders who represented the broad middle of the church, and who in many cases played a prominent role in the Wende. I have paid less attention to theologians and church leaders representing other positions, such as those associated with Christian-Marxist dialogue or with the Christian Democratic Union (CDU), one of the so-called block parties largely allied with the communists. Nor have I described the smaller Roman Catholic Church or the Protestant free churches. Where appropriate, however, I have cited literature that can assist the reader in gaining a more complete picture of church-state relations.

Several institutions are owed particular thanks for their assistance in funding my work. My year of study at the East Berlin seminary was arranged and financed through the World Council of Churches and the Federation of Evangelische Kirchen in the German Democratic Republic (Bund der Evangelischen Kirchen in der DDR). Administrators and faculty at the seminary (the so-called Sprachenkonvikt) were untiring in answering my questions; they were also superb hosts and helped arrange return visits, including the invitation to be a scholar-in-residence in the summer of 1991.

Doane College provided two faculty grants for summer research and writing. The National Endowment for the Humanities supported the work that now appears in chapters 4, 6, and 7.

Several North American scholars have been important critics and conversation partners, commenting on one or more of these chapters in an earlier version. In particular, I owe thanks to John Conway, William Everett, Edward Friedman, William Gleason, Robin Lovin, and Paul Mojzes. I am also grateful to members of the American Academy of Religion who commented on earlier versions of chapters 3 and 6; and to members of the Society of Christian Ethics for their critique of earlier versions of chapters 5 and 8. I am grateful as well to Cynthia Read, my editor at Oxford University Press, and to the anonymous reader who made helpful suggestions both about organization of the book and about particular points of interpretation. Needless to say, these persons have taught me a great deal, even though I have not followed their advice in every case. I alone am responsible for errors of fact or interpretation.

The individual East Germans who assisted me along the way are too numerous to list. Their willingness to guide me through the intricacies of a communist society, and to help me test my observations and reflections, continually encouraged me in my efforts. I am especially thankful to the students with whom I studied at the Sprachenkonvikt in 1984 and 1985.

Permission to Reprint Published Material

I wish to acknowledge permission to reprint the following material:

Chapter 1 is a revised version of "Marxist Perspectives on Religion: Recent Trends in East Germany," *Dialog: A Journal of Theology* 27 (Summer 1988): 196–204; used with permission of the publisher. Copyright © DIALOG, INC. 1988.

Chapter 2 is a revised version of "Die Sprache der Befreiung: Staat und Kirche zum 8. Mai 1985," *Kirche im Sozialismus* 12 (June 1986): 107–116; translated as "The Language of Liberation: Church and State in East Germany Forty Years After the End of World War II," *Occasional Papers on Religion in Eastern Europe* 8, no. 6 (November 1988): 12–35. A shorter, revised version appeared as "Languages of Liberation in East Germany," *Theology Today* 43, no. 2 (July 1986): 249–258. I am thankful to each publisher for permission to reprint this material.

Chapter 3 is a revised version of "Church-State Relations in East Germany: The Church as a 'Religious' and 'Political' Force," *Journal of Church and State* 32 (Winter 1990): 17–35; used by permission.

Chapter 4 is a revised version of "Preparing for the Fall of 1989: Religion and Democratization in East Germany," *Soundings: An Interdisciplinary Journal* 74.1–2 (Spring/Summer 1991): 45–64; used with permission of the publisher.

Chapter 5 is a revised version of "Democratization as a Spiritual-Moral Event: A Study of East German Theological-Political Rhetoric," *Occasional Papers on Religion in Eastern Europe* 12, no. 1 (February 1992): 1–17; used with permission of the publisher.

Chapter 6 is a revised version of "Theologians and the Renewal of

Democratic Political Institutions in Eastern Germany," *Journal of Church and State* 37 (Winter 1995): 87–102; used by permission.

Chapter 7 is an expanded and revised version of "Coming to Terms with the Past: The Church and the Stasi," in *The Uses and Abuses of Knowledge: The Proceedings of the 23rd Annual Scholars' Conference on the Holocaust and the Churches,* ed. Henry F. Knight and Marcia Littell (Lanham, Md.: University Press of America, 1997): 93–108; used by permission of the 23rd Annual Scholars' Conference on the Holocaust and the Churches, Tulsa, Okla., March 1993.

Chapter 8 is a revised version of "Christian Political Involvement in East and West: The Theological Ethics of Wolf Krötke," *The Journal of Religion* 71 (April 1991): 202–216; used with permission of the publisher. © 1991 by The University of Chicago. All rights reserved.

Contents

CHURCH

AND STATE

IN CONTEXT

The Limits of Dialogue

East German Marxist-Leninist Thinkers and the Future of Religion

B y the mid-1980s, it was apparent that East German Marxist-Leninist thinkers saw religion as a problem that they could not easily explain away. Maintaining consistency with earlier Marxist-Leninist thinking, they asserted that religion was a distorted way of interpreting reality and that it would eventually disappear from socialist society. Yet they had reason to feel chastened. No longer could they foresee the quick eradication of religion; rather, it appeared that religion was surviving and even thriving in socialist soil.

In response, some of these thinkers developed new lines of thought, arguing that religion could play an integral role in the development of socialist society. Yet, in contrast to other parts of Eastern Europe, East Germany never developed a genuine Christian-Marxist dialogue.[1] Political expediency, rather than genuine respect, seemed to lie behind the state's emphasis on negotiation with the church; if the church were not going to disappear anytime soon, the state was concerned to avoid a politics of confrontation.

This chapter explores the ambivalence that East German Marxist-Leninist thinkers evidenced in relation to the future of religion. An introductory section examines the legal status of religious communities in East Germany. Subsequent sections seek to answer three questions that dominated East German Marxist-Leninist thinking on religion: (1) Why does religion persist in a socialist society? (2) What does religion contribute to the heritage of a socialist society? and (3) What role does religion play in the development of socialism and communism? In the end, what emerges is a picture of irreconcilable ideological contradictions that paralyzed the state as the church became increasingly involved in political protest.

A note on terminology: *Marxism-Leninism* refers to the official ideology of the Communist Party—in the former East Germany, the Sozialistische Einheitspartei Deutschlands (SED). East German Marxist-Leninists understood East Germany to be a socialist nation, insofar as capitalism had been superseded by placing the means of production in the hands of the workers (under the direction of the party and the state). The intensive economic development and ideological maturity that were believed to characterize communism had not yet been attained.[2]

The Legal Status of the Church

According to the Constitution of the German Democratic Republic (GDR), every citizen had "the right to profess a religious faith and to exercise religious activities" (Article 39). Freedom of conscience was guaranteed. "Every citizen of the GDR has the same rights and duties regardless of his nationality, race, world outlook or religious faith, and social origin or position" (Article 20).

The criminal law book mandated penalties for those who disturbed freedom of conscience or religious expression.[3] The state-approved textbook on constitutional law elaborated on the meaning of religious freedom: The profession of religious faith implied neither social privilege nor disadvantage; no citizen was forced to profess a faith, but believers could join any one of numerous religious communities; and

> the socialist state also secures freedom of religion insofar as it makes generous sums of money available for the preservation of religious cultural monuments, allows church publishing houses, magazines, and commercial businesses, recognizes and supports diaconal work, and finances the training of theological students as well as the research of theological departments at the universities of the GDR.[4]

Freedom of religion was defined, however, within the larger context of Marxism-Leninism. The Constitution stated that "the churches and other religious communities order their affairs and exercise their activities in agreement with the Constitution and legal provisions of the GDR" (Article 39). "The GDR is a socialist state of workers and peasants. It is the political organization of the laborers in city and country under the leadership of the working class and its Marxist-Leninist party" (Article 1). The preamble of the Constitution declared that the people of the GDR understood themselves to be on the way of socialism and communism.

The tension between "freedom of religion" and "leadership of the Marxist-Leninist party" was especially apparent in the area of ideology. The party, while recognizing freedom of religion, promoted the development of a "socialist consciousness." This consciousness would not simply develop spontaneously out of the new economic arrangements of a socialist society; ideological indoctrination was required.

Education was an especially important aspect of the party's ideological work. The schools of the socialist state promoted a "socialist education," which implied the development of a "scientific," in contrast to a religious, point of view.

> The educational system has the task to educate and develop young people who, equipped with solid knowledge and ability, are able to think creatively and act independently, whose world picture, grounded in Marxism-Leninism, penetrates their personal convictions and patterns of behavior.[5]

"Through systematic scientific, atheistic enlightenment and education, the results of science as well as the scientifically grounded Marxist-Leninist world outlook are transmitted to all people in socialism."[6] In the GDR, Marxism-Leninism was understood as essentially atheistic.

The transition of society from capitalism to socialism and communism, and the shaping of a new consciousness, thus implied the gradual death of religion. The Constitution and laws of East Germany embodied an ambiguity that many Christians experienced in practice: While enjoying the right to gather and practice their religion, they sometimes felt like outsiders in a society whose state promoted a scientific, atheistic point of view.

The Persistence of Religion

East German Marxist-Leninists originally argued that religion would gradually disappear as the new socialist order anchored itself in society.[7] They published relatively little on the question of the persistence of religion in socialism, and the standard philosophical dictionary simply noted that although there was no longer a social foundation for religion in a socialist society, religion remained "alive and effective as a consequence of the staying power of tradition and foreign influences."[8]

In 1980, however, the first signs of a rethinking of the issue appeared to take place, when Olof Klohr, a Marxist-Leninist theorist, conceded that there were still objective causes of religion within socialism itself. Insufficient economic, political, and social development had contributed to the ideological, psychological, and moral persistence of religion in so-cialism.[9] Increasingly, East German Marxist-Leninists had to acknowl-edge that religion continued to attract adherents, even among young people who had been born and raised in the socialist order, that religion exerted considerable influence in socialist states, and that it represented a potential and sometimes real political opposition, as in Poland.

Developments in other areas of Marxist-Leninist ideology further un-derscored this line of thinking. Interestingly, some of the most significant developments appeared in East German Marxist-Leninist thinking on the problem of crime. As in the case of religion, Marxist-Leninist thinkers had once held that crime would disappear after capitalism had been erad-icated. Yet crime, like religion, continued to persist in socialist society. While acclaiming the dramatic drop in the crime rate, Marxist-Leninist thinkers had to concede that crime would not soon disappear altogether.

This is not to say that East German Marxist-Leninists equated religion and criminal behavior. Religion was not an inherently negative social factor (i.e., directed against the socialist order) in the same way that crime was. But the roots of the two problems were similar. Both were unexplained "remainders" of the old capitalist system. In this sense, the Marxist-Leninist interpretation of crime had significant implications for the Marxist-Leninist interpretation of religion.

The state-approved university textbook on Marxist-Leninist theory of state and law conceded that previous attempts to account for the persis-tence of crime had been inadequate. Criminal behavior could not simply be dismissed as a moral-psychological defect of the individual. Rather, crime was conditioned by objective and subjective social factors.

The objective factors were both internal to socialism and external to it. The inner objective factors were two fold. First, socialism was not yet communism; it still had "marks" of capitalism. Possible sources of the individualistic attitude that engendered crime included the social contra-diction between rapidly expanding consumer demands, as people strove for a higher standard of living, and the state's inability to satisfy these demands at the present level of production. Second, differences between classes and other social groupings with respect to basic values, concerns, and kinds of work (e.g., physical versus mental) were seen as possible sources of the problem. Nonetheless, it was argued that these marks of the old capitalistic order were no longer essential characteristics of society; they were temporary phenomena that would disappear as socialism matured.

The outer objective factors consisted primarily of the efforts of Western imperialist states to undermine East Bloc socialism. The imperialists sought to exert economic pressure in order to hinder the development of socialist societies. In addition, the Western imperialist states sought to exert ideological influence (e.g., through television and radio, which most East Germans could receive) in order to divert and weaken people's commitment to socialism. Changes in international market conditions as well as natural disasters (such as bad weather reducing anticipated harvests) also constituted outer objective economic disturbances.

The subjective factors had to do primarily with problems in the party's leadership and direction of socialist society. Poor design and faulty implementation of economic policies, as well as inadequate ideological work, nurtured conditions that allowed crime to persist.[10]

In the mid-1980s, it became increasingly apparent to Marxist-Leninists that they would have to make similar arguments to account for the persistence of religion in socialist society. The "staying power of tradition" was no longer an adequate explanation. A host of complex economic, political, and ideological factors was at work.[11]

The question of the relative importance of these different factors generated much discussion in the GDR, especially with the translation and publication of two articles by the Russians A. P. Butenko and V. S. Semyonov in 1983.

A problem far greater than the persistence of petty crime had stimulated the publication of these two articles. They were early attempts to account theoretically for the political turmoil in Poland; they openly acknowledged serious political problems in a socialist society that was supposedly well on the way to communism.

The discussion centered on the role of social "contradictions" *(Widersprüche)* in driving the further development of society. Marxist-Leninist philosophers had generally agreed that a socialist society was driven by "nonantagonistic" contradictions, in contrast to the antagonistic contradictions that were believed to characterize capitalism. These nonantagonistic contradictions did not lead to open conflict and social upheaval; rather, they promoted the dynamic transition of socialism to communism. In relation to the political order, for example, there was an nonantagonistic contradiction between centralism and democracy. The further development of socialism depended both on more efficient central planning and management and on more active participation and involvement of the general populace. Development in one area would spur development in the other. It was the role of the Marxist-Leninist party to analyze the interplay between these contradictions, and to guide their development so that neither would threaten the other.

Butenko argued that those who found only nonantagonistic contradictions in socialist society were forced to account for negative phenomena in terms of the theory of the remainders of capitalism. He found this position inadequate. Remainders of capitalism might well be present in socialism, but the decisive causes of negative phenomena were the subjective factors: mistakes in the party's leadership and in its implementation of state policies. Butenko argued that nonantagonistic contradictions could assume an antagonistic character when socialist leadership and management were weak. When directors of industries pursued their personal good at the expense of society's, they were exhibiting interests antagonistically contradictory to those of their workers. "It must thereby be especially emphasized that that is in no way . . . a 'remainder' of capitalism. The experiences of real socialism demonstrate not only the possibility but also the reality of a retrogressive evolution."[12]

Semyonov emphasized other factors. He recognized that inadequate economic development as well as weak management might hinder the development of socialist society but concluded that the resulting contradictions were not antagonistic. Rather, antagonistic contradictions were generated by the inner and outer enemies of socialism. During the period of transition from capitalism to socialism, and for a considerable time after the establishment of socialism, particular social groups remained attached to the traditions and values of capitalism. Under the right internal conditions, and with assistance from Western imperialistic states, these groups were tempted to seize power, and to try to overthrow the socialist state (e.g., Czechoslovakia in 1968).

According to Semyonov, the one antagonistic contradiction truly internal to socialism lay between those representing social progress and those representing individual egoism (e.g., speculators and criminals). Though the struggle between these two groups would result neither in class war nor in broad social conflict, it would impede social progress, unless society took steps to purge deviant individuals from its midst. While Semyonov failed to identify the specific cause of individual deviancy, he concluded that it had to do with the continuing struggle between capitalism and socialism.[13]

In responding to these two articles, Alfred Kosing, an East German philosopher, refused to acknowledge any antagonistic contradictions in socialist society. For him, the situation in Poland demonstrated not the failure of socialism, but the fact that socialism had never been securely established in the first place. In those sectors of the Polish economy that had resisted integration into the Marxist-Leninist order, a bourgeois mentality, ideology, and way of life had persisted. Poland was apparently still in transition from capitalism to socialism. Poor leadership by the Marxist-Leninist party had contributed to the subsequent rise of social unrest, as had Western imperialistic forces in supporting the counterrevolutionaries in Poland.[14]

These different positions concerning the contradictions in socialism suggested ways that Marxist-Leninists were also rethinking the question of the persistence of religion. One could emphasize "subjective factors" (such as alienation resulting from poor party leadership), "external objective factors" (the imperialist enemies in the West), or "inner objective factors" (such as the incomplete development of socialism). Any explanation that spoke solely of the remainders of capitalism in the socialist consciousness no longer appeared adequate.[15]

The Religious Heritage of a Socialist Society

East German Marxist-Leninists often cited Marx's famous words that religion is both an expression of and a protest against the exploitation that the masses suffer in a class society. Marxist-Leninists saw religion as playing an ambiguous role in world history. On the one hand, the ruling classes had repeatedly used religion to convince the exploited to accept their lot on earth and await their reward in heaven. On the other, religion had sometimes held a revolutionary impulse. It had offered a vision of justice and equality that moved the masses to rebel against their oppressors. To be sure, even here religion masked class interests that were ultimately conditioned by material, economic factors. But "ideas," though secondary, were not powerless. Religion was capable of moving and directing people.[16]

In 1983, the publication of a translation of political tracts by Gerrard Winstanley testified to the East German Marxist-Leninists' growing interest in this second side of religion. Winstanley, the leader of a small group called the Diggers, had tried to effect revolutionary changes in seventeenth-century England: the common use of land, political equality, and the disestablishment of the church. The appearance of the book was not surprising in itself; Winstanley had long been of interest to Marxist scholars.[17] What was remarkable was that the East German Marxist-Leninist editor especially emphasized the revolutionary consequences of Winstanley's religious *ideas*—that is, the fact that he appealed to Scripture to make his arguments against the clergy and its use of religion to maintain and justify oppression of the common people. Moreover, in contrast to earlier Marxist interpreters, the editor suggested that Winstanley's religious concerns did not merely mask fundamentally secular ones. Winstanley had no doubt found in Scripture what he read into it, but his words could not have been so powerful in their time had not Christianity originally been the religion of the oppressed.[18]

Other East German Marxist-Leninists, as we shall see, pointed to the "progressive" and "humanistic" elements of Christianity. Even when religion had been less than revolutionary politically, it had still made important contributions to the cultural development of society.

It was not at first glance obvious that these "positive" elements of religious tradition should find acclaim in a socialist society. According to Marxist-Leninist philosophy, the transition from capitalism to socialism had brought about a decisive break with the past. In contrast to the radical revolutionary movements of the past, the forces of Marxism-Leninism had eradicated the roots of war, exploitation, and oppression and had irrevocably established the basis for peace, progress, and democracy. The new socialist order had sprung from a working class that generally rejected religion.

Yet, by the mid-1980s, East German Marxist-Leninist thinkers, following a dictum first formulated by Lenin, asserted that "socialism in the GDR is the heir and promoter of everything good, progressive, humane, and democratic in history, because it itself embodies progress, democracy, and humanity."[19] With the overthrow of capitalism, the humanistic ideals that its representatives had once advanced could now find complete and genuine realization in socialism. Those prebourgeois and bourgeois revolutionary thinkers who had been possessed by the will to create a world of peace, freedom, equality, and brotherhood for the oppressed and enslaved masses had ideas and teachings worth appropriating.[20] According to the platform of the SED, "everything great and noble, humanistic and revolutionary is preserved and advanced, in that it is set in vibrant relationship to the tasks of the present."[21]

The socialist state also embraced the "humanistic" and "revolutionary" aspects of religion as part of its heritage. Not only the radical vision of a Gerrard Winstanley or a Thomas Müntzer, to whom Marxists had also devoted considerable attention, but the progressive thinking of a Martin Luther deserved honor and celebration as well. In 1983, the state joined with the church to observe the five hundredth anniversary of the birth of Luther. A group of Marxist-Leninist scholars under the leadership of historian Horst Bartel prepared fifteen "theses concerning Martin Luther" in which they argued that:

> Luther laid the theological foundations of a new ideology that had revolutionary impact. For, given the social conditions of the time, the Reformation did not just mean a reform of the church but implied a virtual transformation of society itself. . . . Luther's Reformation left a permanent mark on the nations of Europe. By seeking to solve the basic contradictions in feudal society, it rapidly acquired European proportions as a force that helped to accelerate the transition from feudalism to capitalism. . . . Luther also stimulated the development of a humane ethic by drawing attention to the obligation to serve one's fellow-men, the urge to engage in productive and purposeful work, the necessity to abolish the exploitation of human labour for profit, the need to preserve and protect the family, and the indispensability of virtues such as diligence, industry, thrift, and a sense of duty.[22]

After the anniversary, East German Marxist-Leninist writings on religion continued to appeal to the significance of the state's recognition of Luther. Vera Wrona, a Marxist-Leninist thinker, wrote: "Indeed, the honoring of Luther demonstrated that the work of Luther, as of all those who have contributed to progress, to the development of world culture, finds appreciation in socialism, without regard to their social and class position."[23] Wolfgang Kliem, another Marxist-Leninist thinker, added:

> The history of humankind demonstrates that a religiously motivated ethic can assume different contents and can serve as an intellectual orientation or justification for different social forces. One historical example of outstanding significance are the humanistic, social-ethical ideas of Martin Luther. They . . . still deserve esteem today.[24]

Religion and the Development of Socialism

Because a study of history revealed that religion had sometimes played a socially progressive role, the question arose as to whether religion could also contribute to the development of socialism and the transition to communism. In the mid-1980s, the emerging literature increasingly answered affirmatively and emphasized that Christians and Marxists could cooperate in constructing, and advancing the goals of, a socialist society. Of special interest were articles appearing in the East German *Deutsche Zeitschrift für Philosophie*.

According to these Marxist-Leninist analyses, Christianity was characterized by two strands: the one reactionary and anticommunist, the other progressive and humanistic. This second side had now moved into the foreground in world history. With the rise of socialism, the collapse of colonialism, and the internal crises of imperialism, Christianity had taken an evident "turn to the world." Progressive Christian forces were now seeking to legitimate religion in terms of its immediate contribution to social and political justice, rather than in terms of its relation to otherworldly matters. These Christians were ready to tolerate other progressive groups; differences of weltanschauung were less important than the common social-ethical concerns that united them with Marxist-Leninists. Because both groups valued life itself as the highest earthly good, they could work together to oppose the aggressive policies of Western imperialism. Their ideological differences were said to be secondary to their common struggle for peace.

This call for cooperation between Christians and Marxist-Leninists had several aspects. First, it was believed to be exemplified and justified by the particular historical traditions of the GDR. In the resistance to Hitler, Christians and Marxists had already worked side by side. Ideological differences did not first have to be settled; the exigencies of the moment brought forth a cooperation based on common purpose and mutual respect.

Second, cooperation was believed to have warrants in the classic texts of Marxism-Leninism. East German Marxist-Leninists frequently referred to Lenin's dictum: "The unity of this truly revolutionary struggle of the oppressed class for a paradise on earth is more important to us than a unity of opinion among the proletariat concerning the paradise in heaven." Christians and Marxist-Leninists might have different ways of interpreting ultimate reality, but Marxist-Leninists asserted that the securing of peace and the attainment of the social and political goals of socialism were more important to them than the propagation of atheism and the critique of religion.

Third, East German Marxist-Leninists argued that they shared common humanistic traditions and concerns with Christians. Both groups had a history of striving for justice, equality, and democracy.

What was perhaps most noteworthy about the Marxist-Leninist position was the assertion that cooperation not only was *possible* but also had become *necessary*. Just as Christians in the West now needed to join with Marxist-Leninists to build a worldwide coalition of peace, the future of socialist societies was also requiring Christians and Marxist-Leninists to work together. Kliem and a group of colleagues stated: "The SED proceeds in its policies from the assumption that cooperation with believers is a crucial, life question. For we have to do here with problems that cannot be solved by one party alone nor, needless to say, against each other." [25] Hans Lutter and Olof Klohr, two East German Marxist-Leninist philosophers of religion, argued:

> The widening and deepening of cooperation between communists and believers in the political struggles of our day have become an objective requirement, a historical necessity of such priority that the results of the struggle for peace, democracy, and historical progress are increasingly influenced by it. [26]

According to this Marxist-Leninist interpretation of historical development, the epoch of worldwide transition from capitalism to socialism would be characterized by the growing participation of the masses in the struggle for peace and justice. Since the majority of people in the world continued to believe in a deity, religion would play a crucial role in this process. Lutter and Klohr asserted that one could see cooperation between believers and Marxist-Leninists around the globe: in socialist countries, in the liberation movements of the third world, and in the peace movement in the West. Because this phenomenon was both universal and necessary, it constituted an "objective law." [27]

As already noted, the assertion that Christians and Marxist-Leninists shared common humanistic concerns was central to the latter's new thinking on religion. East German Marxist-Leninists seemed to define humanism as those conceptions of humanity that had human well-being as their chief end. Kliem, for example, defined humanism as the valuation of human life as the highest good. [28] Helmut Seidel, also writing in the *Deutsche Zeitschrift für Philosophie*, argued that humanism included those ideas and strivings that aimed at the well-being and happiness of individuals and their society. Humanism sought to secure the natural and social conditions for humans' free, peaceful, and creative development. The highest purpose of humanity was humanity itself. [29]

The Marxist-Leninist conception of toleration followed from this definition of humanism. Wrona wrote:

> The historical development has proven that the humanistic goal of socialism cannot be attained without the acceptance of points of view that do not agree with the scientifically grounded ones of the working class and are distinguishable from them in various ways, but that aim at the well-being of man. [30]

Because cooperation with Christians was necessary for the further development of socialism, toleration was also necessary, with the qualification, nonetheless, that whatever worked against the attainment of socialism could not be tolerated.

Marxist-Leninists' new thinking on religion emphasized that they did not make ideological conversion a prerequisite for cooperation. Not only could they tolerate religion, but they could also honor a religiously motivated ethic that supported the goals of a socialist society. Kliem asserted, for example, that the state "esteemed" the peace work of the church.[31]

While ideological differences were not wholly irrelevant, they did not need to lead to conflict. Toleration implied open discussion and mutual respect.

> The extensive agreement of concerns and fundamental positions between the Evangelische Kirchen in the GDR and the socialist state with regard to the securing of peace does not rule out differences of opinion over specific questions. Such differences are not at all overlooked by communists. But they proceed from the assumption that these differences can be cleared up through trustful conversation.[32]

Any argument that ideological differences undermined cooperation between Christians and Marxist-Leninists was believed to reflect a misguided effort to enlist religious forces against the socialist state.

The Marxist-Leninist conception of toleration of religion in socialist society rested on the assumption that the state had freed the church to concentrate on its proper tasks. Under capitalism, church and state had cooperated to protect the ruling class and oppress the masses. In socialism, church and state were strictly separated. The state did not require, or ask for, religious legitimation; the church was free to realize its humanistic social-ethical goals. This social commitment of Christians was "derived from the recognition that the socialist society is the first in the history of humankind to provide the possibility of bringing the ethical and humanistic goals of Christianity into harmony with the development and goals of society."[33]

Toleration, however, was qualified in several respects. First, the new Marxist-Leninist writings on religion did not seek to understand religion on its own terms. Religion was esteemed only insofar as it contributed to the further development of socialism.[34] Second, though conceding that socialist society was characterized by a certain kind of socioeconomic order, rather than by "atheism," these writings made it clear that Marxist-Leninists still intended to defend and propagate their ideology.[35] Religion could be tolerated only insofar as it did not call into question

the ideological domination of Marxism-Leninism. Third, the new literature did not dispute the obvious conclusion: The socialist state, because
it was under the direction of the Socialist-Communist Party, would continue to promote a communist, scientific-atheistic point of view.

To many East German Christians, therefore, no genuine conversation
with Marxist-Leninists seemed possible. They could not come as equals
to the table, as long as Marxists-Leninists saw religion as a distorted
consciousness. Some Christians, however, welcomed the new thinking
on religion and aligned themselves with it. Particularly in those circles
associated with the Christian Peace Conference (CPC) (a Prague-based,
state-supported ecumenical organization), the Christian Democratic
Union (CDU) (a political party closely allied with the SED), and the
theologians at several of the state-run universities, the Marxist-Leninist
emphasis on cooperation with believers seemed to vindicate the position
to which they had long been committed. They believed that Marxist-
Leninist thought could help liberate the church from a false understanding of religion; they saw the Marxist-Leninist state as a necessary alternative to the capitalist West; and they called for Christians to help shape
Marxist-Leninist society rather than opposing it or withdrawing from it.[36]

Some in these circles saw a genuine possibility of Christian-Marxist
dialogue and cooperation. Theologians at the University of Rostock organized a series of colloquies with Marxist-Leninist scholars.[37] Theologians
at the Humboldt University in East Berlin encouraged students and faculty to take an active role in state organizations. In both cases, these
theologians saw themselves countering other tendencies in the church:
toward privatizing religion, on the one hand, and toward using it as a
cover for political protest against the state, on the other. They wished to
reconnect piety and social action. While sometimes accused of being too
accommodating toward the regime, they argued that Christians should
contribute to solving the problems of their society. The socialist order
was still imperfect.[38]

The efforts of these circles were never reflective of the church as a
whole. Opportunities for theologians from the church-run seminaries to
participate in this Christian-Marxist "dialogue" were highly limited.[39] Especially in Berlin, the theological faculty at the state university (Humboldt) and the church-run seminary (Sprachenkonvikt) seemed to represent competing approaches to church-state relations. The possibility of a
more inclusive Christian-Marxist dialogue did not emerge until later, and
by then the state was near its end.[40]

Conclusion

The critique of religion played a key role in Marx's critique of bourgeois society. Religion, though ostensibly a private matter, reflected a society driven by practical need, that is, the unbridled egoism of the bourgeois individual. Religion served as opium for the masses suffering under these arrangements; it was a distorted consciousness belonging to a distorted society. Marx believed, therefore, that the critique of religion finally had to issue in the call to revolution. "The critique of religion ends with the doctrine that man is the highest being for man, therefore with the categorical imperative to overturn all arrangements in which man is a degraded, enslaved, abandoned, despicable being."[41]

Marx, especially in his early writings, seemed to believe that a world revolution would soon take place. Humans would shortly be freed from "ideology," that is, from a false consciousness about the true cause of their condition. Lenin later argued that the process of world revolution would proceed more slowly, but he, too, had no doubt that religion would eventually disappear. The new socioeconomic order would remove religion's fundamental causes, and the socialist state would so educate people as to free them from the ignorance on which religion feeds. Persecution was neither necessary nor desirable.

Lenin called for the Russian communists to support those Christians, especially the sectarians, whom the czar had oppressed.[42] But it never occurred to him that cooperation with Christians could still be important after the socialist revolution took place. Both Marx and Lenin had associated the attainment of communism with the development of a radically new consciousness freed of religious influence. East German Marxism-Leninism, in contrast, saw a positive role for Christians in a socialist society and deemphasized the eventual disappearance of religion. However, if the disappearance of religion no longer seemed important, the question posed itself whether East German Marxist-Leninists still believed that the attainment of communism both objectively and subjectively was important or even possible.

Such questions were entirely avoided in the literature that appeared in the mid-1980s in the *Deutsche Zeitschrift für Philosophie*. Yet there was no reason to believe that East German Marxist-Leninists had entirely abandoned their conviction that East German society was on the way to communism. The party still claimed the responsibility to promote a communist education. Moreover, textbook treatments of religion, while calling for cooperation and toleration, continued to note religion's negative aspects. A current political dictionary defined religion as

[a] form of social consciousness with the character of a weltanschauung. A totality of views, emotions, and cultic activities, whose essence consists of a fantastically distorted, illusionary reflection of nature and society in the human consciousness.[43]

Although the new thinking on religion did not speak of the gradual disappearance of religion, neither was the opposite ever asserted. According to all indications, East German Marxist-Leninists were still prepared to argue that religion would not exist under the conditions of communism. The same political dictionary also stated: "The emergence, alteration, and also the gradual dying out of religion proceed necessarily out of the material life-process of man."[44] A 1981 book on the socialist struggle for peace conceded that churches and religious consciousness would still exist for some time in socialist society, but with the gradual attainment of communism, religion would simply vanish.[45]

There was no literature that mediated between the invitation to Christians to enter into dialogue, on the one hand, and the ideological rejection of religion as a fantastically distorted consciousness, on the other. While affirming that Christians could make a positive contribution to the development of socialist society, Marxist-Leninist thinkers continued to hold that the development of that society would lay the foundations for the disappearance of religion. Dialogue would have limits.

It was perhaps not insignificant that East German Marxist-Leninist thinkers did not address these issues head-on. Lenin himself once offered the advice that seemed to account for their silence:

> In the struggle against religious biases, one must proceed with great care. Whoever in this struggle injures the religious sensibility does great harm. . . . If we conduct the struggle with severe methods, we may arouse the masses against us; such a struggle deepens the division of the masses according to the principle of religion, whereas our strength lies rather in unity.[46]

The new thinking on religion may have emphasized cooperation and toleration to guard against Christians' taking offense at the implications of other parts of Marxist-Leninist theory that continued to emphasize religion's gradual demise.

There was perhaps another explanation as well. The initial enthusiasm and idealism that had gripped the party at the founding of the socialist state had diminished. On the one hand, socialism had become more established and secure, therefore conservative. The party was increasingly composed not of committed communists but of people who saw party membership as a way to improve their chances for career advancement. On the other hand, it was apparent that pure communism would not be attained anytime soon. The ambiguity about religion reflected a deeper ambiguity about the very possibility of moving from socialism to communism.

These ambiguities in Marxist-Leninist theory and practice also help to account for the inconsistencies that increasingly emerged in state policies toward the church in the late 1980s. As we shall see, the state acted at times as if it needed the church as a partner to build and maintain socialist society, while at other times it seemed to see the church as an ideological alternative that it needed to combat. These political inconsistencies suggest that the theoretical ambiguity in the Marxist-Leninist understanding of religion paralyzed the state in its relations with the church and eventually contributed to political crisis. The state, unable to comprehend the role of the church in helping to give birth to the democracy movement, failed to respond decisively.

The Language of Liberation

The Church as a Free Space

No genuine dialogue could take place between Christians and Marxist-Leninists in East Germany. Yet the Evangelische Kirche found ways to negotiate with the state and to raise views that implicitly challenged the state-sponsored ideology. The church regularly tested the ideological limits that the state imposed on public discourse. By examining the degree to which the church's language went beyond the official language, this chapter offers some measure of the status of church-state relations in the mid-1980s. While focusing on official church statements and the public pronouncements of church officials, I also refer to groups that wished to go even further in testing the limits of public discourse, reflecting the tack that dissident, alternative groups in the church would take as they began to organize political protest.

In chapter 1, I noted the tension Christians experienced as a "church in socialism." One area where this tension was especially evident was the press. In the GDR, the mass media were organs of party and state. "Freedom of press" was understood in terms of what promoted socialism and communism. On the one hand, the church was not directly subject to the state's regulation of "public language"; "freedom of religion" included the church's right to publish and distribute materials. On the other hand, the state reserved the right to confiscate any publications that grossly violated official standards. Because the church had only a limited amount of paper, it found itself exercising self-censorship.

The church did, however, have other ways to address social issues.

Worship services and church meetings took place openly and freely. Moreover, the church was able to print occasional papers "for use only within the church." Despite the limitations in what it could say in its official publications, the church had considerable ability to raise an alternative voice publicly.

One important facet of church-state relations was the common observance of days of social and political significance. Civic celebrations offered both church and state representatives an opportunity to address public issues.

Particularly significant was May 8, the anniversary of the end of World War II in Europe. In the GDR, May 8 was officially celebrated as the "Day of Liberation"—liberation *from* fascism, liberation *to* socialism and communism. In 1985, the fortieth anniversary, the official rhetoric became especially intense. Party and state coined an official language with which to describe the anniversary's significance. This language consisted of a standardized vocabulary of set words, phrases, and topics.

The Evangelische Kirche also observed May 8, and its language significantly extended the range of public discourse. In form, the church's language seemed less standardized than the state's official language, and in content, it included topics that the official language avoided. Nonetheless, the church respected certain limits. It avoided explicit criticism of party and state. Moreover, the church's language was sometimes vague and abstract. It emphasized general commonalities between church and state rather than concrete differences. Only a few groups in the church pushed further, seeking to expand not only the range of public discourse but also the range of discourse in the church itself.

The Regulation of Language

The country's major daily newspaper, *Neues Deutschland,* carried the official language of party and state. As a publication of the Central Committee of the Marxist-Leninist Socialist Unity Party (SED), *Neues Deutschland* set the accents in the mass media. Because all organizations, with the exception of the church, stood under the direction of party and state, the language of *Neues Deutschland* regulated the language of most of the publications and public speeches in the GDR.

A striking example of such regulation appeared in the weeks leading up to May 8, 1985. Several towns and cities observed the fortieth anniversary of English and American air attacks, and *Neues Deutschland* regularly reported on these state-sponsored observances. In previous years, the air attacks had been described as "Anglo-American terror attacks." In 1985, however, when Erich Honecker, general secretary of the Central Committee of the SED and chairman of the State Council of the GDR, gave a major speech for the occasion in Dresden, he mentioned neither the role of the English and Americans nor the words *terror attack*.

This change appeared to be a new language regulation. Most of the observances and speeches that followed, as reported in *Neues Deutschland*, did not mention the role of the English and Americans. A few articles referred to the "English" or "American" bombers or airplanes.[1] But in no case did one find the formulation *terror attack*, and words like *English* and *American* were employed in a neutral rather than accusatory manner.

It is especially interesting to compare the articles on Magdeburg and Dresden, for the observances in Magdeburg took place before the new accents were set in Dresden. In connection with Magdeburg, one reads of the "Anglo-American" bombers and their "death-bringing load." In the Dresden article, such formulations were missing, and thereafter the word *Anglo-American* entirely disappeared.[2]

The "Day of Liberation"

Similar language regulations governed the interpretation of May 8. On January 11, 1985, party and state issued the terms of public discourse: a "proclamation concerning the fortieth anniversary of the victory over Hitler-fascism and the liberation of the German people." The proclamation, printed on the front page of *Neues Deutschland*, presented the official interpretation of May 8 and delineated the words, phrases, and themes that would appear in later speeches, articles, and reports. Prior to January 11, the topic of the "Day of Liberation" had received scant attention in the press. Afterward, the language of "liberation" appeared every day through May 9 (when the observances of May 8 were reported). Front-page headlines repeatedly mentioned the "Day of Liberation," the "Day of Victory," and "May 8."

Neues Deutschland regularly printed the public speeches of leading party and state officials, who recited the official language.[3] Other articles described key events of forty years ago; aspects of military history; the activities of freedom fighters in the resistance; the gradual liberation of different towns, cities, concentration camps, and countries; and, as previously noted, the destruction of German cities in Allied air attacks. Attention was also devoted to the preparations for May 8 observances in other countries.

Contrasting attitudes toward May 8 in the two Germanies received particular attention. Whereas public debate in West Germany raged over how the nation should understand and observe May 8, *Neues Deutschland* presented the picture of an East Germany fully committed to celebrating the day as the "Day of Liberation." State preparations were reported in full detail: museum exhibitions, contests in factories and places of work, hikes "in the footsteps of the liberators," conferences of scientists and artists, events sponsored by social organizations, new books and films, and special television programs.

May 8 was also a major topic of discussion in the church. Papers were prepared; speeches and sermons were delivered. In some cases *Neues Deutschland* reported on the church's statements; in most cases they were printed by the church "for use only within the church." Leading church officials spoke at several state-sponsored observances commemorating the fortieth anniversary of Allied air attacks—the first time in many cases that they had been given such an opportunity. The church also sponsored its own observances to commemorate the victims of the concentration camps, the losses of the Soviet Union and the Allies, and the death of Dietrich Bonhoeffer. On the evening of May 8, Bishop Johannes Hempel preached in the central cathedral of East Berlin (Hempel, at this time, was the chair of the Konferenz der Evangelischen Kirchenleitungen in der DDR [council of Evangelische Kirchen in the GDR]); the service was broadcast simultaneously over East German television. Despite the domination of the state language in the public sphere, it is reasonable to suppose that the church's language concerning May 8 also reached most East Germans.[4]

In its articles and statements, the party and state raised four major questions: (1) What does "liberation" mean? (2) Who bears the guilt for the events of forty years ago? (3) What role did the Soviet Union play during and after the war? and (4) What does "peace" today mean in light of the events of forty years ago? It is not surprising that the Evangelische Kirche as a "church in socialism" also had these four issues at the center of its statements, reflecting both its social and theological location.

The Meaning of "Liberation"

As already mentioned, the state proclamation of January 11 described May 8, 1985, as "the fortieth anniversary of the victory of the Soviet Union over Hitler-fascism and the liberation of the German people from

Nazi rule." Through such rhetoric, the GDR sought to align itself with the victors rather than the vanquished.

First, it was argued that the GDR had inherited the bequest of the antifascist freedom fighters. While the resistance had united people of different worldviews and nationalities, the German freedom fighters played the leading role, especially the German communists, who were the first victims of fascism.[5] The official language emphasized that the German antifascists embodied the "other" Germany. They represented "the good Germany."[6] They were "the best forces of our people."[7] They saved the honor of the people.[8]

The second reason that the GDR belonged on the side of the victors was because it had taken advantage of the new chance that the liberation had presented. According to the official rhetoric, the GDR had unified the working class, eradicated militarism and the imperialistic roots of war, founded a socialist society, entered into an indestructible alliance with the Soviet Union, and opened the way for all its citizens to work together to build socialism under the direction of the SED.[9]

The official language emphasized that the GDR had broken with the past. It belonged to "the new world of peace and freedom."[10] "Through our republic, her flourishing and thriving in the heart of Europe, the world has become richer in hope. . . . Here the fateful, reactionary past of imperialism and militarism was broken with."[11] The GDR had the chance, "after the liberating deed of the Soviet Union, to introduce a fundamental change in history."[12]

For all these reasons, May 8 was "liberation." The position of the GDR was said to be fundamentally different from that of many leading politicians in West Germany. "Whoever in the BRD [Bundesrepublik Deutschland] speaks of May 8 as a day of mourning, as capitulation rather than liberation, and wishes to alter the map of Europe, places himself outside history and endangers peace in Europe."[13] Whoever in the West intends to observe May 8 as a day of mourning "would have probably preferred to see the fascistic incendiaries win."[14]

The official language of liberation often seemed stilted, formal, or even liturgical. May 8 became more than a historical date. The liberation had significance for all times and all people. "The history of humankind is acquainted with events and times in which the world-altering power of social progress breaks a course beyond all the dark forces of slavery and death."[15] The liberation was the day of victory of humanity over inhumanity.[16] It spared the peoples of the world from extinction and opened a peaceful and happy future to them.[17]

The church's language reflected more reservation and thoughtfulness about the question of "liberation." May 8 was simultaneously judgment, collapse, and liberation. It was judgment or trial: Many Germans experienced imprisonment, flight, hunger, and humiliation.[18] It was collapse—the degree of destruction and horror soon became apparent to all Germans: forty million dead; cities destroyed, above all in the Soviet Union, Poland, France, and Germany; the murder of Jews.[19] The church argued that it was still important for Germans to talk about the suffering and the pain that the end of the war had brought: "Repressed tears lock up mouth and heart. Unacknowledged suffering expresses itself in depression."[20]

In the church's statements, however, "collapse" was not regarded only as negative. Collapse had also meant a new beginning. "For example, trust [in the idea] that the old German virtue of obedience is an eternal virtue broke down. . . . [T]he belief that science in every case means progress broke down, and also [the belief] that weapons bring security."[21] The judgment was "grace" in the sense that "we were awakened out of the stubbornness of our hearts, and our certainty of being holy was smashed."[22]

Church statements differed in their interpretations of this new beginning. One church statement insisted on speaking expressly of liberation.

> Whoever refuses to hear the word "liberation," whoever wishes to speak only about "collapse" and "catastrophe," simply demonstrates that he himself neither suffered under the murderous system nor was ready to see the agonies of others nor to hear their groans.[23]

Other statements were more cautious. Two expressly rejected the designation of May 8 only as "liberation." According to one, "the end had many names, just as the experience was many-sided, as well as the way people were affected."[24] The second was similar in tone:

> This day, the fortieth anniversary of the end of the Second World War, was intensely experienced by many. They ask anew: Where are we coming from? . . . The destinies thereby are very different, and a person's age makes a great deal of difference for the manner of such questions. And above all in this congregation there are also many different answers to that question.[25]

Even if "liberation" was one of these answers, the church's statements reminded people that liberation had come from the outside. "We Germans would not have been able to free ourselves."[26] The liberation, therefore, had been painful.[27] But "looking back, we experience the war's end as liberation to testify anew to God's grace and to serve God's world anew."[28] A statement from Aktion Sühnezeichen (Action Reconciliation), a group active in both Germanies and dedicated to acknowledging German guilt and forging partnerships between Germans and citizens of the nations that Germans had once tried to conquer, argued that the liberation at the end of the war freed Germans from the continuation of the war; an unjust political system; a superman ideology (that devalued other peoples); racial delusion (especially toward the Jews); the extermination of handicapped people; and a planned persecution of Christians.[29]

But the liberation was more than a political event. Christians could see it as embodying God's forgiveness of sins.[30] This "inner liberation" had given Christians new responsibilities.

> Inner liberation assumes in advance that we Germans once again bring to memory what the [National Socialist] regime poisoned: to speak the truth, instead of to lie; to respect justice; to call injustice injustice; to work for those who themselves are unable to procure justice; to make joy, friendship, reconciliation, and peace the sacred bonds between us.[31]

This kind of liberation was a process that would not reach completion until war and mistrust had been overcome.[32] Therefore, "we must ever again ask ourselves whether we have used all the opportunities of this liberation."[33]

The Limits of the Church's Language on Liberation

Both church and state designated May 8 as a day of liberation. But the church's statements also emphasized the suffering, guilt, reconciliation, and new tasks associated with this day. The liberation should not be celebrated simply as victory over fascism; May 8 was also judgment and collapse.

The church's language was more nuanced than the official language, but it did reflect limits that had been set in the official language. First, there were no church statements that directly challenged the official language or pointed to similarities and differences in the church's understanding of liberation.

Second, some groups in the church suggested that it could have said more. During 1985, the research division of the Federation of Evangelische Kirchen collected, edited, and distributed relevant texts by GDR authors addressing themes that the official church language avoided.

These texts included, for example, the following comment by Stephan Hermlin, an East German novelist:

> And then it occurred to our propagandists to employ this strange formula of "victors of history." In itself an absurdity, because there are no victors of history, and there never have been. This formula expresses the conviction that the future belongs to socialism; but it does so in a rather crude way. One designated oneself a victor of history. This formula was immediately extended . . . . [E]very citizen of the GDR could now feel that he was a victor of history. By giving this ridiculous flattery to the people and unburdening them, it was then also easier to rule.[34]

Third, the church's language of liberation was often abstract and unclear. Was liberation something inner or outer? Did it describe an objective fact or a subjective attitude? If liberation was not yet complete, had it ever really taken place? Were there theological grounds for using the term *liberation* more frequently than the term *reconciliation?* (The latter stood at the center of Bishop Hempel's sermon on May 8. He did not use the word *liberation* even once in this major address.) Given that the official language of the GDR mass media spoke exclusively of "liberation," some East German Christians, especially in the emerging alternative groups, asked the church to be clearer about its own use and understanding of the word.

The Question of Guilt

The official language scarcely addressed the question of guilt. Nowhere did one find the suggestion that Germany or the German people bore guilt for their actions. Rather, fascism was responsible. The official language reflected considerable effort to coin special words and phrases to describe the gruesome nature of fascism: It was "pestilence," "barbarism," "criminal aggressor," "the worst enemy of humankind," "superman ideology," "racism," "anti-Semitism," "the brown brute," "the worst reactionary movement since the Middle Ages," "the most frightening tyranny in all history," and "the abhorrence of all humankind."[35]

When the official language went into the question of the cause of Hitler-fascism, it blamed imperialism. "We will never forget what caused this horrible work of extermination and barbarism. It was and is imperialism, the scourge of humankind, which does not shrink from any crime for the sake of profit and in pursuit of world domination."[36] Fascism was the "most reactionary and aggressive monstrosity of German imperialism and militarism."[37]

The official language therefore regarded most Germans as victims of fascism and war. Among the fifty million casualties of the war were six million Germans.[38] Though principally directed against the communists, fascism also attacked democrats and Christians.[39] It "soiled" the entire nation.[40] Eventually the war begun by the Nazis came back home. On the occasion of the fortieth anniversary of the destruction of Dresden, Honecker remarked: "The flames of the Second World War, which went out from Berlin, at that time the capital of the 'Third Reich,' and set the entire world on fire, struck back and also devoured Dresden shortly before the end of the war."[41] But neither he nor the official language ever concretely identified *who* stood behind Hitler-fascism.

The church's statements, too, described the horror of fascism. Fascism was, "in the German context, an unrepeatable, cynical-nihilistic blood and terror regime."[42] Aktion Sühnezeichen called it a political system that through lies and state terror "trampled underfoot the worth, rights, and freedom of people."[43] A victory by Hitler would have meant the end of all human values.[44] In contrast to the official party and state language, however, neither the official church language nor that of church-related groups like Aktion Sühnezeichen employed set formulations especially coined for the occasion.

The church, and especially Aktion Sühnezeichen, addressed the guilt question clearly and directly. The church insisted that one could not ascribe all guilt for the war to fascism. While the official language simply accused imperialism of causing fascism, the church spoke of the failure of the majority of Germans, including the church itself. Aktion Sühnezeichen argued, "the National Socialist regime was sustained by the enthusiastic support of wide circles of the population, from which the churches were no exception. Fascism was not the work of a mere few who had to force themselves on the majority."[45] Several church leaders made similar statements. "The majority of people in Germany at that time . . . were Christians. And we Christians largely faltered before the terror regime of National Socialism."[46] "I think that each person who consciously experienced what was happening in our people at that time must therefore admit his share of guilt because he did too little to change things."[47]

Aktion Sühnezeichen went further than the official church language in pointing to the role of economic interests, especially in the "fateful traditions of our history. . . . [i]n the idolization of nation and state, in anti-Judaism, in education to blind obedience, and in the oppression of social and democratic movements."[48] But Aktion Sühnezeichen was not alone in insisting that it was important for Germans to confess their guilt, if they were to come to terms with the past and to experience a new beginning.[49]

Church statements pointed to three elements of confession. First, one could remember what had occurred and could acknowledge one's part in it. The confession of guilt could be very concrete. In one address, retired Bishop Albrecht Schönherr asked himself:

> Did you then trouble yourself to find out where the masses of people went who were transported off to the East? Did you protest when the SA [Sturmabteilung] men stood before the Jewish shops in April 1933? . . . Did you think that you had suffered enough when your wife one time was sharply criticized . . . because she had bought from Jews?[50]

Superintendent (regional pastor) Joachim Jaeger gave concrete examples of how his town of Nordhausen had been entangled in National Socialism: the mute response when the Jews were driven out of Nordhausen, the town's production of weapons, and citizens' contempt of other peoples, as when a Frenchman in Nordhausen was beaten and killed.[51] Several other church statements also emphasized the special guilt of the Germans toward the Soviet Union, Poland, the Jews, and the communists.[52]

Second, one could affirm that there had been moments of forgiveness and reconciliation. "In amazement have we experienced signs of reconciliation. A new relation to the neighboring peoples has developed through their readiness for reconciliation."[53] "The Allies did not return the same contempt toward our people that had been taught to our people and had been so bloodily practiced by them."[54] Hempel too named signs of reconciliation in his sermon: fellowship with other Christians, with non-Christians, with Marxists within East Germany, with citizens of the neighboring countries to the east, and with members of the churches of the victor countries.[55]

Third, one could affirm that this forgiveness "liberates to a new beginning."[56] Part of this new beginning related to seeing reconciliation as a continuing task. It was acknowledged that over the past forty years the church had sometimes made bad judgments: for example, in failing to acknowledge the reality of two German states, in its prejudice against peoples of the victorious powers, and in its lack of responsibility toward the countries of the third world.[57] The work of peace and justice was as relevant today as yesterday. Again, Aktion Sühnezeichen formulated the position most sharply: "Forty years after Auschwitz, we still stand in our theology and church at the beginning of recognizing our guilt."[58]

Another aspect of the question of guilt had to do with responsibility for the destruction of German cities in air attacks in the last days of the war. While acknowledging that the destruction of German cities had been a consequence of a Nazi-initiated war, the official language questioned the Allies' purpose. The air attacks were not necessary. "The days of the 'Thousand Year Kingdom' had long been counted, the war decided."[59] One newspaper article about Dresden stated: "Altogether, seventy-five thousand homes totally destroyed, forty hospitals and clinics, thirty-five schools. . . . The barracks were not destroyed. The larger freight railway stations were all damaged. Untouched were the headquarters of the air force and the largest armament factories."[60] In general, however, the official language ignored the question of Allied guilt, just as it had ignored German guilt.

The guilt of the Allies was treated differently in the church's language. The destruction even of church buildings was not to be understood as an injustice but as God's judgment. The destruction was senseless, but "whoever carries a senseless war without should not wonder when it strikes back in total senselessness."[61] "We do not have the authorization to calculate the account of our people in comparison to that of other peoples."[62] Moreover, "Reconciliation grows only where we confess our guilt and do not point at others but at ourselves!"[63] This confession had to be both public and corporate.

The Limits of the Church's Language on Guilt

Both church and state dealt with the question of guilt. The official language accused Hitler-fascism of causing the war. By contrast, the church emphasized that the whole people bore guilt. For the church, confession of guilt was central—only after such confession could the experiences and consequences of the war be understood. Yet here again the church's statements avoided openly challenging the official language. Groups like Aktion Sühnezeichen, not the official church, pushed the theme of confession of guilt to the fore. Moreover, these groups again looked to some of the GDR's leading authors to expand the range of public discourse:

> I believe that this mistake of declaring the past to be overcome is very clearly committed among us [i.e., East Germans]. Unfortunately, also by many comrades [i.e., members of the Communist Party] who, with a certain self-satisfaction, say, ["W]e have mastered the past, *those over there*

[i.e., in West Germany] have not, they are, so to speak, still in the middle of it.["] Nobody has the right to say that sort of thing. (Stephan Hermlin)

Thereby an entire generation, and not only one, was deeply damaged in the foundations of its psychological being on this earth. And that is not so easy to repair. It is not over and done with when two years later one says: My goodness, but Marx was right. . . . I do not believe that we have "mastered" the time of fascism in this sense. I am speaking now of the individual coming to terms with his entirely personal past, with that which he personally did and thought and which he cannot blame on another, that for which he also cannot excuse himself along with a mass of people who did the same or worse things. (Christa Wolf)[64]

While church leaders did describe and confess their personal guilt in a couple of cases, most of the church's statements lacked concreteness. The discussion of guilt tended toward repetitious and empty formulas.

The Role of the Soviet Union

The official language concerning the Soviet Union was formulated with special strictness and employed set phrases and words. There were four emphases.

First, the Soviet Union came to Germany as the liberator. Political speeches referred to liberation by the Soviet Union or to the Soviet "deed of liberation." Although the English and American air attacks were sometimes mentioned, crimes of the Soviet troops against the civil population were not. The official assessment of the role of the Soviet Union was overwhelmingly positive. It was said, for example, that "at no time were the Soviet bombardments of cities in the interior of the enemy against nonmilitary objects. The idea and practice of such revengeful attacks upon the German civil population were foreign to the Soviet Union."[65]

Second, the Soviet Union bore the "chief brunt" of the war; the fascists had wanted to eliminate the Soviet Union. Set phrases and words emphasized the heavy losses: The Soviet Union offered a great "sacrifice"; "twenty million sons and daughters of the Soviet Union gave their lives"; it bore the "heaviest burden" of the war.[66]

Third, the Soviet Union was the "chief power" in the Anti-Hitler Coalition. On the one hand, the Anti-Hitler Coalition as an alliance with a shared purpose was a theme of particular prominence in the press reports on the observances in Torgau, where American and Soviet troops had met in the last days of the war. In one speech, the state representative called both the United States and the USSR "our liberators."[67] On the other hand, the state claimed that the war was essentially a struggle between socialism and imperialism. The victory of the Soviet Union "was the proof of the political and moral superiority of the socialistic social and state order over capitalistic exploitation and oppression."[68] "In the violent struggle between imperialism and socialism, socialism showed itself to be superior and undefeatable."[69] This victory of the Soviet Union was said to have altered world political arrangements. Socialism became an international system.[70]

Moreover, the articles about the air attacks never mentioned that the cities to the west of the Elbe River were liberated by the English and the Americans. The liberation, when mentioned at all, was also in this case the deed of the "Soviet Union and its allies."[71] Sometimes, as in the case of the liberation of Karl-Marx Stadt (Chemnitz), the Allies were not even mentioned: "In the midst of the ashes sprung hope, and it sowed friendship to the liberators out of the east."[72]

The official language repeatedly used set phrases and words to emphasize the role of the Soviet army in the war: The Soviet army was "glorious"; the Soviet people demonstrated "mass heroism"; the Soviet Union was on the "chief front" where the decisive battles of the war took place; its victory "determined the subsequent progress of world history" and was the "triumph of humanism, freedom, and human worth"; its victory was the accomplishment of its entire people under the leadership of Stalin and the Communist Party.[73]

Fourth, the Soviet Union helped the Germans immediately after the war. It brought assistance even in the first hours. "The Soviet Union—that was for many the first bread at a time when the flames of battle still blazed."[74] The GDR could thank its present existence to the "assistance and support" of the Soviet Union.[75] The role of the other Allies immediately after the war was entirely ignored.

The official language seemed especially stilted, formal, or liturgical in these references to the Soviet Union, as if to express that the Soviet Union's deed of liberation was eternal and unique. One theme was salvation. The Soviet Union "accomplished an immortal, world historical deed for the salvation of world civilization."[76] Along with the other members of the Anti-Hitler Coalition, the Soviet Union saved humankind from barbarism.[77]

A second theme was thanks. The GDR thanked the Soviet Union, the Anti-Hitler Coalition, and the freedom fighters. These thanks were eternal and always in memory.[78] The desire to thank the Soviet Union was especially prominent. Among the slogans at the state-sponsored demonstrations before and on May 8 were: "Thank you, you Soviet soldiers," "Glory and honor to the sons and daughters of the brave Soviet people," and "Glory and thanks to our liberators."[79]

A third theme was the unique accomplishment of the Soviet Union. "Thanks to the glorious deed of liberation by the Soviet Union . . . our land has been resurrected out of the ruins."[80] The Soviet Union "illumined the noble concepts of freedom, equality, and brotherhood as a greeting to all humankind."[81]

The official language may have helped make the church more attentive to the role of the Soviet Union, but the church's language was less comprehensive and less exaggerated. Only a few church statements confessed the special guilt of the Germans toward the Soviet Union for the heavy losses inflicted.[82] In one instance, the sacrifice of the Soviet Union was memorialized at a church gathering at the Seelower Heights, site of an important battle.[83] In another, the church remembered that the peoples of the Soviet Union "paid the greatest blood ransom."[84]

Like the official language, the church's language did not address the rape and pillage that some Soviet soldiers practiced at the end of the war, and in only one case were they even alluded to, when Hempel asked:

> Are not many of us still so disposed in our perceptions—though it is difficult for us to acknowledge them—that we believe the Western European culture to be more valuable than the Eastern European? And sometimes I think that we still have not forgiven the Soviet soldiers the hardness that they brought along in the execution of victory.[85]

Although Hempel asserted, "We may also speak of our hurts," he himself did not describe them.[86] He touched only indirectly on Soviet guilt, a topic that was completely avoided in the official language. In asking Germans to forgive the Soviets, he gently expanded the range of public discourse; yet by not first speaking openly and concretely about what was to be forgiven, he stayed within limits the state had established.

The Limits of the Church's Language on the Soviet Union

Overall, the church's language concerning the Soviet Union was cautious and restrained. While acknowledging guilt toward the Soviet Union (for the destruction of so many cities and lives) and the church's failure to affirm the genuine achievements of communism, the church's language failed to address Germans' concrete problems and differences with the Soviet Union and the communist order after the war and in the present.

The restraint in the church's language reflected its ambiguous position as a "church in socialism." For those who wished the church to go further in testing the limits of public discourse, it was certainly not a matter of calculating one's own guilt in comparison with others'. But if the church insisted on truth and justice, why was it silent about the Soviet Union? Did its silence suggest that it still stood at the beginning of recognizing its guilt toward the Soviet Union (not only in World War II, but also during the Cold War), or simply that the church wished to avoid controversial themes and unnecessary tensions with the party and the state? Could the church help Germans come to terms with the past if it were unable to speak concretely about political arrangements in the GDR since the war? What were the limits that the church had to respect while not simply succumbing to quiet conformity?

Again, it appeared to these critics that the church could have spoken about the Soviet Union more concretely and with more nuance. Despite its cautious tone, Hempel's sermon did suggest the direction that they wanted the church to go. He described how he himself had experienced the end of the war:

> The eighth of May began for me around four o'clock in the morning in a road trench near the Czech city of Most. It sounds fabricated. I awoke; next to me sat—for the first time in real life—a Russian soldier, scarcely older than my own seventeen years. I know how frightened I was: Now it is going to happen! But he only chewed on his bread and looked at me; [he was] neither friendly nor unfriendly. He broke off a piece of the bread and gave it to me. It was sour. He had not smiled. He said, "*Domoi!* [Go home]." And then he stood up.[87]

Those who wanted the church to risk more to broaden public discourse about the role of the Soviet Union in the war could also point again to some of the East German authors, such as Christa Wolf:

> Only after the war . . . did the Russians become for me concrete persons. But you wouldn't believe how long it takes before an abstract notion about another people—be it as a ghost, be it later as an ideal—fills itself with life, with a bunch of different faces, with relations that mean much to one.[88]

Peace

A concern for peace stood at the center of the official language about the air raids that had destroyed German cities, and about the "Day of Liberation." Three major themes emerged.

First, war could never be allowed to break out again. To highlight this concern, the official statements frequently used religious language. The state-sponsored observances included a "confession" to peace.[89] Speakers referred to the "vow" of "war never again." It was said that the surviving resistance fighters and antifascists took this vow after the liberation, as did the American and Soviet soldiers who met on the Elbe.[90]

Speakers also referred to the "lesson" or "moral" of the war for today. The content of this lesson varied: to bring all forces together to prevent a nuclear inferno; to fight against war before the weapons speak; to secure peace and socialism; to do everything for peace.[91] World War II was a lesson for all "who in their pathological anticommunism slander the Soviet Union as the evil empire."[92]

Finally, the vow from yesterday needed to be sworn again. The lessons of war could continue to admonish people today. A war with atomic weapons would destroy the entire world. In an atomic war, there would be neither victors nor vanquished.[93] There was "nothing more important" than peace.[94] Peace was the "highest" or "most precious" good.[95] Peace was a "commandment."[96]

Second, peace was presently threatened by the West. The West practiced a politics of confrontation. "The most aggressive circles of imperialism, especially the United States and NATO, seek to attain military superiority. . . . They strive for world domination with their policies of atomic armament and extortion. They strive to eliminate socialism violently."[97]

> If world peace is threatened today to the utmost, it is on account of the most reactionary and aggressive circles of monopoly capitalism, this military-industrial complex that determines the policies of the U.S. . . . administration. These circles would like to direct the entire course of world events back into the barbarism of imperialistic domination.[98]

The official language did not expressly call the West fascistic or militaristic, but no doubt was left that its policies had such tendencies. The most aggressive circles of the West were said to threaten all of humankind. "Once again the most aggressive representatives of imperialism threaten to burn the world."[99] The vow of Buchenwald "is today the demand to stop the atomic arms buildup and to disarm those who would obliterate the existence of humankind with Star Wars."[100] Heaven must not become the forecourt of hell.[101]

Third, the GDR intended to strengthen peace. The GDR supported the disarmament negotiations between the United States and the USSR in Geneva.[102] It affirmed the peace initiatives of the Soviet

Union.[103] The GDR was a "peace state" because it had exterminated the roots of war, that is, imperialism and militarism.[104] Peace was "state doctrine."[105]

On the one hand, the GDR emphasized its relations with the Soviet Union, including economic, ideological, political, and military cooperation. Certain words and phrases were repeatedly employed to describe this relationship: The GDR had an "indestructible" friendship with the Soviet Union; this friendship was a "life element," "a matter of the heart"; the GDR and the Soviet Union shared an "inviolable" military alliance; this alliance was "forever and never again otherwise."[106]

On the other hand, the official language asserted that the GDR was ready to cooperate with *all* forces of peace.

> Today it is a matter of unifying ourselves in order to secure peace for humankind and to create a worldwide coalition of reason and realism against the danger of atomic war. Whatever position one holds, whatever way of organizing society he believes to be better, whatever his philosophical and political views on other issues may be, all that must not be an obstacle to a rational interaction of states of different orders next to and with each other.[107]

Socialism and the Soviet Union were the leading peace forces. The Soviet Union had preserved peace in Europe for forty years.[108] Through the growing potential of socialism and the Soviet Union, the forces of peace were becoming even stronger.[109] The GDR stood on the side of the Soviet Union but also cooperated with other peace forces.

The official language betrayed ambivalence on this point, however. It clearly limited the nature of "cooperation" and the extent to which the GDR was ready to accept the position of those peace forces that criticized socialism and the Soviet Union. In the end, the official language attempted to co-opt the other peace forces. It claimed that the peace program of the Soviet Union was for all.[110] Socialism embodied the future.[111]

This ambivalence in the official language extended to the question of those in the West with whom the GDR would cooperate. On the one hand, it was asserted in the official language that the members of the Anti-Hitler Coalition could work together today, despite different worldviews and social systems, because they once again had a common enemy, the danger of an atomic war. The meeting of Soviet and American soldiers in Torgau at the end of the war was symbolic of this coalition.[112] On the other hand, it was emphasized that the nations would have to build a coalition against the American administration. "It is important to unify worldwide all forces of reason, realism, and good will against the dangerous arms buildup and confrontational course of the Reagan administration."[113] "If all peace-loving people . . . work together, the incredibly insane plans for American world rule can still be thwarted before the abyss of war is reached."[114]

Once again, this language was stilted, ritualistic, and liturgical, as reflected in the statement "Peace must and will conquer war."[115] It was said that "today socialism is incomparably stronger, more powerful, and more influential than in the past. Its reality and its politics encourage those throughout the earth whose hearts long for peace and progress."[116] The slogans at the state-sponsored observances also sounded liturgical: "Peace, peace, and once again peace!" "Long live peace for all peoples of this earth!"[117]

Formulations taken directly out of the common political vocabulary of international relations provided a more concrete picture of the peace policies of the GDR; references were mode to "peaceful coexistence"; a peace order for Europe; the special duty of the two German states to prevent war; equality and mutual security; and no military superiority for the most aggressive circles of imperialism.[118]

The church's statements about peace also had three dominant themes. First, it was emphasized that the Christian message proclaims peace. Here the church appealed to biblical or theological language. "The resurrection of Jesus Christ from the dead gives us the certainty that God will help us beyond all guilt to new life in community and peace."[119] "Out of the fullness of the Christian peace witness I remind you that God sent his Son into the world that we might have peace through him. That applies not only to a special sphere of religious experience. It applies to the entirety of our everyday life."[120] In response to the Christian message of God's peace, Christians have "both the freedom and duty to be people of peace."[121] Where peace and justice are concerned, Christ "does not allow his people to withdraw into a corner; they are obligated to the entirety of creation."[122] While the state's official language linked peace with socialism, the church's language emphasized the significance of God's peace for every society and for the whole world.

Second, preserving peace was an urgent task. We live in a "threatened world."[123] "I really don't understand how the arming of space should positively contribute to peace."[124] But the threat to peace came not only from the West. East Germans, too, were entangled in contradictions: "We know that more weapons do not bring more security, but we continually install more weapons because we say that the others do."[125] In contrast to the official language, the church did not simply designate the

GDR as a "peace state." Rather, the church said: "We hope that the prioritization of the military in nearly all spheres will soon come to an end in our country."[126]

Both church and state emphasized that the preservation of peace was more important than anything else. The church's language sometimes showed similarities to certain phrases of the state's official language; for example, the church referred to the "vow" at the end of the war; the "obligation" that war never again begin from German soil; "peaceful co-existence"; a peace order for Europe; the special obligation of both German states; and mutual security.[127]

But the church's language also made a distinctive contribution to defining the present-day task. It condemned a policy of deterrence.[128] Moreover, peace was said to depend on eliminating false images of the enemy and on educating people to peace.[129] The church also emphasized the relationship between peace and other pressing tasks, such as justice, truth, and the well-being of the third world.[130]

Third, the church, like the state, emphasized that Christians were ready to cooperate with all in order to preserve peace. Christians supported the long, difficult work of reconciliation among the different churches, between Christians and Jews, and in families.[131] They supported the deepening of relations between different nations. Governments had to learn to negotiate with one another.[132]

Christians could work together with others whenever it was a matter of peace and justice.[133] Perhaps they could

> be parliamentarians of reconciliation and peace. Those are the people who without weapons, without power, without privileges but with verifiability, accountability, and willingness to take risks go between the fronts and interpret. Interpret, for example, . . . that one must ever again begin with trust, even when it brings so little success.[134]

The church's statements argued that cooperation between church and state had to rest on trust and openness. In a few cases, the church's statements alluded to the difficulties and disadvantages that burdened Christians in the GDR. The church hoped, for example, that "also those who think differently will be able to express their convictions without fear, and to act according to their conscience."[135] But only one church official clearly addressed the problem of living as a Christian in the GDR. He argued that Christians, on the one hand, should remain in the GDR and serve the common good; they had learned that they could work together with Marxists. On the other hand, they should act according to conscience:

> A long time ago a pastor told me that an elder had come to him and said: "I can't hold out any longer. For a month I have been unable to sleep right. Everything that we talk about in the church council, everything that you unsuspectingly tell me, I have to report. I can't continue this living in lies any longer. . . ." To seek "the good of the city" means here very simply: to refuse such demands.[136]

Moreover, cooperation between East German Christians and other people committed to peace would depend on the state expanding the opportunities for travel and personal contact. Here the church directed its concern to the travel restrictions that affected most people in the GDR. "We ask the Allies of the Second World War . . . to promote cultural, economic, and scientific cooperation, as well as the meeting of people over the borders!"[137]

The Limits of the Church's Language on Peace

Like the official language, the church's language put its greatest emphasis on the theme of peace. While acknowledging that the church and the state approached peace from different starting points, the church barely alluded to the implications of these differences. In general, it appeared that the church wished to support dialogue with the state, and to avoid controversy and disagreement.

To be sure, there were only a few words and phrases that *both* church and state employed in their statements, and most of these belonged to the common political vocabulary of East and West. But those within the church who wished it to go further argued that form could not be separated from content. Insofar as the content of the church's language remained general and abstract, its form was not radically different from that of the official language. Both the official language and the church's language, for example, constantly appealed to the word *peace*. According to critics of the church, this word appeared so predictably in state and church statements that it was largely devoid of meaning.

The church's use of language from the common political vocabulary of international relations appeared to pose a different kind of danger. Though this language might at first seem neutral, the state frequently invested it with a specific meaning. The church, for example, employed the phrase "peaceful coexistence" in reference to different countries' peacefully living with and next to each other. But this expression was originally Lenin's and had a very specific meaning in Marxist-Leninist philosophy:

From the Leninist principle of peaceful coexistence it follows that social-ism will be able to triumph over capitalism without war. The socialist states therefore have two historical tasks: (1) to defend the peace against imperialism, which refuses to come to terms with peaceful coexistence and (2) to support the struggle of the international proletariat to eliminate imperialism, and the triumph of the socialistic revolution in individual countries, that is, to develop a special strategy and tactic of fighting impe-rialism that will be effective beyond international relations on a bilateral, international level. The policies that meet both of these objective require-ments are the policies of peaceful coexistence.[138]

Conclusion

I have argued that church-state relations in East Germany in the mid-1980s can be assessed by comparing the language of church and state in relation to events and observances of national significance. An examina-tion of the East German church's language concerning May 8 suggests neither that the state heavily oppressed the church nor that the church conveniently accommodated itself to the state. Rather, the church qui-etly and carefully sought to extend the range of public discussion.

Nonetheless, church-state relations seemed to dictate that the church avoid open confrontation with the state. The church sometimes ad-dressed difficult issues that were ignored in the official language, and it sometimes brought greater nuance and thoughtfulness to issues that the state did address. But the church also respected certain limits set in the official language. Though the East German church had not been reduced to a persecuted remnant, it was nonetheless vulnerable to state pressures, as it lived in the tension between "freedom of religion" and "a society under the leadership of the working class and its Marxist-Leninist party."

In form, the church's language was, for the most part, different from the official language. The church's language was less stilted, ritualistic, and liturgical. Although church statements appealed to biblical and theological language, they had no set words and phrases with which they described liberation, fascism, or the Soviet Union.

In the content of their statements, state and church shared common emphases: liberation, the question of guilt, and peace. Where they dif-fered was in the amount of attention they gave to the role of the Soviet Union in the war, which was not a major concern in the church's state-ments, though it did concentrate on the Soviet Union whenever it ad-dressed the relation between Germany and the Allies.

The shared concerns were developed in very different ways, however; the church statements reflected far greater care and nuance. The church treated "liberation," for example, in the context of "collapse" and regarded it as still incomplete.

The shared emphases were also ordered differently. Whereas the official language placed the most weight on "liberation," the church's language returned again and again to the question of guilt. The church also had other major emphases, such as reconciliation, that did not appear in the official language at all. Sometimes the church cautiously broached topics that were completely ignored in the official statements (as when Hempel commented that Germans had not yet forgiven the Soviet soldiers). But the church rarely levelled direct criticism at either the party or the state.

In no case did church statements openly challenge the official language. Neither the question of language regulations nor the question of language tabus was taken up. Rather, the statements of several GDR authors, which were more open and concrete, represented the stance of those who wished the church to go further.

It appears that the church's language tended to be general and abstract because it feared that more specific and concrete language could lead to confrontation with the state. So long as its language remained general, it could emphasize the common concerns of church and state (for example, the assertion that church and state shared a common concern for peace). Had the church sought to address questions of peace and justice more concretely—for example, by speaking of the disadvantages that Christians suffered educationally and professionally, the militarization of society through paramilitary instruction in the schools, or the censorship of church publications—differences would have been more readily apparent.

In some areas, however, the church's language did speak concretely and therefore represented a significant extension of the state's official language. This extension of language occurred not only in the framework of specifically Christian rituals, such as sermons in worship. In speeches at both church and state ceremonies, church representatives spoke concretely about the suffering that Germans had experienced during the war and about their personal guilt. Such statements acknowledged feelings of sadness, remorse, and humility—feelings that seldom came to expression in the political language of either East or West.

In thus broadening the parameters of public language, the church represented a free space. This free space attracted dissident, alternative groups, and the church's language helped legitimate them and their concern for truth and peace. Yet these groups were critical of the limits that the church respected, and they sought to push the church to speak more openly and concretely about injustices in East German society. As we shall see in part II, these dynamics between the church and its groups helped prepare the way for the radical political changes of 1989.

THE CHURCH

AND THE

PEACEFUL

REVOLUTION

The Church as a Religious and Political Force

By the mid-1980s, the Evangelische Kirche in East Germany consistently represented the major ideological and political alternative to the Communist Party and the socialist state.[1] In a society that had no legal political opposition and offered few opportunities for open discussion of controversial issues, the church represented a significant "free space." It found support not only from those who continued to affiliate and participate, but also from millions of nonmembers who felt that it best represented their political interests.

At the same time, traditional religious life in East Germany had experienced radical decline. Only a minority of East Germans were church members, and only a minority of these were actually active in the sense of receiving instruction in the church's distinctive language and regularly participating in its fundamental rites.

This chapter argues that the church, given this situation, came to find a good deal of its identity not in traditional religious life but as a political alternative to the state. It had greater significance as a political than as a religious force.

The response of the state to this development was ambivalent. On the one hand, the state tried to define the church as merely a religious community with no political interests. On the other, the state tried to define the church's political interests in such a way that the church would police itself and help check more radical impulses that were beginning to emerge among alternative groups in the church's free space. For its part, the church increasingly faced the question of how to ground its political life in a distinctive religious identity.

The Political Character of the Church

The church's political identity went through several stages.[2] Immediately after the war and the division of Germany, church-state relations were largely adversarial. Some church leaders, and many church members, strongly opposed the communist government and hoped that the two Germanies would soon be reunified as a Western democracy.

Tensions came to a head in the early 1950s, when the state conducted a campaign to discredit the church. It accused church youth groups of operating as fronts for Western sabotage and espionage, and banned them. It arrested pastors and raided church properties. Though it eventually backed down from these extreme measures, it continued to pressure Christians—the majority of the population—to withdraw from the church.

In the 1960s, church-state relations gradually improved. The communists, who had predicted that religion would quickly disappear under the new economic order, had to concede that the church continued to enjoy widespread support and might well continue to exist for several generations. The church had to concede, especially after the building of the Berlin Wall in 1961, that the two Germanies would go separate ways for the foreseeable future.

By 1978, church and state were able to hold high-level conversations in which they expressed their mutual commitments: to respect their ideological differences, to cooperate in areas of common social and political concern, and to resolve political differences through dialogue rather than confrontation.[3] Out of this meeting, and later ones, the church won major concessions from the state, such as permission to build churches in new satellite cities and to broadcast programs on state-run television.

By the mid-1980s, the state had increasingly, if not always consistently, articulated and enacted a policy of noninterference in church affairs. The East German Constitution, though securing the leading social and political role of the Marxist-Leninist party, defined the church as an independent organization not under direct control of the party—a position not accorded to any other group in the society.[4] The state endorsed the principle of separation of church and state, and largely allowed the church itself to define the range of its "religious" activities.[5]

These constitutional-legal and policy determinations provided the

East German church with considerably more independence than most churches in the East Bloc. Free from direct government control, it was able to operate its own diaconal institutions, publishing houses, and theological schools. In different ways—including quiet negotiations with the state, public pronouncements, special worship services, the formation of discussion groups, and the commemoration of important civic events—it was also able to play an active, independent political role. It was sometimes able to help win the release of people charged with political crimes, as occurred in 1988 after police raided an East Berlin church and arrested several people connected with the publication of an underground human rights newspaper.[6] It supported improved relations between the two Germanies and planned a church congress to promote "German dialogue."[7] It encouraged the expansion of human rights, including travel to the West and the establishment of alternatives to compulsory military service.[8]

The state did, of course, have ways to exert pressure on the church. Many church projects and proposals required state approval: the invitation of ecumenical guests, travel to conferences in the West, the construction of new churches. Through its propaganda, the state could signal its disapproval of church policies and create a more or less hostile climate for the church. Moreover, state officials could conduct private conversations with church officials and advise them of the state's displeasure with the church's activities.[9] Yet, in general, the state respected the church as an independent entity that would never be wholly integrated into socialist society, at least not until religion itself disappeared.[10]

The church, for its part, increasingly defined itself as a church "within" rather than "against" socialist society. Of particular significance was its decision, in 1969, to separate itself from the West German Evangelische Kirche and become a "church in socialism" (*Kirche im Sozialismus*), neither for nor against the state, but in "critical solidarity" with socialist society.[11] This stance was particularly evident in its peace work. At some points, the church was able to express support for state concerns, such as, in the early 1980s, opposition to the modernization of NATO forces.[12] At other times, however, the church criticized state policies, such as compulsory military education in the schools.[13]

The Religious Character of the Church

Western observers, impressed by the political significance of the East German church, often failed to note that its political strength was not matched by religious strength.[14] By all measures of participation in traditional religious life, East Germany by the mid-1980s was one of the world's most secularized societies.

In one sense, the religious weakness of the East German church was nothing new. The German Evangelische Kirche as a whole had suffered from poor attendance for over a century.[15] Active church participation in both Germanies was small. The numbers for the West German Evangelische Kirche corresponded to those of the East German church—less than 8 percent of the membership of either church regularly attended Sunday worship.[16]

Yet in East Germany church *membership* fell off far more quickly and dramatically than in West Germany. While the West German Evangelische Kirche had lost nearly 15 percent of its membership since 1961, the East German Evangelische Kirche had lost 50 percent.[17]

At the end of World War II, East Germany was 82 percent Protestant. By 1964, membership in the Evangelische Kirche had fallen to under 60 percent of the population, and by 1974 to under 50 percent. By the mid-1980s, the Evangelische Kirche could claim no more than 30–40 percent of the population.[18] Because a majority of the membership was aging, it was predicted that these numbers would decline to 20–25 percent by the turn of the century.[19] It was predicted that the West German Evangelische Kirche, by contrast, would decline more slowly—from slightly over 50 percent of the population at the end of World War II to about 33 percent in the year 2030.[20]

The situation in the larger East German cities looked especially bleak. In 1987, the general superintendent (regional administrative officer) of East Berlin stated that only 7 percent of its population claimed even nominal affiliation with the Evangelische Kirche. In the new satellite cities ringing East Berlin, the rate was even lower—perhaps no more than 3 percent.[21] The situation in West Germany was, again, less dramatic. Even in West Berlin, which had experienced especially high numbers of church withdrawals, about 50 percent of the population continued nonetheless to have nominal affiliation with the Evangelische Kirche.[22]

Other measures of church participation further dramatized the rapid decline of traditional religious life in East Germany. In Saxony, historically a Protestant region, the percentage of marriages conducted by the church fell from 54.7 percent in 1950 to 10.4 percent in 1976. The percentage of children baptized fell from 80.9 percent in 1952 to 17.3 percent in 1976, and in the larger cities the rate was even lower—9.9 percent.[23] Other parts of East Germany recorded similar losses.[24] In

West Germany the declines were more gradual. In 1981, 76 percent of newborns with at least one Protestant parent were baptized in the West German Evangelische Kirche—not far different from the 78 percent recorded in 1961. Of marriages in which at least one partner was Protestant, 45 percent took place in the church (down from 63 percent in 1963)—55 percent if second marriages were excluded (down from 70 percent).[25]

Two sets of factors specific to East Germany help explain why the declines in traditional religious life were far greater there than in West Germany: externally, state pressures on the church; internally, the inability of the traditional "people's church" *(Volkskirche)* model to resist these pressures. Especially in the 1950s and 1960s, direct state measures resulted in massive withdrawals from the church. Parents were pressured not to baptize their children. Children, encouraged to participate in state-sponsored after-school activities, were thereby discouraged from attending the church's Christian education *(Christenlehre)* classes. Schoolteachers sometimes called on children to defend their faith in class. Christian young people were often unable to receive college-preparatory or college education because they were regarded as politically unreliable and intellectually unsound. Christians were excluded from politically sensitive kinds of work and were declared ineligible for promotions to the higher ranks of business leadership.[26] Though no longer as severe by the mid-1980s, these measures were still in place and continued to discourage many East Germans from associating with the church.

The educational system, however, had perhaps the greatest impact on the church. The East German state emphasized the value and necessity of a "scientific education." Religion was at its best a form of philosophical idealism and, at its worst, a crude superstition. One observer noted that the propagation of this scientific worldview had an especially negative impact on the church because of

> conditions that favor secularization, increased apathy and passivity, [and the] growing alienation of nominal Christians from their congregations: the anonymity of people in the large city, frequent changes in career and place of residence, the dissolution of integrative forces such as custom and tradition, [and] increased socialistic cultural and social service offerings.[27]

Internally, the church was too weak to respond to either the challenges of secularization or the pressures of the state. It continued to view its traditional religious rites primarily in terms of their social functions, and it tried to maintain its established parochial system, an extensive church bureaucracy, old church buildings often in need of restoration, and a traditional range of church activities. But the state had managed to weaken the church's social functions, often replacing them with its own rites, such as the socialist youth dedication ceremony (*Jugendweihe*), which effectively displaced confirmation as a social rite of passage.[28] There was no longer any social advantage for those who associated with the church, and often there was disadvantage. Moreover, suffering from declining membership and no longer enjoying stable financing through a state-collected church-tax (a set percentage of one's income tax, which the German state traditionally collected on behalf of the established churches [the Evangelische Kirche and the Catholic Church]; with the division of Germany, this practice continued in the West but not in East Germany), the church found itself burdened by its extensive infrastructure and increasingly came to rely on financing from the West German Evangelische Kirche.[29] The Volkskirche model was no longer viable, and the preoccupation with preserving its remnants further contributed to the church's inability to respond to its circumstances, thereby resulting in still greater membership losses.[30]

Political Identity versus Religious Identity

Even if the *percentage* of church members actively participating remained comparable to that of the West German church, the *absolute numbers* continued to drop dramatically because of continuing overall losses in membership. These steady losses affected the morale and identity of the church. For many East Germans, the decline of traditional religious life meant that external factors—especially social and political circumstances—increasingly gave the church its primary identity.

In particular, East Germans reported that they sought out the church's free space. In contrast to a state that encouraged outward conformity, the church offered a sense of freedom and acceptance that people did not find elsewhere in society. Though they were open to the insights that religion could bring to their lives, they turned to the church primarily in search of a special communal experience characterized by intimate fellowship and open conversation.[31]

Research that could test the nature of the church's free space was limited, but in the mid-1980s an East German researcher, Wolfgang Wesenberg, conducted one study of considerable importance and interest. Employing sociological methods, Wesenberg examined the motivations of young people who belonged to church youth groups (Junge Gemeinden) in East Berlin.[32]

The church youth groups had traditionally consisted of young people from Christian backgrounds. Although, according to Wesenberg, such participants were still in the majority, the East Berlin youth groups increasingly attracted other young people as well. By the mid-1980s, 70 percent were baptized and confirmed, and had parents who paid the church-tax (now a voluntary contribution collected by the church, rather than by the state), but fully 18 percent had had no prior contact with the church.[33] While 90 percent were willing to support the church both financially and through their participation, only 60 percent clearly identified themselves as "believers." 67 percent attended church at least occasionally, but only 33 percent attended regularly.

Even fewer participated in the church youth groups for explicitly religious reasons. Wesenberg found that youth group members had an ambivalent attitude toward the role of religion in their groups. While expecting the church to help clarify issues with which they struggled, they felt that the groups, usually led by a pastor or vicar, placed too much emphasis on religious language and reflection. On the one hand, participants shared a general, latent expectation that the church youth group should be a place in which they could learn something about the church and faith. They acknowledged that the mere fact of meeting in a church, rather than elsewhere, implied this possibility. On the other hand, they did not attend youth group meetings primarily to involve themselves in traditional religious activities, such as worship and instruction, but to enjoy a communal experience that they were unable to find elsewhere in society. Seeking a community that welcomed a high degree of personal involvement and commitment, they attended the group regularly over long periods of time and had strong personal attachments to each other. They saw the group as a community characterized by openness, trust, respect, and mutual affirmation.

Though based on his study of church youth groups, Wesenberg's observations about people's desire to shape an alternative community within the church's free space had wider applicability. Sociologically, traditional religious life no longer stood at the center of many parishes. More people seemed to come to the church in order to enjoy their own group experience than to participate in Sunday worship.[34]

The external and internal factors affecting overall affiliation with the church also helped account for these patterns of participation. External state pressures discouraged formal membership in the church, so people were more apt to appear on the periphery of traditional religious life than in its midst. And because the internal style of traditional religious life associated with the "people's church" encouraged passive receptivity rather than active participation, people were more apt to seek out small, informal groups in which they could have a high degree of involvement than worship and instruction.

Alternative Groups in the Church

These factors prepared the ground for a new development in the early 1980s. Small "alternative" groups emerged in the church's free space. The members of these groups often had even less connection to—or interest in—traditional religious life than other church groups. Moreover, they sought not only to create an alternative community within the church, but to address controversial social and political issues, and to agitate for change. They further contributed to the political character of the church during a time in which traditional religious life was in decline.

In the mid-1970s, East Germany achieved political legitimacy in the eyes of both the West and its own citizens.[35] The two Germanies entered the United Nations as distinct political entities. The United States accorded East Germany diplomatic relations. Moreover, by the mid-1970s, an entire generation of East Germans had grown up thinking of East Germany, not Germany, as their home. Though not always in agreement with their state, these young people, in contrast to their parents, did not dream of a reunified Germany.

In the 1970s and 1980s, East Germany also achieved economic stability. Though continuing to lag behind West Germany, it experienced its own economic miracle. The standard of living was one of the highest in the East Bloc. Massive construction projects provided new, modern housing to hundreds of thousands of people. The beautiful showcase buildings of the past were carefully restored. Extensive trade relations were established with West Germany and, to a lesser extent, with other Western European nations. In addition, East Germany received massive subsidies from West Germany.[36]

Despite these political and economic successes, there was also considerable discontent, especially among young people. In part, their discontent resulted from an educational system that rewarded conformity and repressed individual creativity. In part, it corresponded to that of their Western European counterparts, who, challenging their own political and economic establishment, called for greater consciousness about the perils of nuclear weapons and environmental devastation. Perhaps the single greatest frustration was the limitation on free travel, especially to the West.

This growing discontent expressed itself in several ways. First, it contributed to widespread cynicism and apathy. Many people believed that little or no social change was possible. Adopting an attitude of "inner emigration," they withdrew into themselves. Although they resented the harassments and injustices of daily life, they avoided challenging the state. They were willing to conform outwardly in exchange for the "inner space" in which they could concentrate on their personal living standard.

Second, others who saw little possibility for social change sought "outer emigration." In the 1970s, after signing the Helsinki accords on human rights, the state permitted limited emigration to the West, especially in cases involving family reunification. Growing numbers of people, however, wanted to leave for political and economic reasons. They sometimes waited for years before the state acted on their applications. In the mid-1980s, the state sought to defuse growing social tensions by allowing large numbers of people to emigrate, as many as thirty to forty thousand per year. This policy was not wholly successful, however, as it encouraged thousands of other people, who up to that point had feared the possible repercussions for their careers and their children's educations, to submit emigration applications.[37]

Third, smaller numbers of people expressed their discontent by seeking alternatives within their society. Some joined the Communist Party with the hope that they could bring about social change, though their numbers greatly decreased after the party purged itself of its leading critics in the mid-1970s.[38] Some artistic and intellectual circles provided a forum for alternative expression, and an underground culture slowly developed.

The most apparent alternative was the church and its free space. Because they knew that the state was reluctant to interfere with activities within the church, people seeking social change turned to the church for a measure of security and protection. Some were already members of the church and organized groups from within; in many cases, however, these groups included people from outside the church. In either case, pastors often helped lead them.

Church leaders responded positively to these developments. Even while continuing to express their commitment to dialogue and cooperation with the state in areas of mutual concern, such as diaconal work and peace issues, they insisted that the church had a commission to serve all of society, including people seeking social change.[39] First, because these people often experienced state displeasure and social marginalization, the church wanted to demonstrate tolerance and openness toward them. Second, it realized that its own social vision often corresponded more closely to theirs than to the state's. Third, it increasingly found its own membership calling for support of the issues that they raised.[40]

The new participants did not, for the most part, integrate themselves into traditional church groups, such as the youth groups, but created their own alternative groups. Some of these groups simply adopted the church's symbols, especially those relating to peace, for their own use.[41] Others sought to facilitate careful, thoughtful discussion of controversial social issues—especially concerning peace, the environment, and human rights—not openly discussed elsewhere in society. Still others saw the church as a base from which to launch a protest movement against the state.

The church and the alternative groups were generally able to support each other. Church officials often worked on behalf of activists who were harassed or imprisoned by the state. Moreover, because the church could arrange many activities that other social organizations could not, it was able to give the groups a public presence they would not otherwise have had. Novelists whose works were banned could often hold readings. Controversial exhibitions, performances, and discussions could take place. Though the church had limited opportunities to publicize these events, they had public significance because anyone could attend them.

The alternative groups, for their part, helped the church discover a new range of possibilities for its work. They were willing to test the state's limits on the church. Moreover, they pushed the church to respond more clearly and urgently to issues of peace, the environment, and human rights.[42]

The symbiosis between the church and the alternative groups reached a high point in the Conciliar Process for Peace, Justice, and the Integrity of Creation, an initiative adopted by the World Council of Churches, at the suggestion of the German churches, to encourage widespread grassroots discussion in and among its member churches. In East Germany, numerous congregations and alternative groups participated in regional and national consultations. Representatives developed a series of statements that sketched an alternative vision of society; opposition to the state and its policies was thinly veiled.[43]

At the same time, the emergence of the alternative groups raised special problems. On the one hand, the church sometimes criticized the groups for misusing its free space. The church came under increasing pressure from the state for not policing them better. Eventually, some church leaders asserted that not all groups were welcome in the church.[44] On the other hand, the groups sometimes criticized the church for being too conservative, too accommodating to the state, and too intolerant of new, creative impulses. They sometimes asserted that the church wanted to control them on behalf of the state. In 1987, they pointed to the cancellation of the "peace workshop" (Friedenswerkstatt), an annual meeting of alternative groups from throughout East Germany. Though church leaders argued that they simply wanted a year in which to review the format and future of the event, the groups accused the church of "trading" it for state permission to hold a church congress (Kirchentag) in East Berlin. The frustration in some groups was so high that they saw the church rather than the state as the major obstacle to their work.[45]

These tensions suggest that the church and the alternative groups never fully resolved their relationship. From its side, the church raised questions about the appropriate relationship between political life and traditional religious life. Were the alternative groups "guests" of the church or did they "belong" in some sense to it? Where should the church draw limits to openness and toleration? Did the groups represent an opportunity or a burden? Were they a passing phenomenon, or did they promise the renewal of a tired, tradition-bound church?

From their side, the participants in the alternative groups raised questions about the church's commitment to social justice. Had the church forgotten the radical demands of the gospel? Had it become too concerned with institutional preservation? As domestic state policies slowly relaxed, the alternative groups had more opportunities to meet outside the church, without state interference. Some of their leaders began to suggest that the church was no longer all that important a free space for them.[46]

State Efforts to Define the Church

Even though the church and the alternative groups sometimes represented a political opposition, the state's response to them was ambivalent. At times, the state scolded the church, arguing that its political involvements violated the separation of church and state. At other moments, the state recognized the church as a sociopolitical factor, hoping to define the church's institutional interests in such a way that it would police itself and the groups in its free space. While consistently emphasizing the ideological incompatibility of religion and Marxism-Leninism, the state was less consistent on whether the church should relinquish a sociopolitical role; but the state did try to control and guide this role.

Perhaps key to understanding the state's posture toward the church was the lack of clarity and direction within the Communist Party.

Though East Germany had won political legitimacy, the party had lost revolutionary fervor. The hope that East Germany would soon progress from socialism to communism had faded.

Perhaps most devastating was the party's inability to articulate a distinctive and persuasive national identity. Since the early 1970s, the party had tried to win East Germans' loyalty by improving their living standard. While the party's program put East Germany among the world's leading industrial nations, the party continued to face widespread public apathy, even cynicism, about its policies. East Germans looked to West Germany as the real German success story, and many oriented their lifestyle along the lines of the consumerism that they could daily watch on West German television.

The party found itself caught in a vicious circle. The more people "opted out," whether by inner or outer emigration, the less they contributed to fulfilling the party's ambitious economic goals. The further East Germany fell behind the West, the more dissatisfied people became and the more apt to opt out, thereby making further economic progress even more difficult.

The Soviet Union sought to counter similar economic problems through Mikhail Gorbachev's policies of glasnost and perestroika. The East German leadership, however, was reluctant to follow suit. Publicly it asserted that the East German economy, in contrast to the Soviet, did not need radical restructuring because it was already strong.[47] Privately, it worried that reform could undermine the party's power. East Germans would interpret "democratization" to mean Western-style democracy.[48]

Nonetheless, the East German state increasingly recognized that it too must initiate limited political reform in order to defuse internal discontent and win greater economic achievement from its citizens. Its most drastic move was a radical easing of travel restrictions to the West. In 1985, only sixty thousand visas were issued to persons below retirement age. In 1986 the increase was almost tenfold, and in 1987 more than one million visas were issued.[49]

Seeking to win more support for its programs, the state also turned to the church. Even though church affiliation and participation had radically declined over the previous forty years, the state still regarded the church as a power factor. As the only social organization that stood outside the state's ideological and structural framework, the church continued to attract people seeking an alternative. Moreover, those people who were active in the church, such as the members of the alternative groups, displayed an enthusiasm and commitment that the state could rarely generate for its own programs.

First, the state sought to include Christians more fully in shaping East German society, continuing to emphasize the *necessity* of cooperation with Christians on issues of common social and political concern, especially peace.[50] In 1988, Marxist-Leninist philosophers and Christian theologians engaged in formal dialogue, a first for a state that still regarded Marxism-Leninism as the only true worldview.[51] Cultural journals devoted more space to articles about religious motifs in art, literature, and music. The state press referred to Christians' work morale as a model for all East Germans.[52]

Second, seeking a way for people to vent their discontent without undermining the present political order, the state used the church's free space to test new policies that allowed greater social criticism and experimentation.[53] In 1987, the state began to test glasnost by allowing the church new freedoms to express critical views. Church publications were able to address controversial social and political issues that formerly would have incurred censorship.[54] In late August and early September 1987, the state allowed church groups to participate in the Olaf Palme Peace March, and in some cases to carry banners expressing views critical of state policies, such as those that protested the militarization of school and society and called for the alternative of civilian service for those young men opposed to compulsory military service. Church groups were even able to organize their own independent march between several churches in East Berlin.[55]

The state was able to see the church as a positive sociopolitical factor only so long as its activities remained within bounds that the state could manage. The state seemed to believe that it could best achieve this result by encouraging the church to think and act with an eye to its own institutional interests. The state encouraged the church to police itself and the alternative groups that met in its free space in exchange for the privileges that it had slowly won since 1978.[56]

Conclusion

On the eve of the "peaceful revolution" of 1989, the East German church found itself in the midst of a debate over traditional religious life and the role of the church as a political alternative. It sought a way between various extremes: accommodation and opposition, welcoming those seeking social change and disassociating itself from their activities, providing a free space and controlling what occurred within it. Because the church was more than a social and political alternative, it rightly questioned the activities of some of the alternative groups and their members. Yet, without an identity clearly based in traditional religious life, the church, even apart from these groups, tended to adopt primarily a sociopolitical identity. Some church leaders seemed more concerned with practical politics than with articulating theological grounds for their positions and policies. Church synods more frequently agreed on political issues than on strategies for renewing traditional religious life, as occurred in 1988 when the church strongly appealed to the state to allow more social criticism and freedom of travel but had difficulty finding any clear orientation in its discussion of congregational life.[57] Local congregations sustained the special communities in which East Germans experienced a level of affirmation and openness not characteristic of other social organizations, but traditional religious life continued to experience radical decline.

It is clear that the church did not simply ratify state policies. The church, anxious to preserve the privileges it had won for itself over the years, may have succumbed in some cases to state pressure, but it generally maintained a distinctive political identity. It sought to protect its institutional interests without accommodating itself. Yet it was constantly tempted to define itself primarily in terms set by the state, whether of opposition or partnership.

In the mid-1980s, this situation gave rise to a lively theological debate within the Evangelische Kirche. East German theologians generally agreed that the church could rightly define and sustain its political commitments only if its religious identity was also clearly defined and sustained. Preserving and deepening traditional religious life mattered. These theologians disagreed, however, on the theological implications of the church's free space. Some suggested that "dialogue," "participation," and "community"—characteristics of the church as a free space—were the very heart of the gospel.[58] Others argued that the church's principal task, in response to a secular world, was to articulate the distinctive language, practice, and experience of the Christian faith. The church was a free space that welcomed people into a particular kind of dialogue, shaped by a particular tradition.[59]

Even among those committed to "dialogue," clear differences in emphasis emerged. Some called on the church to be more open to the alternative groups, seeing them as able to renew the whole church. To these theologians, the groups' liberating impulses "reproduced" religion, even if the groups themselves were not necessarily religious in the sense of using traditional religious language.[60] Others, while not necessarily disagreeing, called for the church and its groups to extend their commitment to dialogue to include dialogue with the state and the Communist Party. Most prominently represented in the theological faculties of the state universities, such as East Berlin's Humboldt University, these theologians asked the church to repent of its "anticommunism," and to support the Marxist-Leninist state as a more just sociopolitical order.[61] While not blind to the state's injustices, they believed that Christians could work with the state to realize a more democratic socialism.[62]

This theological debate became all the more critical as public discontent with the Marxist-Leninist state grew. In different ways, both the state and the alternative groups pressured the church to play one kind of political role or another. At stake for the church, however, were not simply pragmatic questions of power and influence but different theological understandings of the church's very nature and purpose.

Preparing for the Fall

The Church and Its Groups

While a host of complex political and economic factors brought about the fall of the East German regime in 1989, the role of religious institutions and ideals has special significance. First, in embodying democratic ideals in its own life and in its relations with the state, the Evangelische Kirche spoke to the hopes and aspirations of much of the general population. Second, the church provided the free space in which alternative groups, though small and seemingly powerless, were able to develop an alternative politics that eventually helped stimulate the emergence of a mass, public opposition. Third, and perhaps most important, religious symbols and themes offered the alternative groups a powerful language and vision for articulating the ultimate importance of democratization.

In contrast to the church's more cautious, diplomatic approach to the state, many of the alternative groups were actively oppositional.[1] By the late 1980s they had become increasingly vocal and public, sometimes publishing underground newspapers and organizing illegal demonstrations. In the spring of 1989, they monitored the East German elections. Their determination that the official returns were fraudulent generated considerable social discontent. In the summer and fall of 1989, distressed about the tens of thousands of people wanting to leave the country—a situation that became critical as Hungary began to let East Germans cross its borders to the West—they were instrumental in founding a national, public opposition.

Others in the church, while not going as far, nonetheless helped organize worship services where people, concerned about their society's future, gathered to express solidarity with each other. The first public demonstrations for political change began after such services in Leipzig,
Dresden, and other cities, and were key to *die Wende* (the turn) that
finally occurred, nonviolently, in October 1989. Church people and people in church-related alternative groups soon found themselves organizing, and participating in, the round tables and citizen committees that
essentially ran the country until the elections of March 18, 1990. In
some cases, these people also emerged as viable candidates. More than
twenty pastors—for the most part, previously associated with alternative
groups—were elected to the new East German Parliament. Several assumed ministerial posts.

A review of recent literature on the democratization of Marxist-
Leninist states provides little insight into why and how religion played
such an important role. Some political theorists associate religion with
traditional, nationalistic forces that tend to emerge as the Communist
Party is delegitimated and loses its hold over repressed cultural impulses.[2]
These theorists would argue that religion is indeed one of the greatest
dangers to the success of democratization in these countries today. At
first glance, one might expect this analysis to apply to German Lutheranism as well, which historically has been a conservative force, supportive
of state authority. In the 1930s and 1940s, for example, broad segments
of the church supported Hitler. A small minority formed the Confessing
Church, but even then in opposition to Hitler's attempts to control the
church, not necessarily in opposition to many of his other programs and
ideas.

Some theories of democratization do help account for the emergence
of alternative groups, but not for religion's importance to them. Hannah
Arendt and, more recently, Adam Michnik and Vaclav Havel all see a
fundamental human desire for truth and freedom that in Marxist-
Leninist states eventually gives rise to small, self-organizing groups and a
"second culture."[3] One can see how these groups might gravitate to the
church if it were able to offer them a free space, as it did in Michnik's
Poland (though not in Havel's Czechoslovakia, where the state effectively controlled the church), but these theories do not explain why in
East Germany the groups not only attached themselves to the church,
but also developed a rhetoric deeply influenced by its symbols and
themes.

Moreover, judging just by the church's decline in social influence and
numerical strength by the 1980s, one would not have expected religion

to play a major role in democratization in East Germany. Nor were the alternative groups that met in the church's free space sizeable; altogether they numbered not more than a few thousand people.[4]

How, under these circumstances, could religion exert the influence that it apparently did? This chapter advances two major arguments. First, the church developed a theology with democratic political impulses that allowed it to challenge the state and offer alternative groups a free space. Second, Christianity offered alternative groups powerful symbols and themes that helped them articulate and organize their democratic concerns. These insights into the process of democratization in one Marxist-Leninist country also suggest the way in which religion might make a contribution to democratization elsewhere in the world.

The East German Church: Theology and Political Ethics

Over the forty years of East Germany's existence, a range of theologies and political ethics characterized different parts of the Evangelische Kirche. The emergence of a democratic political ethic depended on one theological development in particular—an emphasis on openness to the world, concern for the suffering and marginalized, and commitment to personal and social liberation.

The greatest rival to this democratic ethic was a conservative ethic associated with a particular reading of Luther's "two kingdoms" doctrine. Luther had argued that Christians live in two kingdoms: the kingdom of the Spirit and the kingdom of the world. Each kingdom is characterized by different authorities and requirements. The kingdom of the Spirit corresponds to the inner person. It is based on an ethic of love and peace, as practiced and taught by Jesus. Here the radical injunctions of the Sermon on the Mount apply; if one is attacked by one's neighbor, one does not seek revenge or recompense. The kingdom of the world corresponds to the outer person. It is based on an ethic of obedience to human authority, such as the state. In this case, one may indeed be required to use violence, as in the case of the state declaring war. It can be argued that Luther himself intended to keep a dynamic tension between the two kingdoms, but some Lutheran theologians tended to make them into two separate, independent realms.[5]

East German theologians developed this ethic in several directions. Some supported a political quietism. Even though they disagreed with the socialist state, they argued that one should obey it. The deeper meaning of life would be found through personal piety. Others appealed to

Luther to support the state. They argued that the kingdom of the world should be ruled by reason, and that Marxism-Leninism was the most rational political ethic.[6] Religion was limited to mastery of contingency as experienced in the personal realm, such as sickness, loss, and death.[7]

More characteristic of the church as a whole, however, was a theology deeply influenced not only by Luther, but by the thought and example of the Confessing Church. Even though the Confessing Church had an ambivalent attitude toward democracy, it did advance certain theological impulses that could be developed in that direction. Especially important was the Barmen Declaration of 1934, whose chief architect was Karl Barth, the noted Swiss theologian, who had taught in Germany until the rise of Hitler. Barmen argued for the freedom of the church and, while not explicitly calling for political democracy, did envision a church typified by equality and participation. Barth's own theology, moreover, developed the notion that the state, in its sphere, should correspond to the liberating impulses of the gospel, just as the church in its sphere.[8] Dietrich Bonhoeffer's theology also gave important impulses. Bonhoeffer had called for a church "for others," a church open to a world "come of age." He asked the church to be responsibly involved in the world, concerned for the suffering and marginalized, and open to cooperation with non-Christians on matters of common moral concern.[9]

East German theologians developed the implications of the Barmen Declaration, Barth, and Bonhoeffer around three christologically grounded emphases, each of which found some degree of realization in the church's life.[10] The first emphasis was that the church be open to the world.[11] Rather than separating the two kingdoms (inner and outer, religion and reason, personal morality and social justice), this theology emphasized the one kingdom of God, preached and embodied by Jesus. Through his life, death, and resurrection, this kingdom was already breaking into the world.[12] The radical message of the gospel was a possibility, even if never entirely a reality, in history. The church's place, therefore, was in the world.

This emphasis was reflected in the East German church's commitment to addressing those problems most threatening to the world's future.[13] In the early 1980s, the church especially concerned itself with peace, a major issue in both Eastern and Western Europe as the Cold War further escalated the arms race. Justice and the environment then emerged as additional dominant themes.[14]

On all these issues, the church's perspective was broad. It saw the local manifestations of these problems as inseparable from their global context, especially the modern propensity in both East and West to worship modern scientific-technological rationality.[15] The commitment to justice never focused exclusively on the East German context, but included also the third world. Similarly, problems of peace and environmental protection were linked to both national and international priorities. The church criticized the Soviet and American policy of deterrence, even as it opposed the increased militarization of East German society, as reflected in compulsory paramilitary education in school.[16] In addition, the church saw these problems as requiring both personal and social conversion. Peace described both an inner attitude and a concrete, political program. Justice and environmental protection necessitated changes in personal lifestyle as well as social, structural changes. The state alone could never be blamed for all the problems. Every individual shared complicity in and responsibility for the world's problems.

The church's second major emphasis, its special responsibility to the suffering and marginalized, was seen as exemplified by Jesus, who had emptied himself and gone to all people.[17] Even as the East German church increasingly found itself marginalized socially, no longer enjoying the status of a "people's church," it increasingly committed itself to going into the world, rather than expecting the world to come to it.[18] It sought to serve all people, Christian and non-Christian alike, but especially the marginalized, including those marginalized by the state. It saw itself as a free space in which people could gather and freely discuss their problems.

The third emphasis was the church's commitment to personal and social liberation. This liberation was first understood theologically. Christ, through his life, death, and resurrection, had freed people to a new way of life. As a living reality, the risen Christ continued to encounter all human beings and invite them to new life. In recognizing his presence and love, humans experienced "crisis" and "repentance," that is, transformation.

History, too, could be understood in a new way, not as predetermined and unchangeable, but as open to transformative impulses of love and service.[19] The church saw its commitment to "peace, justice, and the integrity of the creation" as grounded in a reality ultimately stronger than the world's ethic of control and manipulation, death and destruction.[20]

The Sermon on the Mount became an especially important expression of the East German church's hope in history.[21] As discussed in chapter 3, East German theologians disagreed on the theological definition and ecclesial application of such words as *openness*, *participation*, and *solidarity*. Yet they were generally able to agree that the Sermon on the Mount helped define a democratic imperative having these characteristics. Indeed, the church argued that such an ethic was a necessity if the world were to find a "survivable" (capable of surviving) form of community.[22]

In practical terms, these three emphases shaped a church that understood itself as a "church in socialism." It found its primary purpose in serving its society, rather than in opposing the Marxist-Leninist government. It supported cooperation and dialogue with the state whenever they would promote social good. Yet its theology provided reason to guard against any form of accommodation or of being co-opted. The church's standard was the kingdom of God, not any particular political ideology or program.[23] Appealing to Bonhoeffer's notion of "deputyship" (*stellvertretendes Handeln*), the church spoke on behalf of the suffering and marginalized.[24] It saw itself as mediating between society and state, and urged the state to address and correct social deficits.

Given the church's self-understanding, it is not surprising that alternative groups were attracted to its free space.[25] Some East German theologians regarded them as potential "covenant communities" living out the radical ethic of Christ. While the church, in support of the common good, would be more open than the groups to society as a whole and to political compromise, the groups reminded it of, and pushed it toward, the radical imperatives of the gospel.[26]

Yet this theology alone cannot wholly account for the role of religion in the democratization process. The church's theology also tended to brake any kind of radical social change.

First, the church was careful not to let itself be defined by either the state or the groups as a political opposition.[27] The church sought to become a positive force *in* socialist society. In doing so, however, it tended to repress the question of whether socialism, that is, Marxism-Leninism, was itself a viable, legitimate political order.[28] Second, because the church resisted identifying itself with any particular political ideology or program, it focused on addressing concrete social needs rather than arguing for a theory of democracy (in contrast, for example, to the American theologian Reinhold Niebuhr, who saw democracy as the closest political approximation to the gospel). Third, the church, though speaking on behalf of the marginalized, saw itself mediating between them and the state, not necessarily agreeing with them or their tactics. Indeed, as the groups became more radical, they and the church experienced increasing tension. The church was concerned that they not misuse its free space, while the groups sometimes accused the church of being as oppressive and undemocratic as the state.[29]

The Alternative Groups

Religion played a major role in democratization in East Germany not only because the institutional church had democratic impulses, but also because the alternative groups in its midst found religious symbols and themes that helped them articulate and organize a powerful social vision.

In a provocative study of these groups, Ehrhart Neubert, an East German Protestant sociologist of religion, argued that Marxist-Leninist society, not the church, reproduced religion.[30] In contrast to the Marxist-Leninist claim that religion would gradually disappear in socialist society, Neubert asserted that religion reappeared in "socializing groups" like the alternative groups that began to flourish in the East German church.

According to Neubert, society is a highly differentiated organism, stable yet evolving. Its health depends on the successful socialization—that is, integration—of individuals. Through socialization, individuals internalize values, learn roles, and develop personalities.[31] Socialization does not simply imply conformity; indeed, society also depends on criticism and innovation.[32]

Neubert argued that socialization normally occurs through a variety of social institutions, reflective of society's cultural complexity and diversity. A Marxist-Leninist state, however, tends to reduce cultural complexity and diversity. Through its dogma and organization, it shapes a unitary culture.[33] Through its unquestioned commitment to science and technology, it rationalizes all areas of life.[34] Correspondingly, it claims an exclusive responsibility for socialization and marginalizes other socializing institutions, such as the church.[35]

Neubert argued that state efforts to socialize individuals, for example, through ideology, were only partially successful. Individuals experienced the state ideology as deterministic, alienating, and closed, with the result that they withdrew into a private sphere. Social apathy and irresponsibility became increasingly pronounced. As a result, the state found itself constantly having to acknowledge and reappropriate selective pieces of the rejected cultural past (as occurred in the 1980s when the East German state "rediscovered" Luther and Bismarck, for example).[36] Moreover, alternative socializing institutions, such as underground cultural and economic structures, spontaneously appeared.[37] Socializing groups in the church shared several key characteristics: (1) They attracted individuals who felt alienated from society; (2) they represented communities of trust and shared experience; (3) they were highly critical of existing social structures and priorities; and (4) they sought to empower their members to change society.[38]

Neubert suggested that these groups accomplished socialization in two major ways. Drawing on Jürgen Habermas, Neubert identified "communicative competency" (*kommunikative Kompetenz*) as the first essential element of successful socialization.[39] If alienated from the public realm, individuals will seek a safe, alternative sphere in which to voice their frustrations and thematize their concerns. In East Germany, individuals gathered in the church because it represented this free space.[40] Socializing groups in the church offered an opportunity for open, genuine communication, which their members understood to rest on certain implicit, fundamental norms, such as equality, freedom, justice, love, and trust.[41] Because they saw these norms as absolute, self-evident truths, they also demanded them of society as a whole. Insofar as they practiced (or at least attempted) "domination-free communication" (*herrschaftsfreie Kommunikation*) among themselves, they regarded it as a real social possibility and program.[42]

Drawing on Niklas Luhmann, a West German sociologist, Neubert identified "contingency mastery" (*Kontingenzbewältigung*) as the second essential element of successful socialization.[43] Individuals feel threatened by contingency, that is, arbitrariness and unpredictability. In response, they find, in the culture itself, powerful symbols that thematize their experience and represent unquestionable, certain, absolute knowledge. Neubert suggested that individuals gathering in socializing groups in East Germany experienced contingency especially in terms of their experience of the state. In response, they claimed peace, justice, and nature as symbols of key importance.

Neubert argued that these symbols bore a cultural meaning, that is, they were not simply defined by Marxist-Leninist ideology but carried connotations and meanings formed over a long historical past and still available to society.[44] First, the symbols helped individuals articulate the way they personally experienced existential anxiety and guilt (their own fear about, and responsibility for, a world threatened by war, injustice, and environmental pollution) and social marginalization (by virtue of their alienation from a state that violated peace, justice, and nature).[45] Second, the symbols helped them articulate the fundamental norms of communication and behavior in their groups (one must speak and act in ways that are peaceful, just, and respectful of nature).[46] Third, the symbols helped them articulate the absolute values that they sought to realize in society as a whole. In this way, argued Neubert, peace, justice, and nature actually functioned as *religious* symbols. They became sacred, transcendent ideals. They demanded that one respond not in terms of scientific-technological rationality, but in terms of the total person. They carried an emotional power capable of evoking considerable passion and commitment. They constituted a new reality to be realized through inno-vative, creative means, in both the groups themselves and society as a whole.[47]

Moreover, Neubert believed that these religious symbols converged with Christian symbols. Because of Christianity's strong historical influ-ence, the culture's religious symbols—in this case, peace, justice, and na-ture—were largely Christian in content. Moreover, Christianity remained the only religious force in East Germany to which emergent sacred sym-bols could be attached. As a result, the socializing groups looked to the church for biblical, theological articulation of their concerns.[48]

Neubert's theory helps explain why the groups had a significant reli-gious dimension even though they did not always actively participate in traditional religious activities. The groups did not separate religion and politics. The emancipatory impulses that they found in Christianity helped them articulate and organize themselves and their larger political program around the democratic concerns of openness, participation, and responsibility.

The Political Rhetoric and Practice of the Alternative Groups

Neubert's theory also helps explain why the groups' rhetoric and practice reflected the emphases characteristic of the church's theology. In many ways, their vision of social change and renewal, even their vocabulary and argumentation, resembled the church's. But the groups were more radical and immediate in their demands. They transformed the church's democratic impulses into an opposition politics.

First, the groups, like the church, emphasized openness to the world and its problems. Their concern for the world was reflected in their call-ing themselves peace groups, two-thirds world groups, or environmental groups. They sought to develop expertise in both the national and inter-national aspects of these problems. They often asked resource people from state offices, as well as from the West, to make presentations at their meetings. Several groups established alternative libraries, such as East Berlin's peace library and environmental library, both housed in churches. Some groups published underground newspapers and calendars and arranged workshops to disseminate information not available from official East German sources. Their creative strategies were remarkable. In 1989, after travel restrictions to the West were liberalized, one environmental newspaper published information provided by several East German women who had asked Western laboratories to measure the level of dangerous chemicals in their breast milk. That same year, an alternative information fair in a Dresden church included a report from groups who, making a street-by-street survey of decaying housing, had found that current state policies would lead to the eventual razing of more dwelling units in Dresden than had been destroyed in World War II.

The groups, like the church, were concerned about the global as well as personal dimension of these problems. They tended to be critical of the West, seeing it as incapable of providing a viable model for a "surviv-able" community.[49] They were innovative in supporting a new personal lifestyle, calling for individual, voluntary reductions in automobile use, as well as asking the state to raise the prices of foodstuffs and utilities to encourage people not to waste them.[50]

Both the church and the groups saw the state as one manifestation of a larger problem of human anxiety and scientific-technological rational-ity.[51] The groups, however, focused the call for repentance on the state, demanding radical political change. Indeed, the imperatives posed by the global problems became a justification for political change at home. The groups complained that bureaucratism, corruption, conformism, dogma-tism, arbitrariness, and condescension were undermining public response to global, life-threatening issues and damaging the socialist promise.[52] They feared that people were losing the "peace potentiality" that the world desperately needed in order to survive.[53]

Second, the groups reflected the church's concern for the suffering and marginalized. While themselves marginalized, they resisted becoming small, sectarian cells. Even when they came under massive pressure from state infiltrators, as did several peace groups in East Berlin in the mid-1980s, they remained committed to welcoming strangers and to seeking out those whom the state marginalized ideologically.[54] They were re-markably inclusive of men and women, Christians and non-Christians, Marxists and non-Marxists. Moreover, several groups organized them-selves to help alcoholics and released prisoners not otherwise assisted by state and church agencies.

The groups, however, increasingly saw *all* of society as suffering and marginalized, and therefore argued for immediate political change. The Initiativkreis (initiative group) for *Absage an Praxis und Prinzip der Ab-grenzung* (Repudiation of the Practice and Principle of Delimitation) was organized in 1987 to oppose the state policy of "delimitation" (Abgren-zung), which included restrictions on travel, contact with foreigners, and democratic participation in government. The group described East German society as "sick" because of its isolation from the rest of the world.[55] Other groups argued for change because East German society was suffering from apathy, resignation, stagnation, denial, and lack of responsibility; indeed, many people were wanting to leave the country.[56] By the fall of 1989, a pastor deeply involved in the alternative scene could describe the emigration issue as a mass psychosis. "We are sick and apparently contagious."[57]

Third, the groups reflected the church's commitment to personal and social liberation. They strongly believed in the possibility of real political change. Their rhetoric drew consistently not only on the ideals of peace, justice, and nature as absolute values, but also on other powerful and more specifically Christian symbols and themes. The groups saw themselves as prophetic, and they easily adopted biblical, prophetic language. In early 1980s, they appropriated a symbol that the church had developed for its own peace program: a man beating swords into plowshares, a reference to an Old Testament prophetic hope (Mic. 4:3). The symbol quickly appeared on patches and buttons, spreading so rapidly that the state, fearing social unrest, banned them, even though the symbol's design, ironically, was based on a statue that the Soviet Union had given to the United Nations.[58] The initiative group against Abgrenzung made a similar appeal to biblical imagery in its initial statement, which bore the words of the prophet Amos (5:24): "But let justice roll down like waters, and righteousness like an everlasting stream."[59] Some groups, echoing John the Baptist and Jesus, called for social "repentance" and "conversion" (Umkehr, "turning around").[60]

Jesus' example and teaching (especially as summarized in the Sermon on the Mount) was especially important to the groups, as to the church. The initiative group against Abgrenzung appealed to Jesus' love of enemies and his willingness to cross all social and cultural borders.[61] Other groups emphasized the new kind of community that Jesus founded: liberated, liberating community characterized by domination-free communication, compassion, solidarity, equality, and responsibility.[62]

The groups even appropriated traditional religious activities for the sake of raising awareness and expressing solidarity. Many groups sponsored worship services on peace, justice, or the environment. In 1988, some organized a special monetary offering in the church to promote awareness of a planned brown coal processing plant in a highly polluted region of the country.[63] In Leipzig, only months before the Wende, others organized a "pilgrimage" from a local church to a polluted river. In 1987 (and again in 1988 and 1989) groups banded together to organize and attend church vigils and "solidarity services" after the state had arrested some of their members.[64]

For some groups, the Lord's Supper was also an important expression of their life together. In 1986, a number of campus ministers asked the church to allow non-Christians to participate in the Lord's Supper, an issue that generated heated theological debate and reflected the degree to which groups were appropriating Christian symbols.[65]

These religious symbols, themes, and rites gave the groups a strong sense of legitimacy and authority. They were important means of inspiring and empowering people to *act* on behalf of peace, justice, and the environment. Yet the very self-certainty of the groups posed a danger that they did not always recognize. Just because these religious symbols and themes did represent absolute values, the groups were tempted to distort and misuse them, to divide the world into forces of good and evil, and to resort to dictatorial action in the name of truth.

This dark, demonic side of religion and the danger of violence, hate, and destruction—all in the name of God (or liberation, or even peace, justice, and the environment)—threatened several times to rear its ugly head in the alternative groups.[66] After they monitored the 1989 elections and discovered that 10 to 20 percent of the electorate had rejected the list of the National Front (whereas the government claimed a 98.85 percent victory), considerable anger broke out.[67] Pastors reported increasing difficulty in keeping some groups from taking to the streets and seeking violent confrontation with authorities. Moreover, as social tension grew, more and more people began pouring into the alternative scene, making control and order increasingly difficult.

Violence, however, was largely averted. At a crucial time, the groups pushed the church to become more than a mediator. The church increasingly assumed a position of leadership in calling for immediate political reform. In 1988, the church's major synod asked the state for dialogue on a host of problems related to education, military service, and bureaucratic procedures.[68] In the fall of 1989, it called for specific social and political changes, including many of the democratic structures and practices that the alternative groups were demanding.[69] At the same time, pastors, sometimes appealing to the example of Martin Luther King, helped organize demonstrations. The church became an active force on behalf of political change and helped channel growing social anger and tension into nonviolent protest.[70]

Moreover, the church contributed a crucial element to democratization by constantly reminding people that their problems belonged in a larger social and theological context. East Germany needed reform not only for its own sake, but for the sake of a "survivable, global community."[71] The church also reminded people that they could not simply scapegoat the state. Again and again, the church's statements included elements of self-examination and confession. In calling on the state for dialogue, the church also acknowledged the need for greater dialogue within the church, among individuals, and before God. In calling for democratic reform, the church acknowledged its own failure, as an institution and as individual Christians, to live as an example of Christ's liberating power. It faulted its way of life for being more oriented toward having than serving, and its lack of community and unity. In responding to the phenomenon of resurging fascism, the church asked people to acknowledge and work through the German guilt of the past.[72] These elements of a higher responsibility and of confession countered the tendencies toward intolerance and self-righteousness that the growing public opposition sometimes displayed.[73]

In retrospect, it appears that in East Germany religion became a force toward democratization rather than reactionary politics because the tension between the church and the groups was creative. The groups continually pushed ahead, calling more loudly than the institutional church for quick and radical reform. The church, for its part, drawing on the very theological elements that braked radical political change, was able to help prevent a violent, revolutionary fanaticism.

Conclusion

An analysis of the role religion played in the process of democratization in East Germany suggests the contribution that religion might yet make to democratization elsewhere in the world. Three elements might be crucial.

First, a particular kind of theology might favor the development of a democratic political ethic. This theology would emphasize openness to the world (in the sense of recognizing and addressing local and global problems that are existentially threatening), a concern for the suffering and marginalized, and a commitment to individual and social liberation. It would include elements of self-examination and confession, as well as a vision of an inclusive, participatory, responsible community.

While Barth and Bonhoeffer gave the church these impulses in the East German context, other Christian theological traditions also seem capable of this contribution. Some political theorists have suggested that Protestantism has made a unique contribution to democratization.[74] The picture seems more complex, however. Every great theological tradition has resources that can be developed in different political directions—one need only think of Calvinism, which has contributed both to the ideology of apartheid and to Puritan theories of democracy. Similarly, Catholicism, though often associated in the past with a conservative political ethic, has spawned liberation theology.

Second, religion might be able to make a contribution to democratization if the institutional church, supported by such a theology, develops a positive relationship with alternative groups committed to democracy. The church may offer a free space, as in the case of East German groups and Latin American base communities. It may also provide leadership, as it did in East Germany, and as the black church did for the civil rights movement in the United States and the anti-apartheid campaign in South Africa.

Third, religion might contribute to democratization if there is a creative tension between the church's theology and the tendency of alternative groups to appropriate religious symbols and themes to legitimate immediate and radical political change. This creative tension is probably most likely in situations where the alternative groups draw on one major religious tradition and look to the church for articulation of symbols and themes of social change and reform. In a more pluralistic situation, it may be easier for radical religious and political tendencies to combine into new forms of fanaticism and intolerance.

Interestingly, the East German case suggests that sheer numbers are relatively unimportant. Both the church and the alternative groups were small enough that the state thought it had them well in hand, yet they clearly represented a transformative potential in society as a whole. Any study of democratization that ignores this religious potential is apt to miss what is most intriguing about it: the *kairos,* the fulfilled moment, in which an entire people suddenly seems filled with charismatic power to shape a new future based on the highest moral and spiritual principles.[75]

The Shape and Limits of the Church's Contributions to Democratization

In retrospect, it appears that the democratization of Eastern Europe and the Soviet Union was historically inevitable. At the time, however, the events beginning with the "new thinking" of Mikhail Gorbachev and coming to symbolic climax in the dismantling of the Berlin Wall took the entire world by surprise, most especially the very people living under communism.

Most scholarly theories of democratization have proved inadequate in their efforts to explain this unexpected fragility of Marxist-Leninist regimes. Zbigniew Brzezinski, for example, argued that democratization of Marxist-Leninist states would occur as their inefficient, command-structure economies faltered. Yet Brzezinski's economic determinism is finally unpersuasive. Writing in 1988, he predicted that countries like economically strong East Germany would be among the last to experience democratization.[1] In reality, its government collapsed as quickly as those of its neighbors.

Brzezinski's model is more generally problematic. Economics was not the major factor to spur democratization. Indeed, the depth of the economic crisis in Marxist-Leninist states was unclear until well after the democratization movements successfully challenged the Communist Party's monopoly on power.

Other political scientists have focused on cultural factors. Ralf Dahrendorf has suggested that democratization depends on the rebuilding of civil society, that is, autonomous, intermediate institutions that allow people to participate in shaping society—institutions that Marxist-Leninist states destroy in order to maintain themselves.[2] But Dahrendorf's reasoning proves circular; one could as well argue that the rebuilding of civil society depends on democratization. Dahrendorf does not account for the rise of the opposition reform movements that seek to rebuild civil society in Marxist-Leninist states—or for the fact that the rebuilding of civil society appears to unleash not only democratic forces but also forces that seek to reclaim primordial identities in association with new forms of authoritarian nationalism.[3]

Yet other scholars, such as Samuel Huntington, have emphasized that, besides economic and cultural preconditions, political factors determine the success of democratization. A political crisis, for example, may force an authoritarian regime to share power: "A central requirement would appear to be that either the established elites within an authoritarian system or the successor elites after an authoritarian system collapses see their interests served by the introduction of democratic institutions."[4] Huntington's approach, however, suggests that a political crisis is most apt to occur where ruling elites have to contend with organized oppositions having sufficient power to force a political crisis if their demands are not met. For this reason, Huntington, writing in 1984, predicted that democratization had its best chances in South America, not in Marxist-Leninist states in Eastern Europe, the Soviet Union, or elsewhere.[5]

While none of these factors alone is sufficient to explain the demise of Marxist-Leninist regimes, together they do suggest the complex dynamics that trigger and sustain democratization. Nor should one underestimate the role that a single leader such as Gorbachev can play. None of these approaches, however, acknowledges what was in fact most important to many of the opposition reform movements themselves. For them, the primary problem in a Marxist-Leninist state was not economic, cultural, or political but was nothing less than what they termed *spiritual,* that is, it had to do with what concerns people's deepest affections and passions and what gives their lives ultimate meaning and dignity. In a closely related way, members of these movements argued that fundamental moral concerns were also at stake, that is, how people express their loyalties and allegiances and what they trust and love and serve as "the good."

These movements did not precisely distinguish spiritual and moral concerns. They could easily appeal to either set of categories to articulate the basis of their opposition to the state. In their view, the Marxist-Leninist state sought to deny any dimension to life outside the scope of its own ideology and power. Because the state masked this ideology in the language of instrumental reason, members of the democracy movements sought to reclaim life's spiritual dimension, especially through the language of art, poetry, and philosophy. They grounded common moral responsibility in universal, humanistic ideals of equality, toleration, and democratic participation.

As noted in chapter 4, some scholars of democratization have recognized this spiritual-moral dimension of democratization, but they have not adequately accounted for the role that religion can play in articulating spiritual-moral concerns. They tend either to ignore religion altogether or to associate it with traditional, authoritarian forces that emerge as the communist state loses its hold over repressed cultural impulses.[6]

As has been shown, however, a significant part of the opposition reform movement in East Germany did emerge in a specifically theological context. This chapter argues that a careful analysis and assessment of the theological-political rhetoric of the East German church demonstrates the validity of interpreting democratization in spiritual-moral terms. Explicitly religious language provided people with a conceptual framework for critiquing the spiritual-moral impoverishment of the Marxist-Leninist state. It helped people examine and challenge their own complicity in the system; it offered them, moreover, a vision of responsible political engagement.

Analysis of the church's theological-political rhetoric also reveals that there were limits to the church's contributions to democratization. While religious language helped impel the emergence of a public opposition, it was never effectively translated into a concrete and persuasive program for a new political order. Religious language was far more useful at the first, rhetorical stage of protesting the Marxist-Leninist regime than at the second, pragmatic stage of building viable political institutions to replace it.

A note on the materials incorporating this distinctive East German rhetoric: Many appeared only in underground publications. Though some have since appeared in West German collections, they are not widely known elsewhere in the West. As scholars begin to analyze the contributions of the East German church and its groups to the democratization process, and to the formulation of a specifically East German vision of a unified Germany, these materials may shed valuable light.

The Spiritual-Moral Crisis of the Marxist-Leninist State

A key theme of East German theological-political thought was the spiritual-moral crisis of the Marxist-Leninist state. Especially representative are the writings of Heino Falcke, an East German theologian and churchman who had close ties to both the world ecumenical movement and the alternative groups that were instrumental in founding a political opposition.

Significantly, Falcke did not separate the spiritual-moral crisis of the Marxist-Leninist state from broader currents in the West. For him, an entire civilization was deep in crisis. In part, the crisis had to do with the way in which many people understood and exercised power as domination and self-assertion. People tried to control reality; they were obsessed with guaranteeing their security, even by means of force; they were driven by acquisition, consumption, and accomplishment; they found identity and purpose by "delimiting" themselves from others (practicing Abgrenzung) and by putting them down.[7]

The result was twofold. First, this kind of power threatened the very existence of the world. Falcke spoke of powers of death: the danger of nuclear war, the widening gap between the world's rich and poor, and the growing threat to the environment. Second, this power, though exercised by humans, caused them to feel profoundly powerless. They were spiritually and morally impoverished, "at their end," and "discontent." In a scientific, technological age, alienation was a widespread phenomenon. Though they were frightened by issues of global survival, people felt powerless to respond.[8]

Falcke located the roots of this crisis in the basic human experience of "anxiety," that is, people's insecurity and fearfulness about the value and worth of their lives. People turn to those "gods" that seem to promise power and security. In the modern world, people especially worship a scientific-technological rationality that promises power through knowledge and manipulation. Yet this very reliance on science and technology has led to the modern crisis. Humans use science and technology in ways that dominate nature and each other. They understand their own worth in terms of "having" rather than "being" and are constantly driven to achieve more power and control. Such an ethic ultimately results in more anxiety rather than relieving it.[9]

According to Falcke, the spiritual-moral crisis of the modern world assumed a special shape in the Marxist-Leninist state. First, in making the "scientific world view" its official ideology, the state denied that alternative ways of envisioning and constructing reality were possible. Second, in asking people to work and sacrifice for the sake of a future kingdom of material wealth, it justified socialist economic arrangements primarily in terms of their supposed ability to satisfy consumer needs. Third, its centralization of power hindered public participation and involvement in political life, resulting in pervasive social attitudes of apathy and irresponsibility.[10]

In sum, Falcke's theological critique of the modern situation in general led him to make a devastating critique of the Marxist-Leninist state in particular. Not only did he argue that its key problem was its spiritual impoverishment, but he suggested that this spiritual impoverishment produced a morally indifferent and immature citizenry. When people understood life only in terms of a narrow, instrumental rationality, they failed to experience and exercise moral passion for any good higher than their own self-interest. They lived only for the satisfaction of material needs and had little sense of a common good. In claiming that it alone defined and shaped reality, the state disempowered people; indeed, it dehumanized them in the sense of denying their capacity for responsible, moral action. East Germans found themselves in a spiritual-moral crisis. The only way out, suggested Falcke, was a new kind of relationship with God, based on confession and repentance.[11]

The Alternative Groups and the Rhetoric of Crisis

The same themes characterized the rhetoric of the alternative groups in the East German church. From the beginning, these groups drew on the church's biblical, theological analysis of the modern situation to critique the spiritual-moral failure of the modern world. Ultimately, they argued, this crisis had to do with the "self-destructive form of civilization" common to the communist East and the West.[12] They asserted that a rationalistic, deterministic ideology, with its roots in the modern world's narrow understanding of power, had become incapable of responding to the threats of nuclear war, social injustice, and environmental pollution.[13]

Yet the groups went further than the church in applying the language of spiritual-moral crisis specifically to circumstances in East Germany. Their rhetoric, as recorded in their underground publications, was direct and sharp.

The groups, for example, did not hesitate to apply their critique to the church itself. In the mid-1980s, some groups argued that the institutional church had become more concerned with maintaining itself than with serving people. They claimed that the church was restricting every expression of people's spontaneity, initiative, and self-determination, and that it was failing to address the urgent existential issues of the day: "the already-occurring war (against people; through armament; against the environment and against the two-thirds world)."[14] Its structures and practices, like the state's, were characterized by bureaucratization, incompetent leadership, the disempowerment of people at the grassroots of society, wasteful expenditures on "objects of self-representation," and a militaristic internal discipline.[15] The church, in appealing to "necessity" and "reality" to limit the groups' political engagement, was simply reflecting the kind of deterministic rationalism typical of modernity.[16]

In critiquing the East German state, the groups identified Abgrenzung (delimitation), which Falcke treated *theologically*, as the nation's key *political* problem. Group members believed that East Germans had become excessively narrow and incapable of openness. Social dialogue, communication, and cooperation had become increasingly impracticable. State and society were characterized by growing fear of each other.[17]

Though the groups were small, they helped articulate the underlying frustrations and resentments of the entire society. At the same time—and perhaps more effectively—the mass exodus of people to the West in the summer and fall of 1989 dramatically awakened the nation to a sense of crisis. In response, the alternative groups began to organize themselves as a national, political opposition. In their public statements, they frequently used words like *loss* and *destruction* to justify their decision to risk the state's displeasure. In their view, people had become so obsessed with the question of whether to leave the country or stay that they were focusing only on themselves rather than more critical social and global issues.[18] Society was falling apart, with the danger that much good would be irretrievably lost. The social achievements of the past—social justice, solidarity in community—were threatened. State policies were destroying the environment as well as the nation's cultural heritage. The moral foundations of society were also threatened, as evidenced by people's ever-increasing lack of social responsibility. The groups' members argued that the government and the people mistrusted each other, to the point that communication between them had completely broken down.[19]

In sum, while not assuming Falcke's theological presuppositions, the groups read the social situation in a way similar to his. The state's rationalistic, deterministic ideology was issuing in spiritual-moral crisis. Spiritual impoverishment had in turn resulted in popular moral failure. People had no sense of a good beyond themselves. They had no moral commitment to changing their society; they were incapable of working for positive political change. Paradoxically, however, the groups argued, this crisis might actually begin to move people to action. Events had reached a breaking point; the crisis had become personally and socially inescapable. Like Falcke, the groups found biblical themes of confession and repentance helpful as they sought to articulate how spiritual-moral crisis might eventually lead to spiritual-moral renewal. No longer could people simply blame the state for their problems. Every individual shared guilt for a preoccupation with personal self-realization that was ignoring, and contributing to, world disaster.[20] Every individual was guilty of practicing Abgrenzung and failing to respond to the larger problems at hand. Every individual had reason to engage in self-examination.[21]

Responding to the Crisis

The church's critique of the spiritual-moral crisis of the Marxist-Leninist state served as the basis for helping people examine and challenge their own complicity in the system. Drawing on powerful religious symbols, church leaders and thinkers developed a distinctive religious rhetoric of "peace, justice, and the integrity of the creation" to analyze the concrete political failings of the established order, to relate spiritual-moral renewal to universal, humanistic ideals, and to envision a new kind of nation and world.

Falcke was again representative. He argued that in the twentieth century, issues of peace, justice, and the environment had become "confessional" because they had to do with the very survival of the world. God's Word had a contribution to make to such a world: nothing less than a hope for its survival.[22]

With the help of Scripture, Falcke developed a Christian social ethic corresponding to this hope. God's Word is Christ, who rules all creation. Christ has entered the human condition, suffered its depths, and been raised to new life. Through his resurrection, his example and teaching (summarized, for Falcke, especially well in the Sermon on the Mount) have become authoritative expressions of the new life available to all.[23]

This christological orientation has important implications for how people can understand and live their lives. Christ is present to every human. Every human therefore has the possibility of encountering Christ and his love. In this encounter, humans become receivers. They discover that their value and worth are ultimately not an achievement, but a gift. Christ's love challenges and changes their lives. It drives them to "crisis" and "repentance" (Umkehr). They are liberated from anxiety and therefore from the obsession with power, and from a world driven by the values of "having," success, and economic growth.[24]

Christian freedom implies social responsibility. Indeed, the Christian ethic is one of "higher responsibility." "Instead of wanting to replace God, humans can correspond with God, responding to him as liberated, responsible partners."[25] Christian freedom includes others' freedom and creation's freedom. This sense of responsibility is fed by hope. Because Christ has entered history, the possibility of conversion and change is not only personal, but social. Christians see history as "an alterable, open process moving toward the kingdom of God."[26] "We then see our world no longer as something set, causally determined . . . and unimprovable."[27] Even when they see little visible success, Christians believe that they can change the world and that the world can surprise them with new possibilities. They live in trust and with a willingness to risk experimentation.[28]

Christian responsibility is also characterized by commitment to community because, "in corresponding with God, humans are relational beings."[29] In describing the nature of this community, Falcke appealed to two important biblical symbols: covenant and the kingdom of God. Both terms bear theological significance. First, they express that God initiates this community.[30] Second, they express that Christ, through his life, death, and resurrection, makes this community a real historical possibility. Third, they express that every human effort to realize this community needs renewal and correction.[31]

Covenant and kingdom help express the community's commitment to peace, justice, and the protection of the creation, and to their integral interconnection. In creating covenant, God gives peace, *shalom*, which the Old Testament prophets describe as living, sound, and therefore just relationship. In the Book of Deuteronomy, God commands Israel to observe every seventh year as a year of covenant renewal and of remission. Debts are forgiven, and relationships characterized by unjust dependency are annulled. Other parts of the Old Testament connect covenant to the integrity of the creation. The year of covenant renewal is the sabbatical year. The land is allowed to rest.[32]

These concerns find new expression and depth in the new covenant established by Christ. Through the Lord's Supper, Christians participate in the new covenant. They repudiate false gods and celebrate God's liberating power. They become a community. The Lord's Supper speaks to life-threatening global issues by, for example, symbolizing the priority of relationship over consumption.[33]

The characteristics of Christian community are also implied in the symbol of the kingdom, which the Sermon on the Mount explicates especially well. The promise of God's kingdom frees people from anxious worry about themselves. First, they are able to practice peace (expressed in loving enemies). Such peace is not simply an absence of war, nor an enforced state of security, but vital, positive community. Second, they are able to practice justice (expressed in the beatitudes, which bless the poor and suffering). Such justice demands a thinking that begins from the perspective of those who suffer, including those who suffer from structures and practices that could eventually threaten humanity itself. Falcke emphasized solidarity with the poor and the third world. He called, moreover, for measuring the impact of science and technology on those who suffer their impact, for example, the inhabitants of industrial areas. Third, the promise of God's kingdom frees people, in their relations with nature, to practice a "solidarity in conflict" (solidarity with nature while in conflict with it), which, though unable to eliminate human manipulation of nature, can limit it and make humans more sensitive to their impact on the environment.[34]

Falcke believed that the church could inspire the world to adopt this ethic only if Christians first exemplified the biblical understanding of liberation and community in their own way of life. The church needed to embody democratic structures and practices. Falcke therefore asked the church, first, to encourage openness. Such a church would not be elitist or exclusive. It would promote openness of discussion and information. Following Bonhoeffer, the church would be "for others," especially those who experienced suffering, including social and ideological marginalization. Just as Jesus associated with outcasts, Christians would seek to exercise love beyond every social boundary (Abgrenzung). Their covenant would be open to all. The Lord's Supper, correspondingly, would also be open to all who sought its promise of peace. Second, the church would encourage participation from below. It would bear with plurality and allow experimentation. It would emphasize consensus and domination-free communication. It would be critical of authoritarian arrangements. It would be open to renewal from the grassroots. Third, the church would seek to nurture interpersonal relationships characterized by commitment but also by tolerance. The church would practice solidarity with the weak and marginalized, and would promote reconciliation between individuals alienated from each other.[35]

The church would also promote these democratic characteristics in society as a whole. With respect to openness, it would encourage widening the public realm. It would oppose a state policy of Abgrenzung based on friend/foe thinking. It would promote contact with other peoples and the idea of a community of peoples. In terms of participation, it would support involvement from below, decentralization, and democratic structures that checked power. It would seek a politics that activated responsibility in all its citizens. In terms of nurturing committed, binding relationships, it would encourage a socialist alternative that recognized the primacy of social justice.[36]

In sum, Falcke drew extensively on Jesus' example and teaching, as well as on biblical concepts of covenant and kingdom, to envision the church as an alternative community. Through his resurrection, Jesus encounters every human being and offers the world peace, justice, and the integrity of the creation as real possibilities, not just distant ideals. Their realization, however, depends on humans first experiencing crisis in such a way that they repent, that is, relinquish their obsession with "having" and "achieving" and assume a higher responsibility for their society and world.

Alternative Groups and Biblical Imagery

The church-related alternative groups also appealed to many of these basic biblical themes as they coined a distinctive, oppositional political rhetoric. As with Falcke, the emphasis fell on the way in which confession and repentance could become the basis of a higher responsibility, that is, a commitment to peace, justice, and the integrity of the creation.

Jesus' example and teaching were central to these groups. Typical of their rhetoric is the assertion that Jesus comes "from below." Born in a stall, he belongs to the lowest social class and lives in opposition to all forms of political, religious, and social domination. His practice of forgiveness offers people freedom from the culture's legalistic morality. His sayings about work (e.g., the parable of the laborers in the vineyard in Matt. 20) challenge the presuppositions of a competitive, achievement-oriented society. Moreover, he appears neither to have money nor to pay taxes. Similarly, his "politics" are apparently "antipolitics," a complete rejection of state power (Mark 10:42).[37]

At times this rhetoric depicts Jesus as nothing less than an alternative group member. "If we were to translate the charges against Jesus into the language of today's laws, they might be: state-hostile agitation . . . [and] state-hostile group building," one underground leaflet declared, in reference to two East German laws to which the state appealed to threaten alternative groups.[38]

This Jesus calls people to repentance, that is, to changing their ways and opposing every form of evil and injustice. He himself constantly challenged every social limit and cultural barrier (Abgrenzung) by going to the weak and marginalized. Christian faith today also needs to seek ways of solidarity and reconciliation "across borders, beyond limits." Christians break tabus and speak the truth. They call for openness, understanding, and trust in place of Abgrenzung. By repudiating the state policy of Abgrenzung, the church would speak a "liberating word" on behalf of the marginalized, promote free and responsible citizenship, and witness to peace. Drawing on the Sermon on the Mount, Christians would see that their "first duty . . . is to overcome enmity . . . enmity that has found political form in the practice and principle of [the state policy of] Abgrenzung."[39] In a world threatened by destruction, to follow Christ, in opposition to Abgrenzung, was to stand for life. Repudiating the state policy of Abgrenzung was a "confessional" matter. Through practicing repentance, people assumed responsibility for radical political reform, and for new moral values equally emphasizing world peace, environmental protection, and third world justice.[40] By acting on a new vision of community, people would address the very crisis of modernity, which the Marxist-Leninist state had embodied rather than resolved.

In sum, the idea of an alternative community, which found considerable development in East German theological-political thought, also became the central focus of the alternative and opposition groups. Though they had little interest in the particular theology underlying the church's social vision, they did appropriate key biblical images and themes, especially those relating to the example and teaching of Jesus. Confession and repentance would become the basis for a higher responsibility both to the nation and to all humanity.

The Limits of Theological-Political Rhetoric

In the fall of 1989, the alternative groups helped found and support opposition parties that challenged the power monopoly of the Communist Party. At first these parties, like the groups that gave birth to them, envisioned an alternative politics. They wished to build a society similar in character to the alternative community that they had discovered in the church.

These parties saw themselves representing a new socialism, a necessary alternative to Western consumerist societies, a "survivable community" in a time of global dangers. Several expressed their commitment to building a "community of solidarity" (*solidarische Gemeinschaft*). In some cases, they also emphasized the need for a new personal lifestyle, for the sake of the social good and the natural environment.[41]

The words *social* (relating to social justice) and *ecological* appeared with particular frequency and emphasis in the rhetoric of the new parties.[42] Peace, the major issue of the early 1980s, though less emphasized (undoubtedly because of the relaxing relations between the superpowers), remained important for characterizing defense matters and international relations.[43] The groups' sense that this social vision had holding power was evident in the way they addressed economic concerns principally in terms of expanding individual freedoms and protecting social and ecological priorities.[44]

In this way, the opposition parties continued to draw on the rhetoric that had shaped the church and its groups. Yet the biblical, theological underpinnings of this rhetoric were no longer evident. While "peace, justice, and the integrity of the creation" still represented powerful ideals, they were now embedded in general political discourse, rather than in the more specific symbols and themes of the church's scriptures and traditions.

Furthermore, the rhetoric that had so effectively voiced public discontent and mobilized public opposition seemed increasingly vapid and unclear to the public as it pushed the new parties to articulate concrete programs. The church and its groups had challenged a world driven by having and achieving. They had argued that East Germany enjoyed a high standard of living; economic concerns should not be at the forefront. Yet as East Germans confronted the practicalities of overhauling an economic system, they discovered just how far the nation had been living beyond its means. Economic concerns in fact quickly came to dominate political discourse. East Germans were increasingly attracted to the West German social market economy, which valued both individual achievement and social welfare and was clearly efficient and productive. They were hesitant to approve a "third way" or any new "socialist" experiments in a democratic East Germany.

The vision of an alternative community, rhetorically so effective under a totalitarian regime, no longer seemed a viable prospect; nor were its advocates able to give it concrete political and economic formulation. An "antipolitical politics" based on a "higher responsibility" had helped people resist the Marxist-Leninist regime; now this understanding of politics appeared incapable of defining new institutions. The cry *Wir sind das Volk* (We are the people) soon became *Wir sind ein Volk* (We are one people); East Germans called for unification with West Germany. Those opposition parties, such as Bündnis '90 (Alliance '90), that remained most connected to the rhetoric of the alternative groups did worst in the elections of 1990. Those, like the Social Democrats, that joined with the West German parties largely relinquished the rhetoric of the past in favor of established political programs.

Nonetheless, the failure of a particular kind of rhetoric to translate itself into the pragmatic task of building new political institutions did not mean that the vision that had once grasped the church and its groups was completely lost. As a new group of East German politicians emerged, several theologians played a leading role, drawing on the East German experience to reflect on the theological-political dimensions of democratization. Some continued to appeal to the particular rhetoric that had characterized the alternative groups; others were more critical of it. Yet, in both cases, they sought to use theological-political categories to articulate the deeper meaning of political life and political responsibility.[45] Again, at this rhetorical level, theology continued to make a genuine, if limited, contribution to political discourse.[46]

Conclusion

The language of spiritual-moral crisis, confession, repentance, and higher responsibility made a significant contribution to Christian social ethics in East Germany. As the two Germanies united, East German church leaders rearticulated these themes as their distinctive contribution to a vision of a new Germany.[47]

The East German theological-political thought of this time suggested three key points of significance to Christian social ethics in both the West and the East. First, Christian social ethics would begin with an analysis of the spiritual impoverishment of the modern situation. It would attend to the degree to which mass, consumer society makes religious claims, that is, emphasizes having and achieving as solutions to anxiety and powerlessness, while in fact creating new forms of anxious dependency and misuse of power. It would critique all ideologies that reduce the meaning of life to a narrow understanding of human reason and control.

Second, Christian social ethics would call people to confession and repentance. Every person in a mass, consumer society succumbs to ideologies of having and achieving at the expense of peace, justice, and the integrity of the creation. Through confession and repentance, one can seek a new way of life. One can become responsible to a good higher than self-interest or group interest.

Third, Christian social ethics would contribute to the building of an alternative community capable of responding to problems of peace, justice, and the integrity of the creation. This task could begin in the church but had implications for society as a whole. In either case, democratic values, such as openness and participation, were not ends in themselves, but means to promoting a higher responsibility for life—individually, socially, and globally.

For each of these three points, the East German theological-political thought of this time demonstrated ways in which Scripture could help describe the nature of Christian democratic responsibility. In particular, the Sermon on the Mount was reclaimed and interpreted not as representing a sectarian vision but as relevant to the sociopolitical order as a whole.

The language of spiritual-moral crisis, confession, repentance, and higher responsibility also found significant parallels in the opposition reform movements that emerged in other Marxist-Leninist states, though these movements did not often use explicitly religious language. A number of prominent East Bloc opposition leaders argued that the crisis of the Marxist-Leninist system was primarily spiritual-moral. People had traded truth and freedom for material security. They had submitted to the state ideology not out of conviction, but out of a need to deceive themselves about the emptiness and crassness of their lives. They had learned to live in a lie.

Vaclav Havel gave especially forceful articulation to the causes and consequences of this way of life.

> The profound crisis of human identity brought on by living within a lie, a crisis which in turn makes such a life possible, . . . appears, among other things, as *a deep moral crisis in society*. A person who has been seduced by the consumer value system, whose identity is dissolved in an amalgam of the accoutrements of mass civilization, and who has no roots in the order of being, no sense of responsibility for anything higher than his or her own personal survival, is a *demoralized* person. The system depends on this demoralization, deepens it, is in fact a projection of it into society.[48]

In response, these movements, like the one in East Germany, called for spiritual-moral renewal. This spiritual-moral imperative took different social forms, however. In China, the tone of the students involved in the Tiananmen Square protests was nationalistic. They saw the Chinese government as caught in feudalistic patterns and unable to advance national interests. They wanted to save the nation.[49] In the Soviet Union, Boris Kagarlitsky, a leading intellectual and dissident, called for reform for the sake of saving Russian culture and renewing the humanistic vision that he found in Marx.[50]

In other cases, intellectuals, in a way more similar to East German theological-political rhetoric, linked spiritual-moral renewal with the very salvation of civilization and the world. Fang Lizhi, the Chinese physicist and dissident, asked intellectuals to have a strong sense of social responsibility and concern for people's physical as well as spiritual-moral needs.[51] Havel called for a new sense of social responsibility in a world threatened by scientific-technological domination.[52]

In calling for social responsibility, these leading dissidents in the communist East also articulated a distinctive notion of national identity. In contrast to those who dismissed Marxism-Leninism as an alien ideology imposed on the nation from without, they called for national repentance, that is, acknowledgement of the entire nation's complicity in the Marxist-Leninist system. In contrast to those who supported a narrow, even reactionary nationalism, they called for a national commitment to universal, humanistic ideals.

This brief review demonstrates that religious language was not the only language that could help articulate the spiritual-moral concerns of the opposition reform movements in the communist East. The fact that religious language did, however, play such a significant role in East Germany undoubtedly had to do with the unique position of the church as a free space in which alternative groups gathered and appropriated religious language. As the groups left the church and were able to organize as a public, political opposition, they too appealed to more general moral formulations to articulate their concerns.

At a time when Americans hear almost exclusively about economic and political reasons for social change, the experience of East Germans and other Eastern Europeans argues for careful investigation of the spiritual-moral dimensions of politics. Part III discusses how the sensitivity to this dimension helped shape a new democratic order in East Germany.

THE CHURCH

AND THE NEW

DEMOCRATIC

ORDER

6

Theologians and the Renewal of Democratic Political Institutions

O n March 18, 1990, East Germans participated in their first and last free elections as East Germans. The party that emerged with the majority in the new Parliament, the Christian Democratic Union (CDU), campaigned on the platform of rapid unification. On October 3, 1990, union became official, and the GDR was a relic of the past.

The subsequent, difficult process of social and economic transition in eastern Germany has obscured the deeply formative political experience that originally accompanied the emergence of a public opposition to and the demise of the Marxist-Leninist state. While few of the new political groups were able to translate their original enthusiasm and idealism into a viable political program, all participated in a lively and significant exchange of views concerning the purpose of government and the nature of popular participation in politics.

Pastors and leaders of the Evangelische Kirche played a significant role in this debate. Some, like Heino Falcke, deliberately refrained from entering electoral politics. They called for a democratization of the church that would draw on the insights of the alternative groups. Others quickly gained prominence in the major German political parties. Even before unification, Manfred Stolpe, formerly the chief administrative officer of the East German Federation of Evangelische Kirchen, had important contacts in the West German Social Democratic Party (SPD). With unification, he won election as a Social Democrat, becoming minister-president of Brandenburg, one of the East's new federal states. Heinrich Fink, formerly the dean of the theological faculty at the Humboldt University—and briefly rector of the university itself—eventually ran for elected office as a member of the Party for Democratic Socialism (PDS), which succeeded the East German Communist Party.

Two Protestant theologians, Wolfgang Ullmann and Richard Schröder, played a particularly significant role in the debate by giving creative and systematic articulation to the issues at stake. Ullmann, born in 1929 in Saxony, part of the Soviet Zone after World War II, served as a parish pastor for nearly a decade, then became professor of church history at the Protestant seminary in Naumburg. In 1978 he was called to teach at the Protestant seminary in East Berlin. Ullmann's interest in the early church fathers, the Radical Reformation, the history of law, and the philosophy of Eugen Rosenstock-Huessy shaped his commitment to an alternative politics.

Schröder, also from Saxony, belonged to a younger generation. Born in 1943, his early memories were not of World War II, but the Cold War, when the East German state was consolidating its power and defining itself over against West Germany. Schröder's Christian upbringing put him at social disadvantage. Whereas Ullmann had been able to study in the West, Schröder did not even receive permission to attend high school. Completing his education in church institutions, he served as a parish pastor for four years, before being called, in 1977, to teach philosophy at the seminaries in Naumburg and East Berlin. Largely self-educated in philosophy, Schröder offered a classical approach that was unavailable at the state universities, where Marxist-Leninist ideology dominated. The Greeks, especially as interpreted through Hannah Arendt, shaped his commitment to politics as a matter of rational debate. He believed that the possibility of such debate depended especially on stable political institutions and on popular participation in politics.

This chapter describes and assesses the role that Ullmann and Schröder played in debating the terms in which democratization should proceed in East Germany. While unification brought about a practical political resolution to the debate, the debate itself remains significant. It illuminates the political attitudes of an entire generation of young East Germans who actively participated in the Wende, and it illustrates the degree to which different understandings of human nature and its capacities for community underlie different understandings of popular participation in government.

Wolfgang Ullmann

As the hard work of shaping and running democratic institutions began in early 1990, the right to self-government unleashed a lively debate, especially among those in the Evangelische Kirche who had led the Wende. Ullmann and Schröder had been colleagues at the seminary in East Berlin. Both had been close to the alternative groups. Both had played a key role in the church's Conciliar Process for Peace, Justice, and the Integrity of the Creation, which had openly criticized the government's human rights record.[1] Yet Ullmann and Schröder developed two very different approaches to politics and came to find themselves in competing camps.

In the late 1980s, Ullmann emerged as a spokesman for the church-related alternative groups and eventually helped found one of the first public opposition groups, Demokratie Jetzt (Democracy Now).[2] During the tumultuous days of 1989, he regularly addressed mass gatherings in the East German churches, as well as the Western media.[3]

With the opening of the Berlin Wall on November 9, 1989, East Germany's future came into question. Economic and political collapse was imminent. The country needed a new government that could win broad political participation and legitimation. Replacing their leaders and initiating reform, the communists desperately fought to retain their power. They were able to win little popular support, however. As a result, the church, as well as prominent leaders of the new political parties, feared the possibility of civil war, and of a political coup, especially if reactionary forces in the military or secret police organized themselves.

In this context, Ullmann played a crucial role in working with church leaders, who alone enjoyed widespread popular support, to organize a national Round Table to bring government and opposition leaders together to negotiate political transition, including revision of the Constitution and preparation for free elections.[4] Leaders of the Evangelische Kirche, together with leaders of the Roman Catholic Church and the Protestant free churches, convened the first Round Table on December 7, 1989, and moderated its meetings until it disbanded on March 12, 1990, shortly before parliamentary elections.[5]

Initially, the government refused to attend. But when Hans Modrow, the new communist premier, attempted to reorganize the hated secret police into a ministry of national security, the Round Table finally gave him an ultimatum. From the middle of January on, he participated in the Round Table, and it essentially assumed legislative powers, both vetoing government proposals and setting forth its own agenda, including measures relating to economic reform, environmental protection, property rights, and immigration.

Ullmann himself served as a minister without portfolio in Modrow's last cabinet. With the nation's first free elections, Ullmann was elected to the East German Parliament, and, within the Parliament, vice-president. With unification, he won a seat in the German Bundestag as a member of a small coalition, Bündnis '90, which was representative of the original opposition groups. While East Germany as a whole quickly distanced itself from these groups (and largely supported the two parties—the Social Democrats and the CDU—that had united with their Western counterparts), Ullmann continued to enjoy considerable respect, and his ideas represented an important, while clearly minority, political position.

Ullmann was deeply impressed by his experience with the Round Table, which included representatives of every major social organization and political party, both old and new. While these groups had varying degrees of public support, the Round Table invited each of them to send the same number of representatives (two), thereby establishing parity among them. Moreover, the Round Table operated on the principle of consensus. While not always attaining complete agreement, the Round Table took pains to allow all voices to speak, and to seek common ground.[6]

Ullmann argued that the Round Table represented a new way of doing politics. First, he saw it as providing for much broader social and political representation than most elected bodies, in which large coalitions rule and smaller groups are either marginalized or unable to attain enough votes to be represented at all. Second, it involved all participants in a search for the common good. It was not an exercise in mere power politics, with different interests competing for superiority, but a common striving for what was just *(Recht)*. It asked participants to speak the truth as best they knew it, confident that consensus would emerge as open, honest dialogue took place. Third, the Round Table was an effort to build and sustain intimate community. It was small enough to allow its members to get to know each other. Despite their differences, they had a sense of common purpose and mutual need.[7]

Prior to unification, members of the Round Table, including Ullmann, prepared and proposed a new East German constitution that incorporated elements of their experience with the Round Table.[8] Because the new East German Parliament was deeply divided on the question of a new constitution and increasingly focused on issues of unification with West Germany, the proposal soon died. Nonetheless, the treaty of unification included a provision for a parliamentary commission to study the possibility of writing a constitution to replace the West German *Grund-*

gesetz (the so-called foundational law that West Germany had adopted after the war in lieu of a constitution, in order to avoid appearing to legitimize the division of the country). In this way, the Round Table proposal stimulated the commission's work, even though the proposal itself found little acceptance.

As a member of the Bundestag, Ullmann continued to argue for the Round Table's proposal, and for alternative political structures that would embody the possibilities of the Round Table model. While recognizing the limitations of the Round Table, especially at the national level, he argued that no state could address and solve major social issues without widespread citizen involvement and support. At the local level, he saw the Round Table model as even more viable.[9]

In part, Ullmann wished to address what he saw as the current political malaise of the Western world. Democratic theory affirms the people's capacity for self-government; in practice, however, many people, even in a democracy, feel alienated or apathetic.[10] They sense that they have little real choice when they go to the polls, and that they elect officials who have little direct accountability to them, at least not until the next election. Ullmann saw the Round Table as a model that could help ameliorate these frustrations and contribute important impulses to democratic renewal.[11]

Ullmann's position rested on a particular theological and philosophical orientation and critique. He argued that Marxism-Leninism had a mechanistic model of power and justice. The state sought to organize society in such a way as to produce equality. The result was the opposite: massive violation of human rights.[12] For Ullmann, the West too was threatened by forms of power politics in which the strongest party imposes its will and calls it justice. Drawing on the example and teaching of Jesus, he argued for conceiving power and justice in terms of equality rather than hierarchy.[13] This vision of a new kind of community was not narrowly political, in the sense of belonging only to the state. On the contrary, it found its ultimate realization in the church. The church, however, could challenge the state to embody this kind of community in its sphere, and to exercise its power in ways that helped individuals claim their fundamental right to self-government.[14]

Ullmann argued against an overly individualistic understanding of rights. People would need to exercise their rights not against each other but for each other. Only by working together would they be able to address and solve the questions that threatened their survival. Ullmann argued that such cooperation could best be achieved in smaller political units. The renewal of democracy would therefore depend on the decentralization of power and population. Only as people live in communities in which they actually know each other can they seek a common good.[15] When people exercise their rights together, they give voice to justice (Recht) together.[16] Law ultimately depends on consensus in community. Ullmann argued that the Sermon on the Mount, while it remains an ideal that criticizes and corrects every earthly reality, finds realization in this kind of political community.[17]

Richard Schröder

To those who had prepared for, and participated in, the Wende, Schröder represented a major alternative to Ullmann. In the mid-1980s, Schröder had organized a reading and discussion group for students from the seminary in East Berlin. Meeting quietly in his home over several years, this group addressed major philosophical questions about the nature of the state, justice, and politics. Eventually, core members of the group began to chart an alternative political course for East Germany, and in the summer of 1989 they founded the East German Social Democratic Party, another of the first public opposition groups.

Schröder joined the Social Democratic Party and, like Ullmann, was elected to the new East German Parliament. He served as head of the Social Democratic faction and helped forge the "great coalition" with the Christian Democrats that prepared the way for unification. With unification itself, he returned to teaching but remained active in politics. A gifted speaker and writer, he became one of the best-known East Germans in the united German SPD.[18]

Schröder agreed with Ullmann that the Round Table had been a necessary institution during a time of national emergency and transition. But he was also critical of its work, arguing that its drive to achieve consensus hindered its ability to confront and challenge the Marxist-Leninist government. Moreover, its control of legislation had been profoundly antidemocratic; none of its representatives had been popularly elected.[19]

Schröder drew a sharp distinction between the private and the public.[20] In the private realm, characterized by such institutions as family and church, people meet each other in varying degrees of intimacy. They reveal themselves to each other. They form their deepest convictions and practices. In the public realm, by contrast, people have a persona; they wear a mask. Their private lives and beliefs are not necessarily relevant to the performance of their public duties.[21]

Schröder saw Ullmann's concerns—dialogue, consensus, intimate community—as belonging to the private realm. They were matters of individual choice and commitment. The state could neither produce nor guarantee them; at most, it could help foster the external circumstances that provided for them. Politics belongs to the public realm. It entails compromise rather than consensus, the possible rather than the ideal, justice rather than love.[22]

Nonetheless, these two realms are not entirely separable: The private conditions the public. If politics is to be more than power politics, it requires people to have a sense of justice. They must come to politics with convictions about what is morally right and wrong. Moreover, their convictions must give them a sense of political responsibility—that is, responsibility to a common good—rather than mere self-interest.[23]

Convictions, however, cannot always find political realization, for politics requires negotiation and compromise, and convictions, though they can be modified, cannot be negotiated or compromised.[24] In this sense, Schröder, like Ullmann, saw the Marxist-Leninist model of power and justice as deeply flawed.[25] Politics is a matter of *poesis*, not of the mechanical application of ideals or an ideology.

In contrast to Ullmann, however, Schröder argued that democracy rested on twin foundations. Ullmann called for the renewal of public life by the introduction of elements of intimate community into it. Schröder called for the renewal of both the public, governmental realm (e.g., through constitutional standards and safeguards, such as the separation of powers) and the private, nongovernmental realm—but apart from each other.[26]

Schröder argued that, in an age in which the social anonymity and instability of mass society seem to undermine intimacy and community, people are tempted to seek intimate community in the public rather than the private realm.[27] He feared that such a politics easily becomes moralistic, imposing a particular set of opinions or feelings as public policy.[28] He called instead for society to recover forms of "binding community" (*verbindliche Gemeinschaft*) in the private realm.[29] As people acquire a sense of right and wrong, as well as skills of arguing, testing, and modifying their convictions, they begin to develop a "political culture," and to overcome the alienation, apathy, and conformity so characteristic of modern life. They slowly become capable of critical thinking, self-government, and political responsibility.[30] This political culture, though private (in Schröder's terms), is the precondition for the renewal of public life.

Rights, too, had a different significance for Schröder than for Ullmann. Ullmann saw rights as reflecting and establishing a fundamental equality among persons. This equality becomes the basis for shared experience, mutual concern, and intimate community. In this way, Ullmann again tended to blur the boundary between the private and the public. For Schröder, by contrast, rights functioned differently in the private and public realms, though they were in both cases grounded in an equality of human beings before God, as established by Christian doctrines of creation and redemption.[31]

This fundamental equality first finds expression in the private realm, especially the church. Christians have the rights of brothers and sisters. They share deep convictions about right and wrong; they seek open, honest discussion of what is true and good; they practice love and forgiveness.

This fundamental equality of human beings before God also has implications for the public realm. If every person has a relationship with God, whether acknowledged or not, others must respect and protect that person's private realm. The experience of the religious wars of the sixteenth and seventeenth centuries convinced people that this equality of conscience would be best protected through the law. Equality before God necessitates equality before the law, expressed in rights that find state protection.[32]

Like Ullmann, Schröder argued that rights always imply duties. One's rights do not simply protect one from others; they require one to respect others. In this sense, rights are the very foundation of community.[33] Unlike Ullmann, Schröder again saw private and public levels of community. The kind of community that one may experience in the church does not provide a model for political life. Nonetheless, the church can make an essential contribution to building the political culture that makes public, political life and democratic government possible.[34]

How, then, can individuals best participate in government? What is required of them, and how can they best represent their interests? In assessing the relationship of intimate community to political community, Ullmann and Schröder engaged in an implicit debate about the parameters of democratization. Their debate suggested that negotiating the rules of participation in the new political system would not simply be a matter of power politics. Nothing less than differing views of human nature and its capacities for community were at stake.

Issues of Popular Political Participation

The members of the church-related alternative groups that helped lead the East German Wende agreed that democracy alone could guarantee people the fundamental political rights that find classic formulation in the American Bill of Rights: freedom of speech, assembly, and press; respect for the integrity of the individual; protection from government interference. Moreover, they shared a common concern that individuals exercise their rights for the sake of social, economic, and political renewal. The Marxist-Leninist state had devastated the nation's political, economic, and cultural life. It had proven itself incapable of addressing issues of both national and global survival, especially in relation to peace, justice, and environmental protection.

People who had once adapted, and even accommodated themselves, to political powerlessness now had the responsibility to reclaim a sense of civic duty. Demokratie Jetzt and Bündnis '90 drew people who argued for a kind of democracy that would provide for a much greater degree of popular participation than they saw in West Germany. Others, such as those who joined the Social Democratic Party or the reformed CDU, argued that the West German political system was basically sound—and, in any case, more desirable than any new experiment in "democratic socialism."

As the new East German political leadership negotiated the terms of democracy and of popular participation in government, three questions came to the fore; Ullmann and Schröder answered each differently:

(1) *How does the question of truth relate to the question of power?* The alternative groups believed that Marxist-Leninist ideology had destroyed political life. People had lost the capacity for critical thinking. They had forgotten or ignored their ability to ask questions of fundamental truth. They had, to borrow Vaclav Havel's phrase, "lived in a lie." In gathering to discuss and examine pressing social issues, the groups saw themselves making the first moves toward "living in truth."

Ullmann further developed this position. The key skill for people who seek to govern themselves is dialogue. Through dialogue, they seek the truth, realizing that each has a contribution to make. Through dialogue, they ultimately come to consensus about the way things are and should be.[35]

Schröder criticized this position. He argued that dialogue about truth, because it involves people's deepest convictions, is essentially a private affair.[36] Politics, as a public affair, begins with, but cannot stop at, dialogue. A government that waits until dialogue becomes consensus will never be able to act quickly or resolutely, for dialogue and consensus require more time than political reality ever allows. Politics is always conditioned by the necessities and limitations of the moment.[37]

To Schröder, Ullmann appeared to imply that those who have the truth have the right to exercise power. Schröder saw this position as problematic in two respects, both of which had parallels in Marxism-Leninism. First, despite Ullmann's rejection of Marxism-Leninism, his position still seemed to assume a mechanistic model of truth, as though truth were something that one simply grasps and applies, with a specific political result in mind.[38] Second, Schröder saw a position like Ullmann's as easily leading to the danger of political elitism. A particular group, in the name of the people, claims to discover and realize a shared truth on their behalf.[39]

(2) *What kind of competency gives one a right to participate in political decisionmaking?* The alternative groups argued for a "competence of the affected" *(Kompetenz der Betroffenheit)*. Insofar as their members felt threatened by global and domestic issues of peace, justice, and the environment, they argued that they had the right and responsibility to act politically. They not only organized seminars and protests, but also called for specific changes in laws and policies.

Ullmann's position drew on these insights. He argued that the state, in addressing major social issues, needed the advice and counsel of as many people as possible. It would want to draw on the insights of those with professional credentials, but also on the insights of those most affected by different courses of action.[40] Indeed, at the local level, affected laypeople bring great motivation to addressing and solving even the most pressing and complex issues, and can quickly develop any necessary expertise.[41]

Schröder argued strongly against the idea of a competence of the affected, maintaining that a politics that measures competency in terms of suffering is potentially "terroristic," imposing one group's opinions and feelings on all society.[42] Because the problems that threaten human survival are highly complex, wise political decisionmaking ultimately depends on consulting primarily those whose competence is based on knowledge and expertise.

Schröder acknowledged that popular discussion of these issues is essential. They affect every person to some degree. But he argued that this kind of discussion should take place in the private realm. True dialogue would depend, moreover, on more than a sharing of mere opinions and feelings. Those who are uninformed have a right to join in the conversation but also a responsibility to educate themselves, at least generally, about the issues that face them locally and globally.[43]

This private conversation nonetheless has public import. By becoming competent participants in the discussion of public issues, laypeople are able to demand accountability from those who, because of their expertise, shape public policy.[44]

Schröder agreed with Ullmann that government at the local level would offer the best opportunities for laypeople who feel "affected" to become involved in policymaking and to develop an expertise that can make a genuine political contribution. In contrast to Ullmann, however, Schröder argued that problems of global and national magnitude—peace, justice, and the environment—are not necessarily best solved at the local level. They are simply too complex.[45]

(3) *What form of representation best respects one's right to participate in political decisionmaking?* The alternative groups practiced direct democracy in shaping their own life; with the fall of the Wall, they envisioned bringing elements of direct democracy into postcommunist political structures. They dismissed established political parties as interest groups that did not necessarily reflect the public will. They saw representative democracy as disempowering ongoing public participation in political decisionmaking. Key to the experience of the alternative groups had been the political awakening of an entire nation, of crowds peacefully gathering in churches and streets, shouting "We are the people" (Wir sind das Volk). As the communist government crumbled, self-organized "citizen committees" had helped to organize and maintain public services, as well as to occupy and secure the buildings of the secret police. The people had demonstrated and proven their right to govern themselves.

Ullmann, too, was deeply impressed by these events. For him, the high point of the revolution was the mass demonstration that took place in East Berlin on November 4, 1989.[46] On that day, only a week before the Wall fell, a million East Germans peacefully gathered at Alexanderplatz, in the heart of the city. Organized by the nation's artists and writers, this demonstration called specifically for the state to respect people's political rights, especially freedom of speech, assembly, and the press.

Inspired by "the people," Ullmann called for a politics that could continue to empower them and to learn from their experience and wisdom.[47] For him, the renewal of democracy meant the reconstruction of politics from the ground up. Local groups, able to organize and govern themselves, would make many of the decisions currently made at the national level.[48] Ullmann also argued for incorporating elements of direct democracy into national decisionmaking. Citizen groups should have the authority to bring bills directly to the Parliament for consideration, and major laws should come to the people for decision by referendum.[49]

Schröder again offered a sharp critique of this position. More clearly than Ullmann and the alternative groups, he saw that the cry for German unification, Wir sind ein Volk (We are one people), would prove more enduring and significant than the earlier Wir sind das Volk (We are the people). He was concerned to draw on the political traditions and experience of the West.

While open to some elements of direct democracy, Schröder argued that its usefulness was limited.[50] In a highly complex world, there can be no return to a romanticized past of radical political decentralization. Moreover, a direct democracy poses the danger that policy will be made by assertion and acclamation, as under Marxism-Leninism, rather than by discussion and negotiation. When the focus is on swaying the masses, politics easily becomes an exercise in demagoguery rather than democracy. Schröder argued that representative democracy actually ensures rather than undercuts accountability. People can know who supports a particular position; a popular referendum leaves no such possibility. For this reason, parties also play an important role in a democracy. They help provide stability and continuity, and they enable the development of clear political positions that can come to public discussion and debate.[51]

Conclusion

Though Ullmann and Schröder never explicitly directed their polemics against each other, they were among the most articulate spokesmen in a debate that shaped East German politics in the brief time between the emergence of a public opposition to the Marxist-Leninist state in 1989 and unification with West Germany in 1990. With unification, the debate lost much of its urgency, for East Germans no longer needed to construct a new state.

Despite this practical resolution to the debate, East Germans have brought elements of it into their new political context. The positions that Ullmann and Schröder represent have found institutional homes nationally—Ullmann's in the recent alliance of Bündnis '90 with the Greens, Schröder's in the SPD. Though Ullmann and Schröder continue largely to represent the concerns of East Germans, they have achieved a degree of national prominence. In the summer of 1994, Ullmann was elected to a seat in the European Parliament. That same year, Schröder ran for the Bundestag, though unsuccessfully. As politicians, they have drawn on the East German experience to articulate a vision of a new Germany in a new Europe.

While it is difficult to gauge the actual political influence of either Ullmann or Schröder, their positions have become part of a larger debate about German politics. With the emergence of parties to the extreme right, the resurgence of the former Communist Party in the eastern part of the country, the growing fragmentation of the political landscape in recent elections, and the relative decline of the Social Democratic and Christian Democratic parties, Germans are asking basic questions about the nature and viability of their democratic institutions. Political discontent with the established parties reflects a growing frustration that politics has become too much the business of professional politicians, rather than providing for popular participation and self-government.[52]

In this context, the areas of agreement between Ullmann and Schröder are more significant than the areas of disagreement. While differing on what the nature of a new constitution should be, both have argued that the renewal of democratic institutions in Germany depends in part on popular ratification of one. While differing on the degree to which a constitution should provide for plebiscites and popular referenda, both have argued for more elements of popular participation in government. Each in his own way has argued that the future of German democracy depends on citizens' taking the political task seriously, and not abandoning it to others.

The Ullmann-Schröder debate also has significance for a deeper understanding of religion and democratization. It is noteworthy in itself that *theologians* played such a significant role in shaping a democratizing nation's political discourse, even if only for a short time, reflecting the unique role of the church in the East German context.

The role of theologians is also remarkable in light of the vulnerability of new democratic regimes to reactionary expressions of primal identities, that is, to new fundamentalisms of nation, ethnicity, and religion.[53] Analysis of the East German situation affirms that religious institutions and ideals can support, as well as impede, democratization. Theologians like Ullmann and Schröder drew on theological categories to connect concerns about individual rights to a vision of a higher responsibility for building and preserving democratic political community.[54]

Yet it is striking that neither Ullmann nor Schröder developed extensive political theologies. Neither was concerned to establish a "Christian" nation. Their appeals to Scripture and theology were limited to rather broad principles of freedom, justice, equality, and responsibility. They addressed issues of religion and politics, and of church and state, primarily to the end of calling for the renewal of a political culture in which people could acquire deep convictions about their political rights and responsibilities. Ullmann and Schröder sought to give political form to the church's free space, so that East Germans might practice the basic skills of critical analysis and debate so necessary for democratic life. Where they differed was in their understanding of the relationship between intimate community and public politics.

In the East German context, the Ullmann-Schröder debate was perhaps most significant in shifting the discussion of popular participation in government away from the enumeration and elucidation of personal rights, which East Germans were so quick to claim for themselves as the Wall fell. Ullmann and Schröder helped focus the debate on the broader issue of what self-government entails and requires. If political rights imply political responsibility, questions of consensus, competency, and representation become crucial. Rights and responsibility might not only support each other but also come into tension, depending on how one defines the nature of popular participation in government.

The Ullmann-Schröder debate seemed to confirm what several political scientists have recently suggested, namely, that democratization is not simply a matter of building new political institutions, such as an independent judiciary or free elections, but is above all the process by which the groups that have opposed the old political system negotiate the rules of participation in the new political system and define the exercise of political rights. The viability of a new democracy depends on the successful completion of such negotiations, and any attempt to short-circuit them risks eventual disillusionment with the idea of democracy.[55] The Ullmann-Schröder debate demonstrated the terms in which such negotiations implicitly proceeded in one country. The renewal of the democratic promise elsewhere in the world will require attention to similar questions.

Coming to Terms with the Past

The Church, the State, and the Stasi

Because the East German Wende had spiritual-moral concerns at its heart, it is not surprising that questions of loyalty and integrity, both personal and corporate, came to the fore as East Germans tried to make sense of the past. *Vergangenheitsbewältigung* (literally, mastery of the past) proved to be one of the most urgent yet difficult tasks of democratization. The battle to shape the future of eastern Germany became a sometimes nasty, politicized fight about its past, that is, about how to interpret the forty years of Marxist-Leninist rule.[1]

Because it played a unique and critical role in the events leading up to the Wende, the Evangelische Kirche in particular came under intense public scrutiny after the Wende. With the opening of the secret police files, some argued that the church, once hailed as the "midwife" of the Wende, had in fact been too accommodating to the regime and had even helped to prop it up.

As a result of these accusations, the church found itself trying to come to terms with the past on two fronts: first, in developing criteria to evaluate pastors and other church leaders who had associations with the secret police; second, in determining how best to assess its institutional past as a "church in socialism."

This chapter explores the factors that made East Germans debate these questions with such urgency and intensity, and identifies and assesses the kinds of arguments that emerged as the church dealt with ministers and members who worked for the secret police. Of particular significance is the theological dimension of these arguments. In coming to terms with the past, the church faced questions of self-understanding. It had to relate its theological commitments to confession, forgiveness, and reconciliation to the practical circumstances of church life.

The Stasi Presence

The Stasi (short for Staatssicherheitsdienst, the state security service or "secret police") was a formidable presence in the GDR. As many as three hundred thousand people (2 percent of the total population) worked officially or unofficially for it, compiling information on several million persons.[2] Moreover, the Stasi assumed mythical proportions.[3] Many East Germans acted as though the Stasi knew everything and had its informants everywhere. Though few people actually had direct dealings with the Stasi, most people constantly understood their lives in terms of its reality.[4]

Visitors from the West did not always appreciate this mysterious yet pervasive presence of the Stasi. At first a Westerner's preconceptions of life in a closed, watched society might find little confirmation. Everyday life in East Germany was strangely familiar: a moderately high standard of living, an ethic of consumption, a Western style of life. Only after one made closer friendships did one understand how the Stasi shaped the popular consciousness, even within the church.

An example is the attitude of theological students at the church-run seminary in East Berlin. Most of these students assumed without question that seminary telephones were bugged. When they received mail, especially from abroad, they looked for tiny tears in the envelopes—evidence, they claimed, of the Stasi's insertion of wire-thin reading devices. The students expressed anxieties that their parents and friends shared but were often more reluctant to express.

On national holidays, the students would point to groups of men loitering at strategic locations in the city: subway station entrances, public squares, bridges. "Stasi," they would say quietly. "They are making sure that no one tries to disrupt the celebrations." The stereotypical image of a Stasi officer was a man in his twenties with a short haircut, wearing a black leather jacket.

Several of the students had been interrogated by the Stasi; nearly all had seen it at work. An alternative group in a Protestant congregation in Pankow, a suburb of East Berlin, came under particular pressure. Out of sixty to seventy people, as many as twenty to twenty-five were with the Stasi, those young men with "that look," as alternative group members put it. These "guests" mostly listened quietly, but sometimes they tried to provoke an argument. They were intimidating simply by their presence, and occasionally they succeeded in unnerving group members.

The mythical presence of the Stasi was also apparent in people's references to the word itself. In private, people sometimes called the Stasi *die Firma* (the firm). In public, people were reluctant to use the word *Stasi* at all. A school director once called the daughter of a seminary professor into his office. A teacher had confiscated a notebook that the girl was passing to a friend; it contained disparaging remarks about the teacher and school. The school director told the girl that she should not write such things because they could end up in the hands of the "wrong people" and get her into "real trouble." It was clear from his tone of voice that he meant the Stasi.[5]

In retrospect, such anecdotes are mildly amusing. As part of the texture of everyday life, the incidents behind them could become oppressive. While people sometimes described East Germany as Prussian communism (as one joke had it, only in Germany could people make communism work in spite of itself), it thrived not on precision and calculation, but on the kind of uncertainty that the Stasi both represented and so successfully propagated.[6]

It was this living with "not knowing" that made the system so pernicious. One waited to the last moment to learn if an application to visit the West would be rejected or approved. One wondered if involvement in the church would eventually bring difficulty with an employer. Not oppressive laws but their arbitrary enforcement drove people mad.

For some East Germans, particularly in the alternative scene, Franz Fühmann, one of East Germany's greatest authors, best captured the feel of life in the GDR. One of his stories is located in a concentration camp. Every morning, the authorities line up the prisoners for roll call. They single out one man in particular, whom they flick on the nose. The act is more humiliating than painful. One day, however, they do not flick him at all. With that, their behavior has become unpredictable, and the man goes mad.[7]

In East Germany, it sometimes took no more than an occasional rumor to give people a flick on the nose, that is, a daily reminder that, in spite of the seeming normality of life, the Stasi could be watching. Many dissidents came to believe that the biggest problem in East German society was the way people censored and policed themselves. "Not knowing" resulted in both personal and social fragmentation. People risked far less than they really could. They spoke in hushed tones about matters that could not possibly concern the Stasi. They avoided striking up a conversation with strangers, not knowing who they might really be. They avoided confronting unjust officials or protesting state policies.

Hannah Arendt speaks of the way totalitarian regimes destroy public life by isolating individuals from each other. Such regimes base themselves on

> loneliness, on the experience of not belonging to the world at all, which is among the most radical and desperate experiences of man. . . . What makes loneliness so unbearable is the loss of one's own self which can be . . . confirmed in its identity only by the trusting and trustworthy company of my equals.[8]

Similarly, Vaclav Havel argues that Marxist-Leninist regimes depended not only on totalitarian domination, but on the demoralized individual who senses no higher responsibility than the self.[9]

In this environment of "not knowing," loneliness, and demoralization, East Germans were constantly tempted to enter into arrangements and compromises with the Stasi. As the Stasi files have been examined, it has become clear just how little money most informants received. They were motivated by something else: a connection to what seemed to them to be ultimate power and meaning. Working for the Stasi gave people a sense that they could know a little bit more, that they could better distinguish what was real from what was not, and that they could become insiders. By providing information about others, thereby perpetuating both the reality and myth of the Stasi, informants won approval from the Stasi and a sense both of community and of higher responsibility.[10]

The Church's Countermyth

The mythical power of the Stasi was sometimes countered by people who drew on religious symbols to construct an alternative way of understanding reality. A particularly vivid example occurred on the twenty-fifth anniversary of the building of the Berlin Wall, on which occasion the East German government sponsored huge celebrations. A student from the East Berlin seminary broke into an abandoned apartment near the Wall, stripped down to his shorts, crawled onto a windowsill, chained himself to the window frame, and stretched out his arms, having unfurled below himself a banner that read "Jesus is dying on the Wall." Within minutes he was arrested and taken to the Stasi for interrogation. His effort to construct a myth to counter the regime's posed an apparent threat to its stability.

This countermyth to the Stasi grounded itself in the special experience of community that the church and its groups offered East Germans. Though the total number of participants in this alternative scene was small, the Stasi spared no effort to watch and harass them.

In a world of "not knowing," one could see no particular logic to the Stasi's strategy. Sometimes they arrested members of alternative groups. At other times their people simply watched, as in Pankow. In every case the Stasi sought to perpetuate fear and isolation and to breed mistrust and dissension.

The groups themselves always reckoned with the possibility that there were informants in their midst. The Pankow group wrestled hard to know what to do about its "guests." Some argued for closing the group; they saw the "guests" as only creating turmoil and destroying the possibility of reasoned, thoughtful conversation. In the end, however, the group decided to keep its meetings open, while forming subgroups that met in members' homes by invitation only. While refusing to identify and purge their "guests," the group did attempt in this way to resist their efforts to sow discord.

This kind of resilience gave the groups a strength beyond their numbers. With the emergence of a mass opposition movement in 1989, their vision of an alternative politics found resonance in the broader population. As the demonstrators grew in numbers and confidence, they began to march past Stasi buildings, placing candles on the doorsteps and windowsills. All that was hidden should now be revealed. In their banners and slogans, the demonstrators shouted the word *Stasi* from the housetops, as though breaking the language tabu could also break the Stasi's power.[11] As they chanted "Wir sind das Volk"—and, within a few weeks, "Wir sind ein Volk"—they called for a rebirth of democratic culture and for the dissolution of the Stasi.[12]

Opening the Files

After the fall of the Wall, church leaders and group members occupied and secured Stasi buildings throughout the country. The Stasi had destroyed some files, but many remained intact. The first freely elected East German Parliament formed a commission to determine the future of the files. Some people feared that opening the files would destabilize the country. Others argued that "living in truth" required opening them.

With unification, this debate continued in the German Bundestag. Public institutions could request a review of the files of persons in legislative, judicial, and civil posts; the question of individual access proved more problematic. Eventually the Bundestag passed a law allowing individuals to view their files, but it regulated the publication of information from the files. Especially significant was a provision for allowing people to know who had spied on them.[13]

Media sensationalism and political posturing accompanied the opening of the files. The public debate sometimes took the tone of a witch hunt, with little sensitivity to the complexities of the issue. While vilifying the Stasi itself, the media tended to treat the files as unquestionably accurate. In some cases, former Stasi officers appeared on television talk shows and before parliamentary commissions, claiming to fill in gaps in the files. In other cases, the media acquired files on the black market. The Stasi question became deeply politicized, with different political interests trying to identify tainted leaders in order to force them to resign from office.[14]

The Case of Heinrich Fink

The case of Heinrich Fink, rector of East Berlin's Humboldt University, was particularly dramatic and controversial, as well as illustrative of the problems of opening the Stasi files. In 1991, the government minister with responsibility for the university dismissed Fink, contending that he had worked as an informant for the Stasi.

Prior to the Wende, Fink had been dean of the theological faculty at the university. He had strong ties to the Christian Peace Conference (CPC) and to groups in the church seeking a Christian-Marxist dialogue. He tended to be supportive of Soviet peace initiatives, sought to forge alliances with third-world church leaders committed to liberation theologies, and argued that cooperation with the East German state offered Christians the best possibilities for representing their concerns. Rather than complaining about the marginalization of Christians in East Germany, he sought to convince both Christians and Marxist-Leninists of the creative contributions that Christians could make to Marxist-Leninist society.

Not an ideologue, Fink made his reputation as an astute politician. He involved church and state officials in efforts to support the small Jewish community in East Berlin. In 1985, he worked with university officials to commemorate Dietrich Bonhoeffer. He was able to protect the interests of the theological faculty while winning influence in the university as a whole.

Fink did not begin to break with the state until relatively late in 1989. In early October, the police cordoned off an East Berlin church in which a group of protesters had gathered, among them Fink's daughter. When he tried to reach her, police shoved him away; the event, captured by West German cameras, propelled Fink into the public spotlight as a possible reformer.

In April 1990, strongly supported by students, Fink was elected to lead the university through a process of democratic renewal. He also won support from the reorganized Communist Party. Critics charged him with protecting the interests of professors who, like himself, had supported the old regime. Supporters, however, saw him as a strong, charismatic leader who was defending East German interests and struggling to save the university from West German politicians.

At the time of his election, government officials cleared Fink of any Stasi connections. In December 1990, however, new evidence emerged. Though the Stasi, a year earlier, had destroyed Fink's own files, other files suggested that Fink had been an IM, or *inoffizieller Mitarbeiter* (unofficial collaborator). It appeared that Fink had worked for the Stasi for twenty years, not only providing information about church officials and policies, but also taking an active role in trying to influence them in favor of the state.

The evidence, however, was circumstantial. The most critical piece of information, a voluntary declaration of cooperation, was never found—if it had ever existed. Fink himself argued that he had never worked for the Stasi, even if the Stasi had possibly regarded him as one of their own. He conceded that the Stasi had sometimes questioned him about students whom it suspected of political disloyalty and about church committees and church-related groups to which he belonged. He pointed out, however, that he had not sought out these meetings; they were no different from the kind of contact with the Stasi that every church leader could expect to have. Since the church was the one social institution relatively independent of state oversight and control, all church officials were of interest to the Stasi.

Ironically, the case pitted different parts of the church against each other. Fink found himself up against another East German theologian, Joachim Gauck, head of the government agency in charge of the Stasi files. As a pastor in East Germany, Gauck had strongly supported the alternative groups. Some now argued that he had political and perhaps even personal reasons to discredit Fink.[15]

Refusing to relinquish his post, Fink went to court to fight the charges. He continued to find wide support from the university's professors and students. Leading East German intellectuals, such as the writers Christa Wolf and Stefan Heym, also came to his defense, seeing him as the victim of a smear campaign.[16] Nonetheless, Fink lost his case, after a protracted legal battle.

The Pervasive Infiltration of the Church

Other cases unleashed further controversy in the church. People's worst fears seemed to be confirmed. The Stasi had thoroughly infiltrated the church. At the end of 1991, a collection of Stasi records published under the title *Pastors, Christians, and Catholics* documented the extent to which the Stasi had sought to manipulate the church.[17] The editors suggested that the church's efforts at rapprochement and "critical solidarity" had simply played into the hands of the state. In response to their interpretation of the evidence, an intense and sometimes acrimonious debate followed.

Similar questions arose after Manfred Stolpe, the minister-president of Brandenburg, admitted that he had held hundreds of secret meetings with the Stasi during his tenure as chief administrative officer of the Federation of Evangelische Kirchen in East Germany. In the next months, the state commission that administers the files revealed that the Stasi had classified Stolpe as an informant. Stolpe claimed that he had used his contacts to try to strengthen the church's position and to win the release of imprisoned dissidents. He denied ever working for the Stasi, and he resisted calls to resign. Eventually, several other leading church officials also admitted to holding unauthorized meetings with the Stasi.[18]

As less prominent individuals examined their files, they, too, found themselves reconstructing the past. Learning who had been associated with the Stasi often had a devastating impact. The church discovered that it was not entirely the kind of community it had believed itself to be. Pastors learned of other pastors who had spied on them. Members of alternative groups learned of other members who had manipulated and used them. Individuals found themselves no longer able to trust their own memory of the past; they were now discovering how things "really" had been. The Stasi continued to cast its shadow into the present; some argued that the opening of the files had sown more suspicion and discord than the Stasi itself ever did.[19]

Ethical Issues

The complexity of these issues called for careful ethical distinctions. When did passing information to the Stasi constitute betrayal? How would the church deal with informants and collaborators? When would it have to demand accountability? When would it be called to practice forgiveness? Did an act of confession make a difference, and under what circumstances? How could the church restore the integrity of "life together" in the church? As the church tried to come to terms with the past, it addressed these questions at three levels: the ecclesiastical, the political, and the moral.[20]

At issue at the *ecclesiastical* level was the question of when passing information to the Stasi violated the special trust that the church had invested in persons by virtue of their office. Some criteria were clear. First, pastoral ethics required pastors not to report private conversations with parishioners. Second, in taking office, East German church leaders pledged not to enter into secret conversations with the Stasi. All attempts to recruit and interrogate them were supposed to be reported to higher church authorities.[21]

Some church leaders had been given a mandate to undertake particular negotiations with the state; they were always aware that Stasi officials might be present at such meetings. With the opening of the files, it appeared that the Stasi had classified some of these persons as informants. To determine whether they actually were or not required additional investigation. Two criteria were key: First, had one signed a formal declaration of intent to work for the Stasi?[22] Second, in giving information to the Stasi, had one betrayed particular individuals or the interests of the church, or had one simply repeated information that was already public in church circles? The files alone could not adequately answer these questions; though of considerable value, they reflected the particular interests and concerns of the Stasi. Because members of the Stasi had been under pressure to prove their success at recruiting informants, they had sometimes classified persons as informants who were not.[23]

The Stolpe case raised particular problems. As the church's chief negotiator with the state, Stolpe had had a wide-ranging mandate. Because he was finally accountable to the church's synod, some argued that he should have reported his meetings with the Stasi to the synod. Yet the synod itself had never asked Stolpe to give an account of all his activities. It had been willing to give him a great deal of freedom, even when it had reason to suspect that he had Stasi connections. The synod trusted his judgments and appreciated his ability to solve problems with the state that pastors and other church leaders could not.[24]

Even more troubling were the cases of other church leaders who had used their contacts with the Stasi to try to protect the church's interests and particular individuals, but whose mandate was more limited than Stolpe's. While the church was generally reluctant to accuse them of betrayal, it did question whether they overstepped their mandate. Some church people called for the establishment of special commissions to investigate these cases on an individual basis and to determine which violations constituted grounds for removal from office.[25]

At issue at the *political* level was the question of what kind of coming to terms with the past would best assist the church in both recovering its moral authority in society and promoting the democratic renewal of society as a whole. It seemed that the Stasi's infiltration of the church had undermined its trustworthiness as a public institution.

Some church people argued that the renewal of the state and of public institutions required legal solutions, that is, it was necessary not only to remove people from office but also to prosecute and punish them.[26] Similarly, they wanted the church to encourage the state to prosecute and punish church people who had worked as informants. Coming to terms with the past in this way, however, required a legal basis, that is, a way to establish whether or not one's passing of information had actually harmed others and violated international law or the laws of the Marxist-Leninist regime.

Other church people emphasized the role of special state commissions in conducting investigations not with legal solutions in mind but in order to document and denounce the crimes of the old regime publicly.[27] In addition, the state would be able to educate people about the past through schools, museums, and publications. The church should support such efforts and take similar steps to investigate and clarify the way in which the Stasi had infiltrated its own life.

At stake in these arguments was the question of which political interests should control the process of interpretation, and for what ends.[28] West Germans—whether in the academy, the media, or the church— were sometimes tempted to impose on East Germans a Western interpretation of East German history, even though most West Germans had no direct experience of either the complexities or the emotions associated with the Stasi's role in East Germany. It became increasingly clear that a broad, scholarly debate, supported by continuing historical research and analysis, would be necessary, and that East Germans should be allowed to debate these matters among themselves, without having to defend themselves before the West.

At issue at the *moral* level was the question of how the church should live out its commitments to confession, forgiveness, and reconciliation when violation of personal trust had occurred. Informants misused their relationships with others; they became victimizers. Such violations were even more intense in the context of the special bonds that people had sought and developed in the East German church. When would reconciliation require the victim to forgive the victimizer? When would it require the victim to hold the victimizer accountable?

One line of argumentation in the church in the former East Germany was that the possibility of forgiveness depended on the victim holding the victimizer accountable. Until the informant had made amends, the victim could not really forgive, nor could the victimizer really receive forgiveness. Repentance needed to precede forgiveness.[29] Others saw difficulties in this position. When victims demanded that repentance be not only in word but also in deed, it was not clear who would determine the actual terms of satisfaction. These critics of "repentance before forgiveness" questioned whether one person could demand repentance of another. They feared that forgiveness and repentance, to the extent that they became human transactions, would become manipulative. The victim would be tempted to find satisfaction in victimizing the victimizer, and the victimizer would be tempted to make a show of confession while remaining unrepentant at heart.

A second line of argumentation was that forgiveness could precede and even evoke repentance. Representatives of this position argued that the victim's word of forgiveness could perhaps move the informant to contrition. They saw the ability to forgive in this way as springing from the victim's coming to understand some of the terrible dilemmas in which informants had found themselves: for example, some had been blackmailed or intimidated or deceived into thinking that they were serving the common good.[30]

Others saw this line of argumentation as tending toward what Bonhoeffer called cheap grace. To forgive too quickly, or to accept forgiveness too quickly, would prevent true reconciliation. Cheap grace was in the best interests of neither victim nor victimizer. Victims might continue to harbor resentments, and victimizers might not have to confront the awfulness of their behavior.[31]

A third line of argumentation was that victims could sometimes forgive the victimizer for their own sake, regardless of whether or not the victimizer showed repentance. Victims could find an inner freedom to forgive their enemy, and to live without a self-destructive desire for either vengeance or justice.[32]

In assessing these different lines of arguments, one found oneself having to assess the nature of the relationship between the victim and the victimizer. Did a relationship of Christian trust exist? Was restoration of this relationship important? If there was no prior relationship, or if its restoration seemed unimportant, coming to terms with the past seemed to suggest the third option—forgiving for one's own sake. If restoring relationship was important, arguments for having victim and victimizer live in the tension between forgiveness and repentance were more compelling. In this case, victim and victimizer would finally have to wait together on transformative possibilities that they alone could not effect, leaving open the hope that forgiveness and repentance could stimulate each other, regardless of which came first.[33]

Investigating Ministers and Members

While the ecclesiastical, political, and moral levels of argument were distinct, they were not entirely separable. For example, the *ecclesiastical* question—whether one had violated the trust invested in one by virtue of one's office—posed moral and political questions of just how much the church should seek to know about these violations. Just as individuals had to decide whether or not to look into their files, the church had to decide whether or not to investigate the files of its ministers and members. The search for just solutions required a careful examination and critique of the moral and political arguments that were made on both sides.[34]

On the *moral* level—what would best contribute to reconciliation among individuals—the argument against having the church research the files was that the church needed to begin with a presumption of innocence and trust toward its ministers and members. It should not investigate individuals unless someone leveled specific charges against them. At the same time, it should encourage guilty individuals to come forward of their own accord and should be prepared to offer them pastoral care and counseling.[35]

In the view of some, this position had problems. They feared that guilty persons would never choose to come forward on their own and would never be exposed. These critics made a moral argument for opening the files: The church had a special commitment to "living in truth." Only the fullest possible disclosure of people's involvement with the Stasi could restore vital, trusting community.

Others argued that the church should not undertake a general investigation of its ministers and members because disclosure of the truth would not necessarily promote reconciliation. On the contrary, such investigations could very easily result in mistrust and anger. It would be too easy for outsiders to misunderstand the plight of individuals who had cooperated with the Stasi. Investigations could too easily become politicized, destroying people's reputations and lives.

Increasingly, people on both sides of these questions had to acknowledge that human justice was always imperfect, efforts at reconciliation would always be uneven, and truth about the past would always be incomplete. The challenge before the church was to strive for the fullest possible disclosure of the truth, while reminding people of the Christian understanding of repentance and forgiveness; and to encourage disclosure of the truth in a way that did not seek to destroy people but opened the way both of acknowledging each other's dilemmas and of finding reconciliation.

In addition, some argued about the *political* dimension to the church's opening or closing the files—the question of what would best contribute to the democratic renewal of the church and society. On the one side were those who believed that conducting investigations of ministers and members would destabilize the church and diminish its moral authority in society. On the other side were those who argued that the institutional church was never an end in itself and that the failures of the past could help a new, more democratic kind of church emerge. If the church was to demonstrate its commitment to the democratic renewal of its structures, and if it was to ensure the integrity of its new leadership, questions of character and leadership mattered.[36] The church should therefore open the files, especially those of church leaders.

In light of these complexities, the church had to exercise great care in its use of the files. Even where church leaders called for a general investigation of their ministers and members, they often conceded that such investigations would have severe limitations. First, the absolute accuracy of the files could never be assumed. Second, some files had been destroyed.

Concerned that the desire for truth, openness, and accountability not impose new injustices, church leaders argued for statutes of limitations and amnesties in some cases. In their view, the rebuilding of trust and the renewal of corporate life were undermined when people lived in perpetual uncertainty about the crimes of the past. These church leaders argued that a time might come for people to leave the past behind for the sake of the common good, even if forgiveness and repentance were still incomplete.[37]

The Limits of Remembering and Forgetting

The complexities of this debate underscored other dangers. As the church attempted to come to terms with the past, it found itself tempted to define its task solely at one level or the other rather than to attend to all three. It faced the challenge of exploring the complex interrelations of the ecclesiastical, the political, and the moral, while providing for continuing, open discussion of the past and its meaning.[38]

On the one hand, some church people appealed almost exclusively to *moral* categories to define the church's *ecclesiastical* and *political* tasks. They argued, for example, that the *moral* category of confession should define the church's dealings with those who violated their office (the *ecclesiastical* question). Those who argued this position often appealed to the work of Alexander Mitscherlich, who held that after World War II the German nation needed to go through a time of *Trauerarbeit* (grief work). Open confession would be cathartic.[39] After the fall of Marxism-Leninism in East Germany, at least one East German psychoanalyst made a similar argument. The real revolution had not yet taken place. What was needed was an inner conversion, a freedom from blind submission to authoritarian structures, and a reclaiming of personal autonomy and democratic culture. If the nation were to experience real renewal, people's feelings needed to be "unplugged."[40] By analogy, it seemed that the church should encourage informants to confess their complicity and should be ready to forgive them. The church should exercise harsher measures, such as removal from office, only if, given this opportunity, one did not confess and were later found out.

Some developed this argument further to define the church's task of *political* renewal. They saw public confession as an important remedy against the supposedly dire consequences of a popular amnesia. In their view, the 1968 student uprisings in West Germany had been fueled by the older generation's refusal to talk publicly (or even privately, in many cases) about the Nazi past. This younger generation had called for the nation to come to terms with a repressed past that was undermining democratic culture. By analogy, it was now argued that if the East German church refused to remember and confess the Stasi past, a future generation might well refuse to invest that church with any moral authority.[41]

Others appealed almost exclusively to *political* categories to define the church's *ecclesiastical* and *moral* tasks. They argued that conversion and repentance depended not on people's unloading emotionally but on how they participated in the new system. What now mattered was one's willingness to support democratic structures and participate in a democratic culture. Since the Wende, historical circumstances had given the church an entirely new situation.

Those who held this position argued that the development and protection of new, democratic structures did not depend on the church's holding individuals morally accountable for their collaboration with the Stasi; by virtue of political and ecclesiastical unification with the West, these structures were firmly established. What mattered now was not whether to remove the morally culpable from church office or demand that they publicly confess their sin, but whether they were willing to work within, and support, the new political structures.[42]

The tension between these two approaches—an exclusive emphasis either on the moral task or the political one—again suggested the inadequacy of either approach alone to come to terms with the past. The moral emphasis on confession did not sufficiently define the church's ecclesiastical and political tasks. Rather, it raised in dramatic and troubling form all the problems associated with wanting people to repent. How much memory of the past could communities afford? Would encouraging people to confess their crimes lead inevitably to politically necessary but morally empty declarations? Would demanding confession affect such a broad segment of the community that people would harbor resentments that reactionary forces could play on to undermine democratic renewal?

Similarly, a politics that emphasized democratic participation but ignored questions about the past obscured the ecclesiastical and moral dimensions of coming to terms with the past. The character question did matter; the integrity of the new structures did depend to some degree on a shared confidence that people had demonstrated integrity in the past. How much forgetfulness, therefore, could a community afford? Did focusing on people's willingness to play by the new democratic rules rather than their previous willingness to play by the rules of the old regime create other kinds of resentments—for example, when the victims of the past continued to find their former victimizers in positions of power and influence, administering the justice that the victims now sought? When was a community ready to grant amnesties, and on what grounds? These questions, which are often raised more generally in relation to nations that undergo democratization, were equally pressing to the post-Wende church in eastern Germany.[43]

Summary Reflections

Without disputing the importance of the church's ecclesiastical and political tasks, one could nonetheless argue that the church had a particular responsibility to focus on the moral task. In post-Nazi Germany, Karl Jaspers noted, "the judge may decide about crimes and the victor about political liability, but moral guilt can truthfully be discussed only in a loving struggle between men who maintain solidarity among themselves."[44] The church continued to be one of the few places in the former East Germany where people and communities would be able to undertake the arduous work of trying to understand the lives that they had lived under the Marxist-Leninist regime—why they did what they did—quite apart from the question of whether or not certain people had violated their office (the ecclesiastical question) or whether or not the church had done enough to regain moral authority in society (the political question).

While the moral task ultimately raised the question of whether or not one had violated personal trust, and whether or not reconciliation would be possible, it needed to begin elsewhere. The most pressing matter was the very process of remembering and interpreting the past, of which the Stasi issue was only one part.[45] Such a process of self-examination could help to answer a people's need to face the truth about itself and its past. It avoided moralizing and scapegoating, which were morally repugnant and politically destabilizing. It did not issue in demands for confession and repentance. Rather, it helped to make confession and repentance possible by helping people, first of all, to acknowledge and examine their mistakes. The church had a special responsibility to provide for a conversation in which people together sought the truth of their lives and of their relations and obligations to one another.[46]

The ability of the church to nurture this kind of community was nonetheless related to its ability to grapple openly with its own failures in the past, a concern that led unavoidably to the ecclesiastical and political dimensions of coming to terms with the past. If coming to terms with the past were not to come simply at the cost of particular individuals who had made mistakes, the church as a whole had to examine where and why it had been, as an institution, too willing to accommodate, compromise, or withdraw. Some church people therefore called for a "pathology of the church in socialism."[47] It was not only a matter of where church leaders had cooperated with the Stasi. It was also a question of whether the church had been too ready to accept the communist state as a legitimate and viable political order. If it had, what in its theology accounted for its failure of nerve? At what points must the church in any society be willing to negotiate with the powers that be, even when they seem diabolic? At what points must it speak a firm no to them?[48]

Whether the church in the former East Germany has succeeded at all in this task is still unclear. There have been many skeptics but also signs of hope, as some church leaders have organized meetings between the victims and the victimizers of the past, between former members of the Stasi and dissidents, and between former schoolteachers and their students; and as church synods and theologians have debated the church's past.[49] While coming to terms with the past will require many more years of discussion, the church could help in modest ways to open a broader conversation in society as a whole.

Church and Politics in a Secular World

The Theology of Wolf Krötke

The tremendous political and social upheavals that rocked the communist world in the late 1980s contain profound lessons about the possibilities and perils of democratization. The transition from totalitarianism to a liberal society was characterized not only by considerable confusion and chaos, but also by high moral idealism. Especially significant was the emergence of mass movements, largely peaceful and nonviolent, that called for popular political participation. People who had seemingly adapted and even accommodated themselves to political powerlessness suddenly reclaimed a deep sense of civic duty.

Some of the intellectuals who helped articulate a renewed sense of a moral, responsible society in these lands have argued that this vision, though springing out of the particular circumstances of the communist and postcommunist East, has continuing significance in the West, imperiled as it is by its own forms of moral apathy and social irresponsibility.[1] In this chapter, I explore the relevance of theological developments in East Germany to questions of church and politics being debated in North America today.

My focus is specifically on the theology of Wolf Krötke, who taught at the church-run seminary in East Berlin and, after the Wende, became the first dean of the reorganized theology faculty at the Humboldt University. While still under the communist regime, Krötke suggested that Christians in East and West, despite their different political settings and histories, stood before a common challenge, namely, secularization.

Christians in both East and West were experiencing a kind of marginalization. Though the church in the West, in contrast to that in the East,
was not suffering under state restrictions prohibiting its members from
assuming positions of social and political influence, Christians in both
East and West were finding that their distinctive values no longer under-
lay much of society.

During this time, Krötke, best known for his systematic work in the
tradition of Barth, Bonhoeffer, and Eberhard Jüngel, represented a major
theological effort to wrestle with the problem of Christianity in such a
world. He called for the grounding of Christian political involvement in
an ecclesiology that would preserve and reflect a distinctive Christian
identity. Though his major essays are not translated into English and are
virtually unknown in the United States, he increasingly won attention
in the German-speaking world, where he was regarded as an emerging
theologian of considerable importance. While my principal concern is to
explicate Krötke's position and its potential contributions to Christian
social ethics, I also offer here a brief critique of its limitations.

The Church in a World of "God-Forgottenness"

Though Krötke claimed to be addressing general theological issues, his
work reflected the secular context of the East German church. Krötke
saw secularization not simply as a matter of losses in church attendance
or membership. Christianity has a distinctive language shaping a distinctive community. Secularization occurs when society no longer uses the
church's language to help give itself identity or to integrate people into
social life.[2]

While scholars working with other definitions of religion came to
other conclusions about the process of secularization in East Germany,
Krötke's argument was quite persuasive.[3] At one time, German society
widely accepted and understood the church's language. Indeed, to many
Germans, to be German meant to be Christian. The church's language
reached into most people's lives—at least when they celebrated society's
major holidays, such as Christmas—or participated in society's major rites
of passage, such as confirmation and marriage. In East Germany, the
church's language now was no longer widely familiar, and social integration no longer depended on it.

Krötke traced this development in part to the Enlightenment, whose
thinkers accused religion of undermining human freedom, and which
gave birth to the theoretical atheism also characteristic of communism.[4]

He suggested, however, that communism had not been the sole factor in the demise of the church's language; even more significant had been the practical atheism that dominated both East and West. Krötke termed this attitude *Gottesvergessenheit* (literally, God-forgottenness). In the modern, scientific-technological world, people seem able to lead their lives without constant reference to God. They have no obvious need for God in a world apparently controlled by human means and ends.[5]

Because its language did not shape socialist society as a whole, the East German church had no significant influence on socialist political structures.[6] On the one hand, Krötke did not entirely lament this development. He argued that the church, whenever it is associated with political power, is tempted to accommodate itself to the world.[7] It tends to abandon its particular identity and ethic and, relinquishing its distinctive language, no longer shapes a distinctive community of witness and service. The German church had succumbed to just this temptation under Hitler.[8]

On the other hand, secularization, characterized by the marginalization of the church and the unintelligibility of its language, results in ethical and political crisis. Krötke argued that the individual in the modern world lacks an ethic by which to unify his or her life. There is no common good to which the individual feels responsible. While society promulgates laws that provide for the general welfare, the individual finds nothing that integrates the different aspects of his or her life into a coherent whole.[9]

Under these conditions of ethical fragmentation, individual freedom seems to be the only absolute. Through exercising his or her freedom, the individual seeks a firm ethical foundation. Without relation to a vision of social responsibility, however, individual freedom threatens to exhaust itself in the search for personal meaning and affirmation. Because the modern world is characterized by a scientific-technological rationality that places life in universal danger, it desperately needs a unifying political ethic. Yet every human ethic of individual freedom finally proves relative only to particular groups. Even when making universal claims, it in fact only serves particular interests in an absolute way.[10]

Individual freedom thus comes to express itself as self-interest and manipulation. People retreat into interest groups that, unable to articulate a common political ethic, ask each individual to create an individual ethic. Following Erich Fromm, Krötke argued that individual freedom becomes nothing more than an acquisitive impulse. The individual seeks personal meaning and affirmation by having "things." The gifts of the natural world—and even other human beings—become mere objects of choice and appropriation. Individuals measure their worth by material possessions. Even the self comes to be regarded as something that one chooses and acquires. But, argued Krötke, one cannot finally "have" others or the self. Individuals only deceive themselves when they attempt to maintain a sense of total control over their lives, and their self-deception ultimately issues in suspicion and violence. The stranger comes to pose a threat to one's own security.[11]

The ethical and political crisis that Krötke described in a communist society has, of course, characterized liberal societies as well. Though Christians in the West may have more opportunities for direct political action than did Christians in East Germany, it is not clear that these opportunities have actually helped them resolve the ethical and political crisis posed by secularization. Krötke's own answer was to call for the church not to try to exercise control over society's power structures but to build community around a common, unifying ethic.

The Church of New Possibilities

In response to the challenge posed by secularization, Krötke asked the church to be a community that would train individuals in ethical judgment: "In a time in which the individual has no ethical orientation, the ability to make ethical judgments is also missing. The Christian community is the offer to train this ability."[12]

To do so, however, the church first had to train people in its distinctive language. In a world of Gottesvergessenheit, even those people who continued to associate with the church suffered from *Sprachlosigkeit* (loss of language), that is, an inability to articulate the basic message of the Christian faith.[13]

For Krötke, this ethical training would begin with worship. Worship lies at the center of the church's life. Through worship, Christians practice hearing God's Word. They learn to discern God's will for their lives. Moreover, worship empowers them to proclaim God's will for others' lives.[14]

The church's ethical orientation follows specifically from the proclamation of God's forgiveness received in faith. Out of their experience of God's mercy and love, Christians, through lives of witness and service, proclaim God's forgiveness to others.[15]

At two points, Krötke modified this apparently traditional Lutheran theology of justification by faith alone. First, in contrast to the Lutheran tendency to separate justification from sanctification, he asserted that faith and morality describe one reality. "We do not first have to make our faith concrete through our deeds or ethical demands. This faith is already concrete. Insofar as we believe, we are simultaneously set into a certain kind of behavior and action."[16]

Second, in contrast to the Lutheran tendency to emphasize individual salvation, Krötke asserted that Christian freedom necessarily implies community. "The freedom to love presupposes the ability to let oneself be loved and to value for oneself others' existence."[17]

The Christian community that Krötke envisioned would invite each member to contribute to its life. He argued that the decline of the Volkskirche actually improved conditions for conversation and involvement. "Everyone can take part in this conversation and use his talents to become active in building up the church."[18] He called on East German Christians to recognize the smaller church as an opportunity for more intense fellowship and study.

The shared task of witness and service would shape a community whose way of life would be strikingly different from that of the world. Krötke contrasted the church's reliance on truth with the world's obsession with power. Whereas the world seeks to control history in order to win identity, the Christian community assumes the identity that Christ bestows on it. Krötke also contrasted the world's "way of having" with the church's "way of being." Because the modern ethic of freedom presupposes that individuals make themselves by acquiring and manipulating things, individuals compete against each other. This ethic ultimately results in a desperate attempt to secure oneself at the expense of others. But Christians know that God, through Christ, affirms them not because of what they do or have, but because of who they are before God. Life in Christ frees people from seeking to control and coerce others. Freedom no longer realizes itself as the freedom for individuals to choose whatever they desire, but as the freedom for them to love and forgive. Christians, able to relinquish control of their lives, reach out to others.[19]

The Christian community, therefore, has a sense of new possibilities. Krötke argued that God, by coming to us in Christ, "assumes all our failures and thus makes new life possible for us."[20] Through Christ, we discover the possibilities of our original, true nature.[21] Jesus' Sermon on the Mount helps describe these possibilities, which do "not spare us from the kind of behavior which the world holds to be 'impossible' and 'utopian.' "[22]

This sense of new possibilities would be especially clear in the church's freedom from the violence that characterizes the world's life, since the church rejects the use of force. The Christian community is "inspired by the mandate of the love of enemy and by the way of power-lessness among persons."[23]

The church is ultimately a place of joy, imagination, and peace. It does not acquiesce in social structures or attitudes that engender resigna-tion or fatalism. The love that accompanies the freedom experienced in Christ "does not rest complacent with the fact that the world now func-tions according to the law of injustice and punishment, of separation and retribution."[24] Through prayer, Christians seek alternatives. "Christians, who pray, are thus not in the final analysis subject to the judgment of others and to the criterion of worldly success. . . . For in prayer is made present the fullness of the possibilities of the new life."[25]

The church's distinctive language thus shapes a distinctive commu-nity, an alternative community. The church does not seek to exercise control over society's power structures, but to live out of God's love and forgiveness. It is a community characterized by new possibilities for wit-ness and service to the world. In this way, Krötke framed the church's political task first of all in terms of its ecclesiology.

The Church and Politics

According to Krötke, the openness that the church is to display in its own life should also characterize its relations with those outside its fold. The church does not accommodate itself to the world, but neither does it withdraw from the world. It is not concerned with securing and pre-serving itself, but with doing whatever it can to help others.[26] Following Bonhoeffer, Krötke called the church a church "for others."[27]

Krötke argued that the church could be open to the world because of God's universality, that is, God's reality for all human beings. He asserted that natural theology, the effort to know God through reason, tries to demonstrate God's universality but inevitably reduces God to a function of human existence.[28] He therefore argued for understanding God's uni-versality as an expression of God's freedom. Indeed, Krötke's theology ultimately rested on the central insight that God, though radically "other," demonstrates his universal presence by freely giving himself, through Christ, to all human beings, whether they are religious or not. "God's reality in the sense of the Christian faith is an event that encoun-ters every human being."[29] "In reality there is no 'god-less' human being."[30]

From this perspective, the Christian proclamation is not simply for the church. "As the God who comes and addresses humans, God is himself the source of a free Christian proclamation."[31] The church is free from every worldly master, but also free to approach every human being. "It indeed knows that every human being is suited to hear God's Word simply because he or she is a human being, that is, a creature to whom God is present and by whom God remains."[32] Christians proclaim the God who encounters and forgives every human being. They proclaim the Christ who reconciles the entire world to himself.[33]

The church's openness to the world has important implications for Christian political involvement. According to Krötke, Christians are always directed outward. They see God at work throughout the world. "The [church in its] proclamation [of the gospel] is therefore empowered to see all human behavior always concretely in the light of this event and then to ask what it means in this light."[34]

Christian political involvement begins as a matter of displaying an alternative to the world but then becomes a matter of actively shaping the world to reflect the reality of the God who encounters it. "Christians stand in all areas of life in a position of responsibility for affirming the life of all that God has created."[35] "Christians will therefore responsibly support all decisions that serve to affirm God's creatures, and they will criticize those arrangements that stand in contradiction to Christ."[36]

First, the church declares that all people, regardless of the particular story that they tell about themselves, have a responsibility for the common good. "The Christian community . . . realizes the claim of Jesus Christ as a truth that is valid for all creatures. All human beings, because they are creatures of this God, bear responsibility for the true creaturehood and humanity of humans."[37]

Second, the church through its own way of life represents new political possibilities, new ways of ordering community, for society as a whole also. Though the church initially manifests these possibilities apart from the world, it always understands its way of life as witness and service to the world. Especially the task of proclamation, according to Krötke, shapes a community that, by the nature of its own life, also reflects God's will for the world. Christians will work for social realization of the possibilities that they discover among themselves, even as they encourage others, especially the state, to do so.

In three areas, Krötke was able to make specific recommendations about life in the church and, by analogy, about life in society as a whole. First, he called for the church to be a community in which people share power with each other. Without attempting to derive particulars of church order directly from Scripture, he argued that the gospel defines

Christian proclamation as a task belonging to the entire church. This common task shapes a "community of brothers and sisters."[38] The church should resist organizing itself according to hierarchical principles. The purpose of church order is to enable each member to serve and enrich the others.[39]

This way of life together in the church would also be a form of political witness to the world. Indeed, "it is only when the responsibility for everyone is taken seriously in the [Christian] community itself that the community can credibly advocate those structures in society that encourage and strengthen such responsibility as a truly human stance."[40] By the nature of its own way of life, the church witnesses to the world that "the principal means by which the state can be true to its responsibility is by enabling and advancing the responsibility of all for the common good, and thereby for justice and peace."[41] Christians should encourage the state to provide opportunities for each citizen to participate responsibly in the task of government.

Second, Krötke called for the church to be a community in which people learn from each other. The task of proclamation implies dialogue in the church. Together the members of the Christian community are to seek to discern God's will in each new moment. The church is open to, and concerned about, every question of ethical responsibility.[42] It also considers every possible answer and welcomes new, alternative solutions, even while recognizing both their shortcomings and the limitations that each concrete situation imposes on them.[43]

The church's commitment to dialogue is also a form of political witness to the world. "Through its own exemplary conduct [the church] will also point to the fact that the dialogue about such alternative ways of life can contribute to the benefit of our humanity."[44] Christians will encourage the state to recognize how society as a whole can benefit from the "potential for openness to the future which is provided by every community that is devoted to its Lord."[45]

Third, Krötke called for the church to be a community in which people practice peace and justice among each other. The task of proclamation shapes a church that seeks new, unforeseen possibilities, especially the possibilities of peace. This way of life in the church also witnesses to the way of life that God makes possible for all human beings. Christians should encourage the state to realize social and political arrangements that correspond to God's shalom.[46] Krötke acknowledged the responsibility of the state to exercise authority and use force in order to avoid social anarchy. But war between nations could be justified only in the "emer-

gency case," such as the Nazi threat. Moreover, with the advent of nuclear weapons, the question arose whether there could ever again be justification for war under any circumstances.[47]

In sum, Krötke called for a church characterized by democratic participation, dialogue, and the way of peace and justice. It would represent an
alternative community with a political vision for society as a whole.
Moreover, these three characteristics would help define the particular
way in which the church would relate to the state. Open to the world,
the church would participate in political affairs, seek dialogue with the
state, and help create social and political structures that reflected the
reality of God's encounter with all human beings.

The Implications for the Church in the West

Krötke's position has obvious similarities to that of certain theologians
in the West, such as Stanley Hauerwas and John Howard Yoder. They,
too, see the church as a distinctive community shaped by a distinctive
language. They, too, ground Christian political involvement in a vision
of the church as an alternative community. Some brief comparisons,
therefore, may suggest points at which current North American debates
about church and culture parallel Krötke's position.

Krötke suggested that liberal and communist societies, despite their
differences, embody a common ethic of individual freedom. Neither political order has offered people a compelling vision of the common good.
Associated with this ethic of individual freedom is the belief that human
beings control their own destiny, and this belief ultimately leads to self-
deception and violence.

Hauerwas, too, sees a world that lacks a common, unifying ethic. In
describing the world's ethic of individual freedom, he says: "It matters
not *what* we desire, but *that* we desire. Our task is to become free, not
through the acquisition of virtue, but by preventing ourselves from being
determined, so that we can always keep our 'options open.' "[48] Hauerwas
argues that the arbitrary desires defining our lives finally expose the inadequacy of this freedom. Like Krötke, he concludes that society is characterized by ethical and political crisis. We no longer know what to do
with our freedom, and we deeply long for moral absolutes and ethical
foundations. Without them, we increasingly rely on self-deception, manipulation, and violence to maintain a sense of control over our lives.[49]

Krötke argued that the church's response to this situation rests on how
its distinctive language defines a distinctive community. The church lives

not out of an effort to control history, but out of God's mercy. Its alternative way of existence represents a political witness to the world.

Hauerwas, too, emphasizes that the church has a distinctive language. It has a distinctive narrative, the story of Jesus Christ, and this story is the basis for a distinctive kind of community. Characterized by freedom and nonviolence, the church represents an alternative to the social and political structures of the world. Through its way of life, the church makes a distinctive political contribution. As Hauerwas likes to say: "The church does not *have* a social ethic; the church *is* a social ethic."[50] The church shows the world a new way of life based on service rather than domination.

> By taking seriously its task to be an alternative polity, the church might well help us to experience what a politics of trust can be like. Such communities should be the source for imaginative alternatives for social policies that not only require us to trust one another, but chart forms of life for the development of virtue and character as public concerns.[51]

While seeing the church's way of life as a political witness *to* the world, Krötke also argued that the church's distinctive characteristics define the nature of Christian political involvement *in* the world. Even as it draws its members together into a special kind of community, the church is open to the world and seeks opportunities to participate in social and political affairs, engage in dialogue with public leaders, and create institutional structures that provide for peace and justice.

Hauerwas, again, makes a similar point. In response to his critics, he argues that the Christian commitment to nonviolence, for example, is profoundly political.

> Once one disavows the use of violence, it means one has a high stake in developing political processes through which agreement is reached without the necessity of coercion. As Christians, we, of course, want to make our societies as open as possible to the voice of dissent.[52]

Hauerwas's theology draws extensively on Yoder's. Indeed, Yoder makes for especially fruitful comparison with Krötke. In calling for the church to represent an alternative community, Yoder, like Krötke, demonstrates how Christians will encourage the state to act in ways that correspond to the possibilities set forth in the gospel. Yoder develops "middle axioms" that "translate" the gospel's witness to Christ into political imperatives, including respect of persons, minimal use of force, and basic obligations of justice.[53]

Implications for Christian Social Ethics

These possibilities for setting Krötke in conversation with Hauerwas and Yoder highlight two points at which Krötke's theology suggests constructive possibilities for Christian social ethics. The first is methodological, a response to the reality of secularization; the second theological, an understanding of Christ.

Krötke asked Christian social ethicists to take secularization seriously. To be sure, secularization remains a problematic term. Sociologists and theologians continue to question whether or not such a phenomenon really exists and, if so, in what way it characterizes the modern world. Some, like Harvey Cox in The Secular City, have celebrated the possibilities of a secularized Christianity. Others, like Peter Berger, have pointed to organized religion's unexpected resiliency in the modern world.[54] Still others have asserted that all human experience, including that in the modern world, has a religious dimension, even though it may manifest itself in forms unrelated to traditional religious communities.[55]

As described earlier, Krötke saw secularization in terms of a loss of language. East Germans no longer used widely or even recognized the distinctive vocabulary and narrative of the Christian church. Recent sociological research suggests that one could apply Krötke's observations to the contemporary American scene as well. Even if one argues that there is something like a religious, transcendental horizon to all human experience, mainline Protestant churches have experienced a general trend toward disaffiliation from the church.[56]

This loss of language has implications for Christian social ethics. Hauerwas has argued that when the church relinquishes its distinctive vocabulary, it is no longer able to resist buying into the secular ethic of the nation-state. In conflating its language with general ethical concepts, supposedly accessible to all people, the church seems to gain a public, relevant voice but loses its ability to critique the manipulation, violence, and dishonesty of the modern world. While Krötke might have agreed with Hauerwas's way of contrasting the Christian ethic with that of the world, he was not concerned primarily with a church that has relinquished its language, but with a church whose language no longer makes sense to most of society. Whereas Hauerwas begins with the confidence that the church has a distinctive language, Krötke asked Christian social ethicists to consider a prior question: How can the church make its language understandable to people, beginning with its own members?

Hauerwas and Krötke might agree that people learn this language as they learn the practices and virtues of the community to which it belongs.[57] But Krötke emphasized the degree to which the church had become unsure of its own practices, even its most basic rites. He argued that there was great need for Christians to receive training in the language and practice of worship and prayer. The responsibility for such training should fall not only on the shoulders of a few gifted clerics or lay leaders. If Christian political involvement were to grow out of the distinctive language and practice of the church, Christian social ethicists would also have the responsibility to interpret basic Christian concepts and relate them to the church's social vision.

During the late 1980s, Krötke's own work increasingly took this direction and suggested a rich programmatic direction for Christian social ethics. The last book that he wrote under the communist regime, simply entitled *Beten Heute (Prayer Today)*, began with the assertion that prayer, while the most characteristic of religious practices, no longer makes sense to most people in the modern world. As he explored the distinctive Christian understanding of prayer, Krötke was also able to show its implications for social ethics. He argued, for example, that Christian prayer, which asks God to be present to all human beings, is only honest and genuine to the degree that the church works to realize those conditions that sustain human life in all its dimensions, such as justice, peace, and environmental protection.[58]

Krötke also focused on the Christian doctrine of God. Because the very word *God* had become strange and confusing in a secular world, Christian practice and language would make little sense until people had some understanding of it.[59]

Clearly, then, Krötke believed that Christian social ethics in the modern world must be *theological* ethics, written, moreover, not simply for scholars, but for the Christian community as a whole, as well as for those who want to learn about the church and its way of life. Christian theological ethics would train people in the church's distinctive language by helping them to understand the church's most basic concepts and practices. And in doing so, it would also be *social* ethics. As people would learn the church's language, they would also find themselves participating in an alternative community that makes a political witness to the world.

This political witness includes dialogue with the world. Both Hauerwas and Yoder have been careful to emphasize that their position is not a sectarianism that withdraws from the world.[60] They are open to dialogue with the world (and Yoder's middle axioms demonstrate one way in which it might proceed). Indeed, their understanding of Christ demands openness to dialogue. Hauerwas emphasizes that Christians show hospitality to the stranger because "the community itself was formed by the presence of the ultimate stranger, Jesus Christ."[61] Yoder emphasizes how Christ, through his life and death, breaks down the walls that people erect between each other and empowers Christians to be open to and concerned about the stranger.[62]

Krötke, too, emphasized that the church's dialogue with the world has a distinctively christological foundation. He developed this point, however, somewhat differently from Hauerwas and Yoder. Christians, according to Krötke, seek dialogue with the world because God, through Christ, encounters all human beings and invites them to become aware of God's presence and love. If Christian social ethics, in reaction to secularization, must begin methodologically by explicating the distinctive concepts and practices of the Christian community, its understanding of Christ also gives it theological reason to do so.

Krötke's Christology establishes a second programmatic point for Christian social ethics. Besides interpreting basic Christian concepts and practices and relating them to the church's social vision, Christian social ethics has the duty to engage in dialogue with the world—not simply to witness to the alternative way of life embodied by the Christian community, but also to shape the world to reflect the reality of the God who, through Christ, encounters it. God, through Christ, promises his presence and love in all dimensions of human life. Christian social ethics will therefore seek to understand, test, and support all sociopolitical positions that improve human well-being.[63]

Concluding Reflections and Questions

With unification, the church in eastern Germany faced a new situation. The political disadvantages associated with church membership were gone. The church was once again able to finance its operations with a state-collected church-tax. In many areas, religious education was reintroduced in the public schools.

Yet unification did not bring about a resurgence of affiliation with the church; on the contrary, with the church's efforts to update its rolls, many people left the church to avoid paying the church-tax. It was clear that secularization would remain the dominant social reality. No more than 10 to 20 percent of the population had even nominal affiliation with the church.

The situation in western Germany was similar. Despite much higher rates of affiliation with the church, disaffiliation was growing; in many regions the church faced financial shortfalls. It was just one voice among many. As in eastern Germany, the church found itself having to come to terms with a secular society.[64]

In such an age, the German church faced in a new way the question of how it was to relate to the world. Was Krötke's theology a possible resource?

On the one hand, Krötke's theology, though developed in East Germany, has a compelling vision for the church in a secular society, whether in North America, Germany, or elsewhere. Krötke would remind the church that God himself, through Christ, enters the world. Christians can, therefore, work for policies, both in the church itself and in the world, that reflect God's presence in the world, even when the world does not know or accept the language by which Christians proclaim God's universal reality.

Yet, as the church in North America and in both parts of Germany faces the reality of cultural disestablishment, Krötke's position also has limitations. First, it shares some of the same weaknesses as Hauerwas's position. While neither Krötke nor Hauerwas would see himself as succumbing to sectarianism, critics have charged that they focus too exclusively on life inside the church and fail to see the way in which God may work outside the church, for example, in popular movements of liberation.[65] Krötke's theology was inadequate to explain the emergence of the East German democracy movement, a point that he himself has acknowledged since the Wende. While the church helped lead the Wende and articulate its deeper, spiritual-moral meaning, the church was not the only factor and, in retrospect, not the major factor in bringing about the peaceful revolution.[66] Krötke never developed a political theology that took the full complexity of the situation into account.

Second, it is not clear that either Krötke's theology or the lessons of the church in eastern Germany are applicable to the church in the West as it seeks a vision for the way ahead. In many respects, the special role of the church in East Germany was determined as much by oppressive state policies as by a compelling vision of the gospel. It is much harder for the church to represent an alternative community in a democratic, pluralistic society. People no longer need its free space. Even when they do gather in the church, they no longer experience the intensity and depth of relationships that once characterized the alternative groups in the East German church. It appears that one cannot directly apply the lessons of the "church in socialism" to the church in the secular West.

Krötke's work, nonetheless, reminds Western theologians of the ways in which some theologians in the former East Bloc attempted to rethink issues of religion and culture, church and politics. Moreover, it represents the kinds of questions and concerns that East German Christians, especially in a younger generation, continued to ponder as they tried to make sense of life in a reunified Germany. Even if the theology that Krötke developed in East Germany should prove to be of limited value for the church in the West today, it provides continuing insight into the religious impulses that helped shape the distinctive process of democratization in East Germany.

Epilogue

After the Wall

The Evangelische Kirche played a critical role in the process of democratization in East Germany. First, at a sociopolitical level, the church represented the only institution not under the direct control of the Communist Party. It offered a free space in which an alternative politics could emerge. Second, at a theological level, the church articulated an understanding of the faith that lifted up the democratic impulses of the gospel and the Christian tradition. The church insisted that this vision of democracy was to find realization first in the church's own way of life, but then in the church's witness to the world. As a result, the church committed itself to shaping the socialist political order to become more democratic. Third, at a cultural-religious, spiritual-moral level, the church offered alternative groups a reservoir of symbols, images, and practices on which they could draw to give power and depth to their democratic, egalitarian ideals. The church's theology shaped their thought, but they went further than the church, radicalizing its theology and giving it direct political application.

These three factors supported each other to such an extent that by the mid-1980s the church had become the symbol of resistance to the communist state. Yet, in retrospect, it is clear that the role of the church in the process of democratization was not inevitable. A host of political, economic, and cultural factors, most of which had nothing to do with religion, were at work. The rise of Gorbachev, economic dependence on the West, and the unrest and expectations of a younger generation, especially in relation to freedom of travel and self-expression, were critical, and they interacted in complex ways with the religious factors. Indeed, to some observers, these nonreligious factors seem to offer better explanations for the Wende than the religious factors.

For this reason, historians will debate for many years to come the significance and nature of the church's role. Was the church in fact the midwife of the peaceful revolution, as many claimed after the Wall fell? Or was it simply the birth canal through which democracy came to light in East Germany, expelled by deeper contractions of social and political crisis that gripped all of the East Bloc?

If the church was able to play a significant role in the Wende, it was in part because the Communist Party failed to see the degree to which religion could harbor and stimulate a democratic potential. The party believed that it could manage the church for its own purposes. The church could function as an escape valve for pent-up social frustrations; it could be taught to police the alternative groups in its midst in exchange for social privileges; it could be lulled into cooperating with the state in building the truly human society that the state envisaged. The party never understood how a church of dwindling numbers, declining in social influence, continued to be able to call the party's legitimacy into question and to exert power against it politically. The party was therefore never able to take effective measures to counter the church.

Perhaps more important, the party failed to see how the continuing existence of religion called its own ideological commitments into question. The persistence of religion in socialist society could have served as an early warning signal that all was not well. It could have pushed the party into looking more realistically at a host of contradictions that it was trying to strait-jacket into rigid, ideological categories. A truly creative Marxist-Christian dialogue might have emerged and given birth to a renewed—and revised—vision of socialist democracy.

Yet it is also the case that the church, at times, played a significant role in the events leading up to the Wende in spite of itself. It rarely pushed the limits set by state and party. It remained overwhelmingly committed to being a "church in socialism," not over against the socialist order. It sought to reason and negotiate with the state and to encourage reform from within. The alternative groups in its midst posed it as much of a problem as an opportunity. To some church leaders, the groups seemed to be going too far, too fast; they appeared to be driven by politics, not the gospel.

Ironically, even within the alternative groups, few dissidents wanted a revolution. They too believed that communism was reformable; indeed, they often hoped that the communist East could become a more attractive, viable alternative to the West, where they saw powerful economic and political forces undermining democratic ideals.

When the peaceful revolution finally came, many East Germans and East German Christians hailed it as a vindication of the church and the alternative groups. In those first days of elation, few paused to ask what exactly in the church was being vindicated. The real tensions that had existed between church officials and alternative group members were briefly obscured, as were the different visions of democracy represented by different parts of the church.

When these differences came into plain view again, their clash was all the more explosive. Individuals and groups representing different political interests and different parts of the church battled each other for power in church and state, and accused each other of having collaborated with, or having failed to stand up to, the communist state.

Among these different voices were those Christians, especially in the alternative groups or close to them, who insisted that the lessons of the "church in socialism" should make a distinctive contribution to the renewal of church and society in a new Germany. They hoped that a reunified German church would rethink its relation to church and society. They believed that the East German church had learned the value of maintaining a critical distance from the state; it had learned to survive in a post-Christendom era; it had taken seriously what it meant to be Christian in a secular world. The West German church seemed, by contrast, locked in the patterns of the past, unable to see the realities of the present.

In the end, these Christians found themselves mostly disappointed in their efforts to bring this kind of distinctive East German identity into a new Germany. They soon had to concede that the lessons of the "church in socialism" were not immediately applicable to the reunified German church.

One issue was church financing. While the West German church relied on a state-collected church-tax, the East German church had depended on voluntary contributions. While West German pastors were well paid and their congregations could afford to renovate their buildings to the most modern standards, the East German church had learned to live with less. Some East German Christians hoped that the reunified church might develop new models of financing. They wanted to preserve the church's independence, as well as a greater level of equity in the salaries of pastors and other church workers than seemed to be the case in West Germany.

Yet East German Christians soon learned the extent to which their church had been living off of West German financing, not its own. With the fall of the Wall, the West German church insisted that the East German church pay its own way. Reintroduction of the church-tax appeared to be the only practicable solution. Even with its reintroduction, the church in eastern Germany faced massive financial shortfalls. Numerous churches in rural areas were closed; in several Landeskirchen, church leaders spoke of a need to eliminate up to a third of the pastoral positions.

A similar dynamic characterized other issues. Some East German Christians hoped that the church might continue to think of itself as an alternative community representing ideals of truth, justice, and peace over against a state and a society driven by power politics and economic greed. They resisted the notion of reinstating religious instruction in the public schools. They called for the church to support new kinds of alternative groups and citizen initiatives.

Yet they soon learned that the circumstances of the West presented a different set of challenges. In a pluralistic, democratic society, the church was only one alternative among many. It had to compete with a whole range of interest groups and government initiatives. It was not the only space in which democratic impulses could arise and find public articulation.

As a result, what difference the East German experience made for the present was unclear. As East Germans and East German Christians adjusted to a new way of life, many of them fell silent, unable to say exactly who they were and where they fit in a new Germany. While the Wall itself had mostly disappeared, except for a few graffiti-covered segments that memorialized the events of 1989, some observers asserted that walls still existed in Germans' heads. Coming to terms with the past would involve not only the questions of the Stasi but also differences in mentality and history between East and West.

The East German story, nonetheless, holds profound lessons. First, it reminds us that religion is not inevitably co-opted by the reactionary nationalisms and tribalisms that emerge with the fall of totalitarian states; rather, religion can play a significant and creative role in the democratization process. The East German situation suggests some of the theological developments, as well as social conditions, that enabled the church to contribute to that process. Investigation of the role of religious communities in other democratizing countries may shed additional light on when and why religion contributes to democratization or political reaction.

Second, the East German story reminds us that politics can have a spiritual-moral dimension. At stake in Marxist-Leninist societies, and then in the democratization movements, were people's fundamental commitments and loyalties, not simply matters of economics or personal liberty. In East Germany, religious ideals and symbols helped people give voice to their concerns about peace, justice, and the creation. Religious language and practice contributed to a renewed vision of human responsibility for the common good.

Third, the East Germany story lifts up key issues in contemporary Christian social ethics: the impact of secularization on the church and its way of life, the ability of the church to represent an alternative community, and the relationship of the church to popular movements of liberation. While Christian social ethics in East Germany broke little new ground, it did demonstrate in a particularly vivid way that these questions were more than scholarly matters; the very life of the church seemed to be at stake. Theological and ethical reflection sprang out of the concrete challenges that the church faced and helped shape the church's response.

Finally, the East Germany story is worth knowing because it helps us better understand the people who lived through these momentous events and are now trying to find their way into the future. Their hopes and disappointments, dreams and failures, are not determined by the past, but neither do they make sense without reference to the past. East Germany no longer exists, but its history will shape the culture and politics of the new Germany. The silence into which East Germans have presently fallen may be necessary if they are someday to dream new dreams. One can only be amazed and thankful that they have already taught us so much.

Notes

Chapter 1. The Limits of Dialogue: East German Marxist-Leninist Thinkers and the Future of Religion

1. See Paul Mojzes, *Christian-Marxist Dialogue in Eastern Europe* (Minneapolis: Augsburg, 1981); and Götz Planer-Friedrich, "Worum geht es den Freidenkern?" *Kirche im Sozialismus* 15 (April 1989): 45–48.

2. In a socialist society, for example, pay was to be determined according to the "principle of achievement." It was believed that in communism each would receive according to need.

3. Ministerium der Justiz, *Strafgesetzbuch der Deutschen Demokratischen Republik* (Berlin: Staatsverlag der Deutschen Demokratischen Republik, 1984), section 1, paragraph 133.40.

4. Akademie für Staats- und Rechtswissenschaft der DDR, *Staatsrecht der DDR—Lehrbuch*, 2nd ed. (Berlin: Staatsverlag der Deutschen Demokratischen Republik, 1984), 200–201.

5. IX. Parteitag der Sozialistischen Einheitspartei Deutschlands, "Entwicklung der Volksbildung und kommunistische Erziehung der Jugend," in *Programm der Sozialistischen Einheitspartei Deutschlands* (Berlin: Dietz Verlag, 1985), 66.

6. Kollektiv von Mitarbeitern des Dietz Verlages, "Atheismus," in *Kleines Politisches Wörterbuch*, 4th ed. (Berlin: Dietz Verlag, 1983), 98.

7. Ruth Zander, "Zusammenarbeit—Kommunisten und Gläubige in der sozialistischen Gesellschaft," in *Ausser der Reihe: Beiträge zur Meinungsbildung in der Kirche*, ed. Theologische Studienabteilung beim Bund der Evangelischen Kirchen in der DDR (Berlin: Theologische Studienabteilung beim Bund der Evangelischen Kirchen in der DDR, 1984), 24.

8. Manfred Buhr and Alfred Kosing, "Religion," in *Kleines Wörterbuch der*

marxistisch-leninistischen Philosophie, ed. Buhr and Kosing, 7th ed. (Berlin: Dietz Verlag, 1984), 282.

9. Olof Klohr, "Anmerkungen zur Rolle der Religion in der sozialistischen Gesellschaft," report at the Güstrow Symposium ll, discussed by Almut Engelien, "Die theoretische Auseinandersetzung der SED mit der Religion," in *Die Evangelischen Kirchen in der DDR*, ed. Reinhard Henkys (Munich: Chr. Kaiser Verlag, 1982), 137.

10. Institut für Theorie des Staates und des Rechts der Akademie der Wissenschaften der DDR, *Marxistisch-leninistische Staats- und Rechtstheorie—Lehrbuch* (Berlin: Staatsverlag der Deutschen Demokratischen Republik, 1980), 605–608.

11. See G. J. Gleserman, *Der historische Materialismus und die Entwicklung der sozialistischen Gesellschaft*, trans. Regina Delorme and Klaus Ziermann, 2nd ed. (Berlin: Dietz Verlag, 1973), 282–311.

12. A. P. Butenko, "Noch einmal über die Widersprüche im Sozialismus," *Sowjetwissenschaft—Gesellschaftswissenschaftliche Beiträge* 37 (1984): 36. See also A. P. Butenko, "Widersprüche der Entwicklung des Sozialismus als Gesellschaftsordnung," *Sowjetwissenschaft—Gesellschaftswissenschaftliche Beiträge* 36 (1983): 226–242.

13. W. S. Semjonow, "Zur theoretischen Vertiefung und Konkretisierung des Widerspruchsproblems im entwickelten Sozialismus," *Sowjetwissenschaft—Gesellschaftswissenschaftliche Beiträge* 37 (1984): 378.

14. Alfred Kosing, "Über die Widersprüche der sozialistischen Gesellschaft," *Deutsche Zeitschrift für Philosophie* 32 (1984): 727–736.

15. See also the discussion by Engelien, "Die theoretische Auseinandersetzung," 135–137.

16. As I discuss in the concluding part of this chapter, this understanding of religion does not accurately represent Marx's own position.

17. See, for example, Christopher Hill, *Introduction to Winstanley: The Law of Freedom and Other Writings*, by Gerrard Winstanley (Cambridge: Cambridge University Press, 1983).

18. Gerrard Winstanley, *Gleichheit im Reiche der Freiheit*, ed. Hermann Klenner, trans. Klaus Udo Szudra (Leipzig: Verlag Phillip Reclam jun., 1983), 330.

19. Vera Wrona, "Sozialismus—Humanismus—Toleranz," *Deutsche Zeitschrift für Philosophie* 32 (1984): 756.

20. Akademie für Staats- und Rechtswissenschaft der DDR, *Staatsrecht der DDR*, 184.

21. IX. Parteitag der Sozialistischen Einheitspartei Deutschlands, *Programm der SED*, 72.

22. GDR Academy of Sciences under chairmanship of Horst Bartel, *Theses Concerning Martin Luther*, trans. Intertext (Dresden: Verlag Zeit im Bild, 1983), 8 (thesis 2), 21 (thesis 8), and 24 (thesis 9). Rudolph Mau, an East German church historian, offered a thoughtful analysis of the new Marxist-Leninist interpretation of Luther: "Die marxistischen Luther-Thesen der DDR," *Berliner Theologische Zeitschrift* 1 (1984): 27–44.

23. Wrona, "Sozialismus," 765.

24. Wolfgang Kliem, "Kommunisten und Christen gemeinsam im Kampf um den Frieden," *Deutsche Zeitschrift für Philosophie* 32 (1984): 773.

25. Heinz Buske et al., *Bündnis Politik im Sozialismus* (Berlin: Dietz Verlag, 1981), 252–253.

26. Hans Lutter and Olof Klohr, "Aktuelle Probleme der Zusammenarbeit von Marxisten und Christen," *Deutsche Zeitschrift für Philosophie* 33 (1985): 875.

27. Ibid., 878.

28. Kliem, "Kommunisten und Christen," 771.

29. Helmut Seidel, "Gedanken zum Begriff und zur Geschichte des Humanismus," *Deutsche Zeitschrift für Philosophie* 32 (1984): 750–751.

30. Wrona, "Sozialismus," 759.

31. Wolfgang Kliem, "Religion und Friedenskampf in unserer Zeit," in author collective under the direction of W. Scheler, *Die Philosophie des Friedens im Kampf gegen die Ideologie des Krieges* ed. Erich Hocke, issued by Militärakademie Friedrich Engels (Berlin: Dietz Verlag, 1984), 238.

32. Ibid., 240.

33. Lutter and Klohr, "Aktuelle Probleme," 881.

34. Zander wrote: "Church and theology are understood functionally as a social factor. Apparently the Marxists can imagine a positive change in the church only as an adaptation to socialist thought"; "Zusammenarbeit," 30.

35. Lutter and Klohr, "Aktuelle Probleme," 879.

36. Particularly significant for their role in articulating this position were the theologians associated with the Weissensee Work Group (Weissenseer Arbeitskreis), an outgrowth of the "church brotherhoods" (kirchliche Bruderschaften) of the Confessing Church, organized in 1958 in opposition to Bishop Otto Dibelius, who refused to recognize East Germany as a legitimate state and supported conservative, Western policies. See *Die Weissenseer Blätter* 4 (1988).

The East German branch of the Gossner-Mission (named after Johannes Gossner, missionary to Russia in the early nineteenth century) played a similar role in promoting the possibilities of Christian-Marxist dialogue and cooperation. See Bruno Schottstädt, *Konkret—Verbindlich: Notizen aus der DDR* (Hamburg: Herbert Reich, Evangelischer Verlag, 1971).

For a thoughtful reflection generally supportive of the contributions of the CDU, the CPC, and the Weissensee Work Group to church-state relations, see Johannes Althausen, "The Churches in the GDR between Accommodation and Resistance," *Religion in Eastern Europe* 13 (December 1993): 21–35. For the important role of the CDU in church-state relations, see Robert F. Goeckel, "Die Rolle der CDU in der Kirchenpolitik der DDR," in *Die Rolle der Kirchen in der DDR: Eine erste Bilanz*, ed. Horst Dähn (Munich: Olzog Verlag, 1993), 92–103.

37. See Helmut Fritzsche, "Christian-Marxist Cooperation in the German Democratic Republic since 1945," *Occasional Papers on Religion in Eastern Europe* 7 (June 1987): 1–13. In 1987, Fritzsche announced the founding of a research

center at the University of Rostock for "peace, society, and Christian-Marxist dialogue," to include faculty from the departments of theology, Marxism-Leninism, and Latin American studies; this was the first time in the GDR since the 1970s that the term "Christian-Marxist dialogue" appeared in any kind of official way. See Planer-Friedrich, "Worum geht es," 46.

38. See Helmut Fritzsche, "The Current Status of the Dialogue between Christians and Marxists in the GDR Concerning Ethics," *Occasional Papers on Religion in Eastern Europe* 10 (February 1990): 17–31. See also Manfred Punge, "An der Schwelle des Dialogs: Zum Gespräch zwischen Marxisten und Christen in der DDR," *Kirche im Sozialismus* 14 (April 1988): 49–54. For a collection of texts, with commentary, that documents state efforts to influence the theological faculty at the Humboldt University, see Dietmar Linke, *Theologiestudenten der Humboldt-Universität: Zwischen Hörsaal und Anklagebank, Darstellung der parteipolitischen Einflussnahme auf eine Theologische Fakultät in der DDR anhand von Dokumenten* (Neukirchen-Vluyn: Neukirchener, 1994).

39. Prior to 1989, the most important opportunity was not within the GDR itself, but at the International Conference of Systematic Theologians of Socialist Countries in Debrecen, Hungary. In 1989, Marxist-Leninists from the Humboldt University and representatives of the Federation of Evangelische Kirchen in the GDR were able to hold several rounds of meetings. See Richard Schröder, *Denken im Zwielicht: Vorträge und Aufsätze aus der Alten DDR* (Tubingen: Mohr, 1990), x–xi.

40. See Althausen, "The Churches in the GDR," 31.

41. Karl Marx, "Zur Kritik der Hegelischen Rechtsphilosophie," *Marx-Engels Werke*, ed. Institut für Marxismus-Leninismus beim ZK der SED (Berlin: Dietz Verlag, 1957), 385.

42. W. I. Lenin, *Was Tun?* (Berlin: Dietz Verlag, 1984), 101.

43. Buhr and Kosing, "Religion," 809.

44. Ibid.

45. Akademie für Gesellschaftswissenschaften beim ZK der SED, *Denken gegen die Zeit: Die geistige Krise des Imperialismus* (Berlin: Akademie für Gesellschaftswissenschaften beim ZK der SED, 1981), 110.

46. W. I. Lenin, "Rede auf dem I. Gesamtrussischen Arbeiterinnenkongress," in *Über die Religion* (Berlin: Dietz Verlag, 1982), 95.

Chapter 2. The Language of Liberation: The Church as a Free Space

1. See the newspaper articles in *Neues Deutschland* about the state-sponsored observances in Halberstadt (Käthe Aebi, "Friedenskundgebung auf Halberstädter Domplatz," April 9, 1985), Plauen (Gunther Wendekomm, "30000 Bürger Plauens unterstützen neue Friedensinitiative der UdSSR," April 11, 1985), Potsdam (Heiner Schultz, "Einwohner Potsdams unterstützen die sowjetische Friedensinitiative," April 15, 1985), Wismar (Hans Jordan, "Einmütige Unterstützung für UdSSR-Friedensinitiative," April 16, 1985), and Zerbst (Käthe Aebi,

"Eindrucksvolles Bekenntnis zu den Vorschlägen der UdSSR," April 17, 1985). The role of the English and Americans was not mentioned at all in the articles about Cottbus ("Cottbuser gedachten der Zerstörung ihrer Stadt," February 16–17, 1985), Karl-Marx Stadt ("Eindrucksvolles Bekenntnis zu Frieden und Sozialismus," March 6, 1985), Dessau ("Friedenskundgebung mit über 60000 Bürgern auf Dessauer Rathausplatz," March 8, 1985), Jena ("Über 20000 auf eindrucksvoller Manifestation für den Frieden," March 20, 1985), and Nordhausen (Margrit Böhm, "Nordhausener gedachten Zerstörung ihrer Stadt," April 6–7, 1985.)

2. See the newspaper articles in *Neues Deutschland* about the state-sponsored observances in Magdeburg ("80000 auf eindrucksvoller Manifestation des Friedens," January 17, 1985) and Dresden (Jochen Zimmermann and Horst Richter, "Dresden ist Mahnung und Verpflichtung zum Frieden," February 14, 1985).

3. My analysis is restricted to the proclamation of January 11, the most important political speeches about the liberation, the articles about the fortieth anniversary of the destruction of German cities in Allied air attacks, and the most important church statements.

4. Since most East Germans received West German television and radio, they would also have heard Western reports about the East German church's commemoration.

5. Zentralkomitee der Sozialistischen Einheitspartei Deutschlands, Ministerrat der DDR, Staatsrat der DDR, Nationalrat der Nationalen Front der DDR, "Aufruf zum 40. Jahrestag des Sieges über den Hitlerfaschismus und der Befreiung des deutschen Volkes," *Neues Deutschland* (January 11, 1985).

6. Horst Sindermann, "Im Kampf für den Frieden als treuer Verbündeter an der Seite der Sowjetunion," *Neues Deutschland* (May 9, 1985).

7. Harry Tisch, "Mit hohen Leistungen für das Wohl und das Glück unseres Volkes," *Neues Deutschland* (May 2, 1985).

8. Erich Honecker, "In unserem Land lebt die Einheit des Antifaschisten fort," *Neues Deutschland* (May 6, 1985).

9. Zentralkomitee, "Aufruf zum 40. Jahrestag."

10. Horst Sindermann, "Menschheit siegte über die Barberei," *Neues Deutschland* (April 15, 1985).

11. Erich Honecker, "Die DDR verkörpert die Ideale des antifaschistischen Kampfes," *Neues Deutschland* (April 29, 1985).

12. "Cottbuser gedachten der Zerstörung."

13. Zentralkomitee, "Aufruf zum 40. Jahrestag."

14. Heinz Hoffmann, "Unsere Freundschaft hat tiefe Wurzeln geschlagen," *Neues Deutschland* (April 17, 1985).

15. Hermann Axen, "Schwur von Buchenwald in der DDR in Ehren erfüllt," *Neues Deutschland* (April 15, 1985).

16. Sindermann, "Menschheit siegte."

17. Erich Honecker, "Der welthistorische Sieg für den Frieden und eine glückliche Zukunft der Menschheit," *Neues Deutschland* (May 9, 1985).

18. Bund der Evangelischen Kirchen (GDR) and Evangelische Kirchen (West

Germany), "Wort zum Frieden," declaration on the occasion of the fortieth anniversary of the end of World War II, March 19, 1985; also published in *Zeichen der Zeit* 39 (May 1985): 126–127.

19. Ibid.

20. Bishop Christoph Stier, "Ansprache auf dem Waldfriedhof Halbe," address at the forest cemetery (May 10, 1985; Halbe), Press-Information no. 21, appendix 3 (Berlin: Bund der Evangelischen Kirchen in der DDR, 1985).

21. Bishop Johannes Hempel, "Predigt über 2. Korinther 5, 19–20," sermon from the worship service commemorating the fortieth anniversary of the end of World War II (May 8, 1985; Marienkirche, East Berlin), Press-Information no. 21, appendix 1 (Berlin: Bund der Evangelischen Kirchen in der DDR, 1985).

22. Bishop Christoph Demke, "Predigt im Friedensgottesdienst in Torgau, Psalm 85" (April 25, 1985; Torgau), unpublished manuscript, sermon from worship service for peace.

23. Retired Bishop Albrecht Schönherr, "Ansprache in Buchenwald" (March 30, 1985; Buchenwald), unpublished manuscript, address at the ceremonies in Buchenwald to commemorate Dietrich Bonhoeffer.

24. Demke, "Predigt im Friedensgottesdienst."

25. Hempel, "Predigt über 2. Korinther 5."

26. Schönherr, "Ansprache in Buchenwald."

27. Aktion Sühnezeichen (GDR) and Aktion Sühnezeichen/Friedensdienste (West Berlin), "Zeichen des Friedens und der Versöhnung setzen," joint statement concerning May 8, 1985, no date of publication listed; also published in *Zeichen der Zeit* 39 (May 1985): 127–128.

28. Bund der Evangelischen Kirchen, "Wort zum Frieden."

29. Aktion Sühnezeichen, "Zeichen des Friedens."

30. Schönherr, "Ansprache in Buchenwald."

31. Ibid.

32. Demke, "Predigt im Friedensgottesdienst."

33. Superintendent Joachim Jaeger, "Aus der Ansprache auf dem Marktplatz in Nordhausen anlässlich einer Gedenkveranstaltung zum 40. Jahrestag der Zerstörung Nordhausens" (April 4, 1985; Nordhausen) in *8. Mai,* ed. Evangelisches Konsistorium Magdeburg (Magdeburg: Evangelisches Konsistorium Magdeburg, 1985), 15–17, mimeographed booklet, address on the occasion of the ceremonies commemorating the fortieth anniversary of the destruction of Nordhausen.

34. Stephan Hermlin, excerpt from *Äusserungen 1944–1982* (Berlin and Weimar: n.p., 1983), 398, in *8. Mai 1945–1985: Texte zum Nachdenken,* Informationen und Texte no. 13, ed. Referat Weltanschauungsfragen, Theologische Studienabteilung beim Bund der Evangelischen Kirchen in der DDR (Berlin: Theologische Studienabteilung beim Bund der Evangelischen Kirchen in der DDR, 1985), 3.

35. Zentralkomitee "Aufruf zum 40. Jahrestag"; Erich Honecker, "Eine welthistorische Tat, die auch das deutsche Volk befreite," *Neues Deutschland* (March

23–24, 1985); Axen, "Schwur von Buchenwald"; Sindermann, "Im Kampf für den Frieden"; and Honecker, "Der welthistorische Sieg."

36. "80000 auf eindrucksvoller Manifestation."

37. Honecker, "Eine welthistorische Tat"; Honecker, "Der welthistorische Sieg."

38. Zentralkomitee, "Aufruf zum 40. Jahrestag"; Sindermann, "Im Kampf für den Frieden."

39. Sindermann, "Im Kampf für den Frieden."

40. Honecker, "In unserem Land."

41. Erich Honecker, "Es geht heute um das Überleben der Menschheit und um die Existenz unserer Erde," *Neues Deutschland* (February 14, 1985).

42. Schönherr, "Ansprache in Buchenwald."

43. Aktion Sühnezeichen, "Zeichen des Friedens."

44. Ibid.

45. Ibid.

46. Jaeger, "Aus der Ansprache auf dem Marktplatz."

47. Bishop Gottfried Forck, "Ansprache im Konzentrationslager Sachsenhausen" (May 10, 1985; Sachsenhausen), address at Sachsenhausen concentration camp, Press-Information no. 21, appendix 5 (Berlin: Bund der Evangelischen Kirchen in der DDR, 1985).

48. Aktion Sühnezeichen, "Zeichen des Friedens."

49. Schönherr, "Ansprache in Buchenwald."

50. Retired Bishop Albrecht Schönherr, "Ansprache am Gedenkstein für das jüdische Altersheim" (May 10, 1985; East Berlin), address at the memorial for the Jewish retirement home, Press-Information no. 21, appendix 2a (Berlin: Bund der Evangelischen Kirchen in der DDR, 1985).

51. Jaeger, "Aus der Ansprache auf dem Marktplatz."

52. Bund der Evangelischen Kirchen, "Wort zum Frieden"; Aktion Sühnezeichen, "Zeichen des Friedens"; Schönherr, "Ansprache in Buchenwald"; Schönherr, "Ansprache am Gedenkstein"; and Demke, "Predigt im Friedensgottesdienst."

53. Bund der Evangelischen Kirchen, "Wort zum Frieden."

54. Demke, "Predigt im Friedensgottesdienst."

55. Hempel, "Predigt über 2. Korinther 5."

56. Bund der Evangelischen Kirchen, "Wort zum Frieden."

57. Ibid.

58. Aktion Sühnezeichen, "Zeichen des Friedens."

59. Jochen General, "Die Stadt des Friedens mahnt," *Neues Deutschland* (February 2–3, 1985).

60. Hajo Herbell, "Dresden—40 Jahre danach," *Neues Deutschland* (February 9–10, 1985).

61. Jaeger, "Aus der Ansprache auf dem Marktplatz."

62. Schönherr, "Ansprache am Gedenkstein."

63. Jaeger, "Aus der Ansprache auf dem Marktplatz."

64. Stephan Hermlin, excerpt from *Äusserungen 1944–1982*, 399 (8. *Mai 1945–1985*, 11); Christa Wolf, excerpt from *Fortgesetzer Versuch: Aufsätze, Gespräche, Essays* (Leipzig: n.p., 1979), 119, in 8. *Mai 1945–1985*, 7; and Wolf, excerpt from *Fortgesetzer Versuch*, 109 (8. *Mai 1945–1985*, 6–7).

65. Herbell, "Dresden—40 Jahre danach."

66. Zentralkomitee, "Aufruf zum 40 Jahrestag"; Honecker, "Eine welthistorische Tat"; Honecker, "Der welthistorische Sieg"; and Honecker, "In unserem Land."

67. Horst Sindermann, "Bündnis aller Kräfte des Friedens ist heute notwendiger denn je," *Neues Deutschland* (April 26, 1985). See also Zentralkomitee, "Aufruf zum 40. Jahrestag"; and Tisch, "Mit hohen Leistungen."

68. Zentralkomitee, "Aufruf zum 40. Jahrestag."

69. Honecker, "Eine welthistorische Tat."

70. Zentralkomitee, "Aufruf zum 40. Jahrestag."

71. Aebi, "Friedenskundgebung auf Halberstädter Domplatz."

72. "Eindrucksvolles Bekenntnis."

73. Zentralkomitee, "Aufruf zum 40. Jahrestag." See also Honecker, "Eine welthistorische Tat"; Honecker, "Die DDR verkörpert die Ideale"; Honecker, "In unserem Land"; Sindermann, "Im Kampf für den Frieden"; Hoffmann, "Unsere Freundschaft"; and Erich Honecker, "Bewegende Manifestation unserer Kampfgemeinschaft," *Neues Deutschland* (May 6, 1985).

74. Zentralkomitee, "Aufruf zum 40. Jahrestag."

75. "Eindrucksvolles Bekenntnis."

76. Kurt Hager, "Die DDR ist ein stabiler Friedensfaktor in Europa," *Neues Deutschland* (April 22, 1985).

77. Honecker, "Die DDR verkörpert die Ideale."

78. Sindermann, "Menschheit siegte"; Sindermann, "Im Kampf für den Frieden"; and Honecker, "Die DDR verkörpert die Ideale."

79. Hager, "Die DDR ist ein stabiler Friedensfaktor"; Axen, "Schwur von Buchenwald"; and Honecker, "Bewegende Manifestation."

80. Axen, "Schwur von Buchenwald."

81. Sindermann, "Im Kampf für den Frieden."

82. Bund der Evangelischen Kirchen, "Wort zum Frieden"; Aktion Sühnezeichen, "Zeichen des Friedens"; Schönherr, "Ansprache in Buchenwald"; and Demke, "Predigt im Friedensgottesdienst."

83. Bishop Christoph Demke, "Ansprache an der Gedenkstätte auf den Seelower Höhen" (May 10, 1985; memorial on the Seelower Heights), Press-Information no. 21, appendix 4 (Berlin: Bund der Evangelischen Kirchen in der DDR, 1985).

84. Schönherr, "Ansprache in Buchenwald."

85. Hempel, "Predigt über 2. Korinther 5."

86. Ibid.

87. Ibid.

88. Wolf, excerpt from *Fortgesetzer Versuch*, 155 (8. *Mai 1945–1985*, 5–6).

89. See the newspaper articles in *Neues Deutschland* about state-sponsored observances in Magdeburg ("80000 auf eindrucksvoller Manifestation"), Dresden (Zimmermann and Richter, "Dresden ist Mahnung und Verpflichtung"), and Potsdam (Schultz, "Einwohner Potsdams unterstützen die sowjetische Friedensinitiative").

90. Sindermann, "Menschheit siegte"; Sindermann, "Bündnis aller Kräfte"; Axen, "Schwur von Buchenwald"; Hager, "Die DDR ist ein stabiler Friedensfaktor"; and Honecker, "Die DDR verkörpert die Ideale."

91. Zentralkomitee, "Aufruf zum 40. Jahrestag"; Honecker, "Eine welthistorische Tat"; Honecker, "Die DDR verkörpert die Ideale"; Honecker, "Der welthistorische Sieg"; and Hager, "Die DDR ist ein stabiler Friedensfaktor."

92. Sindermann, "Im Kampf für den Frieden."

93. Zentralkomitee, "Aufruf zum 40. Jahrestag."

94. Honecker, "Es geht heute um das Überleben."

95. Hoffmann, "Unsere Freundschaft"; and Honecker, "Eine welthistorische Tat."

96. Honecker, "Der welthistorische Sieg."

97. Zentralkomitee, "Aufruf zum 40. Jahrestag."

98. Sindermann, "Im Kampf für den Frieden."

99. Axen, "Schwur von Buchenwald."

100. Sindermann, "Menschheit siegte."

101. Honecker, "Die DDR verkörpert die Ideale"; and Honecker, "Der welthistorische Sieg."

102. Zentralkomitee, "Aufruf zum 40. Jahrestag"; Hager, "Die DDR ist ein stabiler Friedensfaktor"; Honecker, "Die DDR verkörpert die Ideale"; and Sindermann, "Im Kampf für den Frieden."

103. Zentralkomitee, "Aufruf zum 40. Jahrestag"; Hoffmann, "Unsere Freundschaft"; and Honecker, "Die DDR verkörpert die Ideale." See also the newspaper articles in *Neues Deutschland* about the state-sponsored observances on the anniversary of Allied air attacks on German cities (cited in nn. 1–2).

104. Zentralkomitee, "Aufruf zum 40. Jahrestag."

105. Hager, "Die DDR ist ein stabiler Friedensfaktor"; and Tisch, "Mit hohen Leistungen."

106. Honecker, "Bewegende Manifestation"; Honecker, "Der welthistorische Sieg"; and Hoffmann, "Unsere Freundschaft."

107. Honecker, "Die DDR verkörpert die Ideale."

108. Honecker, "Eine welthistorische Tat"; and Hager, "Die DDR ist ein stabiler Friedensfaktor."

109. Honecker, "Bewegende Manifestation."

110. Sindermann, "Im Kampf für den Frieden."

111. Honecker, "Der welthistorische Sieg."

112. Sindermann, "Bündnis aller Kräfte"; and Honecker, "Die DDR verkörpert die Ideale."

113. Hoffmann, "Unsere Freundschaft."

114. Axen, "Schwur von Buchenwald."

115. Hager, "Die DDR ist ein stabiler Friedensfaktor."

116. Honecker, "Der welthistorische Sieg."

117. Honecker, "Eine welthistorische Tat"; Sindermann, "Menschheit siegte"; Sindermann, "Im Kampf für den Frieden"; Axen, "Schwur von Buchenwald"; and Hoffmann, "Unsere Freundschaft."

118. Honecker, "Eine welthistorische Tat"; Honecker, "Bewegende Manifestation"; Zentralkomitee, "Aufruf zum 40. Jahrestag;" Sindermann, "Menschheit siegte"; and Sindermann, "Im Kampf für den Frieden." See also Honecker, "Die DDR verkörpert die Ideale"; and Honecker, "Der welthistorische Sieg."

119. Bund der Evangelischen Kirchen, "Wort zum Frieden."

120. Church President Eberhard Natho, "Beitrag von Kirchenpräsident Natho zum 7. März 1985 in Dessau" (March 7, 1985; Dessau), General Communication 9/85, Der Landeskirchenrat, Evangelische Landeskirche Anhalts (March 8, 1985), mimeographed paper, address in Dessau on the occasion of the observances of the fortieth anniversary of the destruction of Dessau.

121. Superintendent Gebhard von Biela, "Bei der Kundgebung auf dem Halberstädter Domplatz" (April 8, 1985; Halberstadt) in 8. *Mai*, 17–18, address in Halberstadt on the occasion of the observances of the fortieth anniversary of the destruction of Halberstadt.

122. Schönherr, "Ansprache in Buchenwald."

123. V. Biela, "Bei der Kundgebung."

124. Hempel, "Predigt über 2. Korinther 5."

125. Demke, "Predigt im Friedensgottesdienst."

126. V. Biela, "Bei der Kundgebung."

127. Aktion Sühnezeichen, "Zeichen des Friedens," Demke, "Predigt im Friedensgottesdienst"; and Bund der Evangelischen Kirchen, "Wort zum Frieden."

128. Bund der Evangelischen Kirchen, "Wort zum Frieden"; Hempel, "Predigt über 2. Korinther 5"; Stier, "Ansprache auf dem Waldfriedhof Halbe"; and Demke, "Ansprache an der Gedenkstätte."

129. Bund der Evangelischen Kirchen, "Wort zum Frieden." See also v. Biela, "Bei der Kundgebung."

130. Bund der Evangelischen Kirchen, "Wort zum Frieden"; Schönherr, "Ansprache in Buchenwald"; and Demke, "Predigt im Friedensgottesdienst."

131. Hempel, "Predigt über 2. Korinther 5"; Stier, "Ansprache auf dem Waldfriedhof Halbe"; Aktion Sühnezeichen, "Zeichen des Friedens"; and Schönherr, "Ansprache am Gedenkstein."

132. Bund der Evangelischen Kirchen, "Wort zum Frieden."

133. Schönherr, "Ansprache in Buchenwald."

134. Hempel, "Predigt über 2. Korinther 5."

135. V. Biela, "Bei der Kundgebung."

136. Retired Bishop Werner Krusche, "Aus der Predigt über Jeremia 29, 4–14a" (February 10, 1985; Kreuzkirche, Dresden), in 8. *Mai*, 14–15, sermon given in the Church of the Cross in Dresden.

137. Bund der Evangelischen Kirchen, "Wort zum Frieden."

138. "Friedliche Koexistenz," *Philosophisches Wörterbuch,* ed. Georg Klaus and Manfred Buhr (Leipzig: VEB Bibliographisches Institut, 1974), 435.

Chapter 3. The Church as a Religious and Political Force

1. The Catholic Church was smaller and also less significant as a political and religious force, as were the Protestant free churches.

2. For a good overview of the development of church-state relations, see Horst Dähn, *Konfrontation oder Kooperation? Das Verhältnis Staat und Kirche in der SBZ/DDR 1945–1980* (Opladen: Westdeutscher Verlag, 1982); Trevor Beeson, *Discretion and Valour,* rev. ed. (Philadelphia: Fortress Press, 1982), 193–218; and Robert F. Goeckel, *The Lutheran Church and the East German State: Political Conflict and Change under Ulbricht and Honecker* (Ithaca, N.Y.: Cornell University Press, 1990).

3. Bishop Albrecht Schönherr, a member of the Confessing Church and for a time associated with the Weissensee Work Group, was instrumental in leading the church into and through these negotiations. For two statements of his position, see Albrecht Schönherr, *Zum Weg der Evangelischen Kirchen in der DDR* (Berlin: Union Verlag, 1986); and Albrecht Schönherr, "Weder Opportunismus noch Opposition," *Die Zeit* (February 14, 1992).

4. The Constitution of the GDR, Article 39.2.

5. See Reinhard Henkys, "Kirche—Staat—Gesellschaft," in *Die Evangelischen Kirchen in der DDR: Beiträge zu einem Bestandsaufnahme,* ed. Reinhard Henkys (Munich: Chr. Kaiser Verlag, 1982).

6. Charles Yerkes, "Protestants and Perestroika in the German Democratic Republic," *Christian Century* 105 (October 5, 1988): 871.

7. "Kirchentag will 'Deutschen Dialog' fortsetzen," *Kirche im Sozialismus* 13 (October 1987): 171.

8. See, for example, the report of a synod in Saxony: "Chronik: 21. bis 25. März 1987," *Kirche im Sozialismus* 13 (April 1987): 82.

9. For one case, see Reinhard Henkys, "Wenig Zukunftweisendes," *Kirche im Sozialismus* 14 (April 1988): 42.

10. See Henkys, "Kirche—Staat—Gesellschaft."

11. For one explication of "critical solidarity," see " 'Kirche für andere' in der DDR: Gespräch mit dem Erfurter Propst Falcke zur Bedeutung Bonhoeffers für den Weg der Kirche," *Kirche im Sozialismus* 12 (April 1986): 59–63.

12. Pedro Ramet, *Cross and Commissar: The Politics of Religion in Eastern Europe and the USSR* (Bloomington: Indiana University Press, 1987), 89.

13. Ibid., 84. See also chapter 2 of this book.

14. Ramet, for example, barely touches on the impact of secularization in his chapter on East Germany in *Cross and Commissar.*

15. See Hugh McLeod, *Religion and the People of Western Europe* (New York: Oxford University Press, 1981), 101.

16. For the West German statistics, see Dieter Rohde, "Kirchliche Statistik," *Kirchliches Jahrbuch für die Evangelische Kirche in Deutschland 1981–1982*, vol. 108–109, ed. Wolf-Dieter Hauschild and Erwin Wilkins in association with Georg Kretschmar, Harmut Löwe, and Eduard Lohse (Gütersloh: Gütersloher Verlagshaus Gerd Mohn, 1985), 376–378; and Gerhard Schmidtchen, *Gottesdienst in einer rationalen Welt* (Stuttgart: Calwer, 1973), 201. For East Germany, see William E. Downey, "GDR Protestants: Numbers Down, Social Services Grow," *Lutheran World Information* 8 (1987): 9. These numbers are also comparable to those of other Western European churches. See McLeod, *Religion and the People of Western Europe*.

17. For West Germany, see Rohde, "Kirchliche Statistik," 363. For East Germany, see Wolfgang Büscher, "Unterwegs zur Minderheit: Eine Auswertung Konfessionsstatisticher Daten," in Henkys, *Die Evangelischen Kirchen in der DDR*, 423.

18. "Unter 40 Prozent," *Kirche im Sozialismus* 13 (April 1987): 37–38.

19. "Von der Mitläuferkirche zur Freiwilligkeitskirche," *Kirche im Sozialismus* 13 (April 1987): 37.

20. William E. Downey, "Study Predicts Lutheran Drop to Minority Status in West Germany," *Lutheran World Information* 21 (1986): 20.

21. Günter Krusche, "Minderheitskirche in der Grossstadt: Zur Lage der Evangelischen Kirche in Ost-Berlin," *Kirche im Sozialismus* 13 (April 1987): 45.

22. In 1981, West Berlin had 977,000 *evangelisch* members out of a total population of 1,879,000. Rohde, "Kirchliche Statistik," 403.

23. "Kirche im Socialismus," *Kirchliches Jahrbuch für die Evangelische Kirche in Deutschland 1976–1977*, vol. 103–104, ed. Wolf-Dieter Hauschild and Erwin Wilkins in association with Georg Kretschmar and Eduard Lohse (Gütersloh: Gütersloher Verlagshaus Gerd Mohn, 1981), 517.

24. See Büscher, "Unterwegs zur Minderheit," 422–435; and Dähn, *Konfrontation oder Kooperation?* 84–88.

25. Rohde, "Kirchliche Statistik," 365, 372. The West German Evangelische Kirche compiled statistics only on its own membership.

26. See Dähn, *Konfrontation oder Kooperation?* 107–124; and Beeson, *Discretion and Valour*, 208–210.

27. Dähn, *Konfrontation oder Kooperation?* 86.

28. McLeod, *Religion and the People of Western Europe*, 136. By the mid-1980s, more than 97 percent of young people were participating.

29. William E. Downey, "Some GDR Churches Dependent on Western Churches for Funding," *Lutheran World Information* 2 (1987): 7–8.

30. For an examination of the church's failure to reform its traditional structures, see Reinhard Henkys, "Konzentration auf die Oasen?" *Kirche im Sozialismus* 13 (April 1987): 41–42; Heino Falcke, "Neues Denken," *Kirche im Sozialismus* 13 (April 1987): 62; and Dietrich Mendt, "Salz der Erde: Ein Vortrag zur Lage der Kirche in der DDR," *Kirche im Sozialismus* 13 (June 1987): 107.

31. In West Germany, in contrast, people viewed the church largely as *not*

representing and advancing their political and social values. See Schmidtchen, *Gottesdienst*, 138–144.

32. Wolfgang Wesenberg, "Jugend in der Ortsgemeinde: Ansätze einer gemeindepädagogisch konzipierten Theorie und Praxis kirchlicher Jugendarbeit in Anschluss an eine sozialwissenschaftliche Untersuchung des Junge Gemeinde-Abends in Berlin" (1987). I worked from a summary that the author provided me, which he hoped to have accepted as a doctoral dissertation at Karl Marx University in Leipzig.

33. A study of the church's youth work in another area of East Germany came to similar results, suggesting that approximately 25 percent of the young people with whom the church worked had no religious background; Johannes Lohmann, "Frühdiagnosestation Jugendarbeit: Die Arbeit mit jungen Menschen im Zusammenhang gesamtkirchlicher Aufgaben," *Kirche im Sozialismus* 13 (December 1987): 233.

34. During my own extended research stays in East Germany, I spent time with congregations that had only thirty people on the average in Sunday worship, but more than two hundred people involved in various groups during the week. Some of these groups had a strong religious component (such as Christian education classes); others primarily provided an opportunity for open conversation. Even when attending the more explicitly religious activities, people often reported doing so more for the sense of community than for worship or instruction.

35. For a good overview of East Germany's political and economic development, see David Childs, *The GDR: Moscow's German Ally* (London: Allen and Unwin, 1983).

36. Since reunification, it has become clear just how much the East German economic miracle depended on special economic arrangements with West Germany, and on West German subsidies. The East German economy was fragile and close to collapse at the time of the opening of the Berlin Wall in 1989.

37. Peter Lewis, "A Swelling Exodus to Freedom," *Maclean's* 80 (April 16, 1984): 32–33.

38. Childs, *GDR*, 223–227.

39. Bonhoeffer's idea of a "church for others" was especially influential in this regard. See " 'Kirche für andere,' " 59–63.

40. Heino Falcke elaborated on the church's response to the alternative groups in "Unsere Kirche und ihre Gruppen," *Kirche im Sozialismus* 11 (August 1985): 145–152.

41. See chapter 4.

42. See Falcke, "Unsere Kirche," 149–151.

43. See Ökumenische Versammlung von Kirchen und Christen in der DDR zu Gerechtigkeit, Frieden und Bewahrung der Schöpfung, *Ökumenische Versammlung für Gerechtigkeit, Frieden und Bewahrung der Schöpfung, Dresden-Magdeburg-Dresden: Eine Dokumentation* (Berlin: Aktion Sühnezeichen, 1990).

44. See Helga Hirsch, Marlies Menge, Joachim Nawrocki, and Gerhard Spörl,

"Mit Glasnost gegen die alte Garde," *Die Zeit* (February 12, 1988); and "Macht-kampf um Honecker?" *Die Zeit* (March 18, 1988).

45. For articles analyzing these incidents, see "Zur Dokumentation: Friedens-werkstatt," *Kirche im Sozialismus* 12 (December 1986): 238–240; Hans-Jürgen Röder, "Rebellische Kirchenbasis," *Kirche im Sozialismus* 13 (June 1987): 87–88; and Rüdiger Rosenthal, "Grössere Freiräume für Basisgruppen," *Kirche im Sozialismus* 13 (October 1987): 189. After further negotiation, the church allowed the peace workshop to take place. But a number of groups, upset with the church leadership and unsatisfied with the shape of the church congress, organized an alternative church congress.

46. Rosenthal, "Grössere Freiräume," 189–191.

47. Henry Kamm, "East Germany's Official Lips Say No to Glasnost," *New York Times* (March 8, 1989).

48. Elizabeth Pond, "East German Leader Winces at Soviet Leader's Call for 'Democracy,' " *Christian Science Monitor* (February 23, 1987).

49. Theo Sommer, "Ein gutes Ende—kein neuer Anfang," *Die Zeit* (February 12, 1988).

50. See chapter 1.

51. See Manfred Punge, "An der Schwelle des Dialogs: Zum Gespräch zwischen Marxisten und Christen in der DDR," *Kirche im Sozialismus* 14 (April 1988): 49–54.

52. There was even evidence to suggest that the state sought to learn from the church how to make aspects of its own work more effective and compel-ling. In 1986, several representatives of the state's mass youth organizations told me that they had observed church youth work in order to implement more cre-ative programming in their own groups. Similarly, state health officials acknowl-edged the efficacy of the church's resources for dealing with sickness and death. See "Nachdenken über Sterben und Tod," *Kirche im Sozialismus* 13 (April 1987): 64.

53. See Reinhard Henkys, "Deutliche Signale," *Kirche im Sozialismus* 13 (De-cember 1987): 221–222.

54. Matthias Hartmann, "Glasnost im Gemeindeblatt," *Kirche im Sozialismus* 13 (December 1987): 224–226. Nonetheless, new tensions in church-state rela-tions led the state to exercise censorship measures again a year later. The limits of glasnost had been reached. See Hans-Jürgen Röder, "Offenheit hatte auf den Kirchentagen Vorrang," *Kirche im Sozialismus* 14 (August 1988): 129–130.

55. Manfred Herrmann, "Ein Stück 'Glasnost'—um des Friedens willen: Olaf-Palme-Friedensmarsch mit ungewöhnlichen kirchlichen Akzenten," *Kirche im Sozialismus* 13 (October 1987): 181–184. The state, however, reminded the alter-native groups that there were still limits to their activities, arresting people who attempted to carry their own signs in other state-sponsored marches. See Hirsch et al., "Mit Glasnost"; and Yerkes, "Protestants and *Perestroika*," 870–872.

56. For one view of the government's strategy, see Vladimir Tismaneanu, "Na-

scent Civil Society in the German Democratic Republic," *Problems of Communism* (March–June 1989): 98.

57. See "Als Gemeinde Leben" and "Die Bundessynode zu Fragen des innengesellschaftlichen Dialogs," *Kirche im Sozialismus* 14 (October 1988): 168, 170–171.

58. See Jens Langer, "Gesellschaftliche Kooperation: Ein Beitrag aus der DDR zur Zusammenarbeit von Christen und Marxisten," *Kirche im Sozialismus* 13 (February 1987): 18–19; Jens Langer, "Die grossen 'kleinen Leute': Gegenwart und Zukunft des 6. März 1978," *Kirche im Sozialismus* 13 (April 1987): 69–70; and Jens Langer, *Evangelium, Frieden und Gerechtigkeit: Grundfragen der Ökumene im Prisma zeitgenössischer theologischer Ansätze* (Berlin: Union Verlag, 1988). Langer called for dialogue within the church and between church and society, including Marxists. In his own writings he tried to put different theologies and philosophies into conversation.

59. For a critique of those positions that reduce the gospel to open conversation, see Wolf Krötke, "Christsein in der Gesellschaft," *Kirche im Sozialismus* 14 (April 1988): 59–63.

60. See chapter 4.

61. The GDR had six theological faculties at state-run universities and three independent church-run seminaries.

62. For a helpful overview, see James E. Will, "Protestant Theology in Eastern Europe prior to 1989," *Occasional Papers on Religion in Eastern Europe* 11 (October 1991): 40–44.

Chapter 4. Preparing for the Fall: The Church and Its Groups

1. It is, of course, impossible to draw a clear line between the institutional church and the alternative groups. For my purposes here, I use the term *alternative groups* in a broad sense to include all political rhetoric and activism from groups at the grassroots of the church, as well as from pastors active in the alternative scene.

2. Two such analyses, representing different parts of the political spectrum, are Zbigniew Brzezinski, *The Grand Failure* (New York: Scribner's, 1989), 93; and Regis Debray, "What's Left of the Left?" *New Progressive Quarterly* (Spring 1990): 28.

3. See Hannah Arendt, "Epilogue: Reflections on the Hungarian Revolution," in Hannah Arendt, *Origins of Totalitarianism*, 2d., ed., enl. (New York: Meridian, 1958), 480–510; Vaclav Havel, "The Power of the Powerless," trans. Paul Wilson, in *The Power of the Powerless: Citizens against the State in Central-Eastern Europe*, ed. Vaclav Havel (London: Hutchinson, 1988), 23–96; Adam Michnik, "Notes on the Revolution," trans. Klara Glowczewski, *New York Times Magazine* (March 11, 1990): 38–45; and Adam Michnik, *Letters from Prison and Other Essays*, trans. Maya Latynski (Berkeley: University of California Press, 1985), 88–91.

4. In 1988, for example, it was estimated that there were about one hundred environmental groups, ranging in size from six to sixty members. See "Grünes Netzwerk 'arche,' " *Kirche im Sozialismus* 14 (August 1988): 128.

5. For Luther's view, see Martin Luther, "Secular Authority: To What Extent It Should Be Obeyed," in *Martin Luther: Selections from His Writings*, ed. John Dillenberger (Garden City, N.Y.: Doubleday, 1961), 363–402. For one review of the problems and possibilities of the two kingdoms doctrine, see Joachim Rogge and Helmut Zeddies, eds., *Kirchengemeinschaft und politische Ethik*, (Berlin: Evangelische Verlagsanstalt, 1980).

6. See Heino Falcke's description of this position in Heino Falcke, *Mit Gott Schritt halten: Reden und Aufsätze eines Theologen in der DDR aus zwanzig Jahren* (Berlin: Wichern Verlag, 1986), 31. Though this position was often associated with the CDU, the CPC, and several members of theological faculties at the state universities, the leading theologians in these circles saw themselves as in fact resisting a church that had too often used the two kingdoms doctrine to justify a crude anticommunism. While supportive of the Marxist-Leninist state, they would have placed themselves in the tradition of Barth and Bonhoeffer. See "Die Barmer Theologische Erklärung von 1934 und unser Christusbekenntnis von 1984" (booklet of papers from a conference organized by Kirchliche Bruderschaft Sachsens and held March 30–April 1, 1984; booklet published 1984); and Johannes Althausen, "The Churches in the GDR between Accommodation and Resistance," *Religion in Eastern Europe* 13 (December 1993): 27–29. The theology of Hanfried Müller, one of the leading theologians at the Humboldt University, is especially illustrative of these issues. For a penetrating analysis, see James S. Currie, "Christianity and Marxism: A Historical Perspective on the Role of Ideology in the Thought of Hanfried Müller" (Ph.D. diss., Rice University, forthcoming).

7. See Hans Moritz, "Religion und Gesellschaft in der DDR," *Theologische Literaturzeitung* 110 (1985): 577.

8. See, for example, Karl Barth, "The Christian Community and the Civil Community," in Karl Barth, *Community, State, and Church* (Garden City, N.Y.: Doubleday, 1960), 149–189.

9. See especially his *Ethics*, ed. Eberhard Bethge (New York: Macmillan, 1955); and Dietrich Bonhoeffer, *Letters and Papers from Prison*, ed. Eberhard Bethge, enl. ed., (New York: Macmillan, 1971). For a penetrating analysis of the democratic implications of Bonhoeffer's position, see Robin Lovin, *Christian Faith and Public Choices: The Social Ethics of Barth, Brunner, and Bonhoeffer* (Philadelphia: Fortress, 1984).

10. Especially important are Heino Falcke and Wolf Krötke, whose theologies inform this analysis. While one could also analyze official church declarations, Falcke and Krötke provide a more systematic approach. Both their positions are analyzed in greater detail later: Falcke in chapter 5, Krötke in chapter 8.

11. For Krötke's christological grounding of the church's openness to the

world, see Wolf Krötke, *Gottes Kommen und menschliches Verhalten: Aufsätze und Vorträge zum Problem des theologischen Verständnisses von Religion und Religionslosigkeit* (Berlin: Evangelische Verlagsanstalt, 1984), 8; and Wolf Krötke, *Bekennen— Verkündigen—Leben: Barmer Theologische Erklärung und Gemeindepraxis* (Berlin: Evangelische Verlagsanstalt, 1986), 26, 30, 45.

12. See Falcke, *Mit Gott Schritt halten*, 90.

13. The best source for tracing these developments in the East German church was the West Berlin journal *Kirche im Sozialismus* (after 1989 renamed *Übergänge*).

14. All these themes are extensively addressed in Falcke, *Mit Gott Schritt halten*. Also, see Wolf Krötke, *Beten Heute* (Munich: Kösel Verlag, 1987), 69–77.

15. See Falcke, *Mit Gott Schritt halten*, 96, 165.

16. See Pedro Ramet, *Cross and Commissar: The Politics of Religion in Eastern Europe and the USSR* (Bloomington: Indiana University Press, 1987), 84.

17. This theme is particularly important to Falcke. See Falcke, *Mit Gott Schritt halten*, 25, 123; and Falcke, " 'Neues Denken,' " *Kirche im Sozialismus* 13 (April 1987): 63. Though Krötke does not single out a special responsibility to the suffering and marginalized, his writings consistently emphasize the church's openness to *all*.

18. This stance is especially clear in documents included in Sekretariat des Bundes der Evangelischen Kirchen in der DDR, *Kirche als Lerngemeinschaft: Dokumente aus der Arbeit des Bundes der Evangelischen Kirchen in der DDR* (Berlin: Evangelische Verlagsanstalt, 1981).

19. See Falcke, *Mit Gott Schritt halten*, 94; and Falcke, " 'Neues Denken,' " 62.

20. See, for example, Krötke, *Beten Heute*, 100. The phrase "peace, justice, and the integrity of the creation" was central to the church's political rhetoric and was picked up by the World Council of Churches.

21. See Heino Falcke, "Die Bergpredigt als Grund der politischen Verantwortung des Christen und der Kirche," in Falcke, *Mit Gott Schritt halten*, 88–109; and Wolf Krötke, "The Sermon on the Mount and Christian Responsibility for the World," trans. Douglas L. Clark, *Bangalore Theological Forum* 18 (January–March 1985): 23–40.

22. See Falcke, *Mit Gott Schritt halten*, 97–98.

23. Ibid., 12–15.

24. See Bonhoeffer, *Ethics*, 224–227; and Heino Falcke, "Stellvertretendes Handeln: 'Kirche im Sozialismus' am Beispiel der DDR," *Kirche im Sozialismus* 15 (December 1989): 232–238.

25. While the state urged the church to police these groups, it was reluctant to strain relations with the church by disbanding them.

26. See Falcke, *Mit Gott Schritt halten*, 107, 120; and Heino Falcke, "Unsere Kirche und ihre Gruppen," *Kirche im Sozialismus* 11 (August 1985): 149–151.

27. Barth had urged East German Christians not simply to equate communism with fascism, as though they were equally evil. See Karl Barth, "Letter to a Pastor in the German Democratic Republic," in Karl Barth and Johannes Hamel,

How to Serve God in a Marxist Land, trans. Thomas Weiser (New York: Association Press, 1959), 45–80.

28. See the debate about the East German church's formula "Kirche im Sozialismus" in Richard Schröder, "Was kann 'Kirche im Sozialismus' sinnvoll heissen? Diskussionsbeiträge zur Standortbestimmung der Christen in der DDR," *Kirche im Sozialismus* 14 (August 1988): 135–137; and in Heino Falcke, "Stellvertretenes Handeln: 'Kirche im Sozialismus' am Beispiel der DDR' " (232–238), Richard Schröder, "Nochmals 'Kirche im Sozialismus' " (238–243), and Walter Bindemann, "Dimensionen einer Formel: Theologische Überlegungen zu 'Kirche im Sozialismus' " (243–247), *Kirche im Sozialismus* 15 (December 1989).

29. One vivid illustration of this tension occurred in 1987 when alternative groups organized a Kirchentag von unten (Church Congress from Below) in protest of the church's official congress, which they believed excluded them and their concerns. See Hans-Jürgen Röder, "Rebellische Kirchenbasis," *Kirche im Sozialismus* 3 (June 1987): 87–88.

30. Ehrhart Neubert, *Reproduktion von Religion in der DDR Gesellschaft* (Berlin: Theologische Studienabteilung beim Bund der Evangelischen Kirchen in der DDR, 1986). A brief summary appears as Ehrhart Neubert, "Religion in der DDR Gesellschaft," *Kirche im Sozialismus* 11 (June 1985): 99–103.

31. Neubert, *Reproduktion von Religion*, 19.

32. Ibid., 26.

33. Ibid., 5–6.

34. Ibid., 9–10.

35. Ibid., 20–26.

36. Ibid., 5–6.

37. Ibid., 16.

38. Ibid., 31–42.

39. Ibid., 47.

40. Ibid., 52.

41. Ibid., 50.

42. Ibid., 54.

43. Ibid., 55.

44. Ibid., 64–66.

45. Ibid., 56.

46. Ibid., 50, 68.

47. Ibid., 50–51, 63–65, 67–68.

48. Ibid., 72–74.

49. See, for example, the remarks of Friedrich Schorlemmer, a pastor active in the alternative scene: Friedrich Schorlemmer, "Lasst uns die Wahl!" in *Die Opposition in der DDR: Entwürfe für einen anderen Sozialismus*, ed. Gerhard Rein (Berlin: Wichern Verlag, 1989), 149. Falcke, too, argues for a "socialist" alternative, in Heino Falcke, "Die Kirchen sind jetzt die Politik nicht los," in Rein, *Die Opposition in der DDR*, 228–229.

50. Some of these concerns are powerfully expressed in the "Twenty Theses

from Wittenberg." See Wittenberger Kirchengemeinden unter Leitung von Pfarrer Friedrich Schorlemmer, "Thesen zur gesellschaftlichen Erneuerung," *Kirche im Sozialismus* 14 (August 1988): 131–133.

51. See Schorlemmer, "Lasst uns die Wahl!" 140–141.

52. See Wittenberger Kirchengemeinden, "Thesen zur gesellschaftlichen Erneuerung."

53. Hans-Jürgen Fischbeck, "Gedanken zur Einbringung des Antrags in die Synode Berlin-Brandenburg," in *Aufrisse: Absage an Praxis und Prinzip der Abgrenzung*, ed. Stephan Bickhardt, Reinhard Lampe, and Ludwig Mehlhorn, 1987 (mimeographed), 9. An edition was published in the West as *Recht ströme wie Wasser: Ein Arbeitsbuch aus der DDR* (Berlin: Wichern Verlag, 1988).

54. See my article "Christian Options in East Germany," *Christian Century* 103 (January 22, 1986): 72–73.

55. Stephan Bickhardt, Reinhard Lampe, and Ludwig Mehlhorn, "Vorwort," in Bickhardt, Lampe, and Mehlhorn, *Aufrisse*, 4.

56. See Wittenberger Kirchengemeinden, "Thesen zur gesellschaftlichen Erneuerung."

57. Schorlemmer, "Lasst uns die Wahl!" 140.

58. For one description of this incident, see Ramet, *Cross and Commissar*, 88–90. Indeed, the power of "swords to plowshares" may have been less in its biblical origin and more in the successful effort to reclaim a symbol that the communists had tried to appropriate for their own purposes.

59. Bickhardt, Lampe, and Mehlhorn, "Vorwort," 4.

60. See Wolfgang Ullmann, "Absage—theologisch, kirchengeschichtlich, politisch: Drei Antworten auf drei Fragen," in Bickhardt, Lampe, and Mehlhorn, *Aufrisse*, 13; and Wittenberger Kirchengemeinden, "Thesen zur gesellschaftlichen Erneuerung."

61. Hans-Jochen Tschiche, "Horizonte unserer Kirche," in Bickhardt, Lampe, and Mehlhorn, *Aufrisse*, 18–19.

62. Wittenberger Kirchengemeinden, "Thesen zur gesellschaftlichen Erneuerung." See also Initiative Kirchentag von unten, *Kirchentag von unten: Fliegendes Papier* 4 (June 1987, mimeographed).

63. See W. Christian Steinbach, "Unsere Zukunft hat schon begonnen: Widerstand gegen die schleichende Katastrophe von Espenhain," in *Über das Nein hinaus: Aufrisse zwei*, ed. Stephan Bickhardt, Reinhard Lampe, and Ludwig Mehlhorn (October 8, 1988, mimeographed), 95.

64. Regular reports on these events appeared in *Kirche im Sozialismus*. See, for example, Richard Henkys, "Deutliche Signale," *Kirche im Sozialismus* 13 (December 1987): 221–222; Karl-Heinz Baum, "Der Marsch um die Festung Jericho," *Kirche im Sozialismus* 14 (February 1988): 12–14; and the "Chronik" at the end of each issue of *Kirche im Sozialismus*, which tracked activities throughout the church.

One of the most important gathering points for weekly prayer and protest was the Nikolaikirche in Leipzig. For a collection of documents, with a forward that analyzes the significance of the prayer services for the democracy movement in Leipzig, see Christian Dietrich and Uwe Schwabe, eds., im Auftrag des "Archiv Bürgerbewegung e.V." Leipzig, with a foreword by Harald Wagner, *Freunde und Feinde: Friedensgebete in Leipzig zwischen 1981 und dem 9. Oktober 1989: Dokumentation* (Leipzig: Evangelische Verlagsanstalt, 1994).

65. See Evangelische Studentengemeinde Berlin, "Im Reich Gottes ist noch Platz!" *Zeichen der Zeit* 39 (November 1985): 288–291; and "Die Bedeutung der Taufe für die Zulassung zum Abendmahl" (Kommission für theologische Grundsatzfragen des Bundes der Evangelischen Kirchen in der DDR, 105. Tagung der Konferenz der Evangelischen Kirchenleitungen in der DDR, May 9–10, 1986).

66. Perhaps the best twentieth-century interpreter of the demonic potential of religious symbols is Paul Tillich. See, for example, Paul Tillich, *Systematic Theology*, vol. 3 (Chicago: University of Chicago Press, 1963), 102–106.

67. For a commentary on the returns, see Hans-Jürgen Röder, "Signale der Entschüchterung," *Kirche im Sozialismus* 15 (June 1989): 83–84.

68. See Synode des Bundes der Evangelischen Kirchen in der DDR, "Bundessynode 1988: Aufruf zum Dialog," in Rein, *Die Opposition in der DDR*, 202–204.

69. See Synode des Bundes der Evangelischen Kirchen in der DDR, "Bundessynode 1989: Was nötig ist," in Rein, *Die Opposition in der DDR*, 214–217. Also significant was the statement coming out of the Conciliar Process for Peace, Justice, and the Integrity of Creation. See Ökumenische Versammlung von Kirchen und Christen in der DDR zu Gerechtigkeit, Frieden und Bewahrung der Schöpfung, "Ökumenische Versammlung: Mehr Gerechtigkeit in der DDR," in Rein, *Die Opposition in der DDR*, 205–213. This statement powerfully articulated the convergence of church theology and alternative group rhetoric around the three themes of openness to the world, concern for the marginalized, and commitment to personal and social liberation.

70. Falcke suggested the possibility of nonviolent resistance, after the example of King, in Falcke, "Stellvertretendes Handeln," 237. For a description of a pastor helping to organize a demonstration according to these principles, see my "Church in East Germany Helps Create 'die Wende,' " *Christian Century* 106 (December 6, 1989): 1140.

71. Synode des Bundes, "Bundessynode 1988," 202.

72. See Synode des Bundes, "Bundessynode 1988" and "Bundessynode 1989."

73. These elements are also strongly represented in the theologies of Falcke and Krötke. See Falcke, "Die Kirchen sind jetzt," 218–229, in which he argues for the need for the entire nation to confess complicity in the East German past; and Krötke, *Beten Heute*, 80–81.

74. For a study noting this position, as well as the relationship of other religious traditions to democracy, see Samuel P. Huntington, "Will More Countries Become Democratic?" *Political Science Quarterly* 99 (Summer 1984): 207–209.

75. The notion of kairos (fulfilled time) as a transformative, self-transcending historical moment is explored in Tillich, *Systematic Theology*, 369–372.

Chapter 5. The Shape and Limits of the Church's Contributions to Democratization

1. Zbigniew Brzezinski, *The Grand Failure: The Birth and Death of Communism in the Twentieth Century* (New York: Scribner's, 1989), 234, 249.

2. Ralf Dahrendorf, "Has the East Joined the West?" *New Progressive Quarterly* (Spring 1990): 41–43.

3. See Boris Kagarlitsky, *The Thinking Reed: Intellectuals and the Soviet State from 1917 to the Present*, trans. Brian Pearce (London: Verso, 1988), 221–222.

4. Samuel P. Huntington, "Will More Countries Become Democratic?" *Political Science Quarterly* 99 (Summer 1984): 214.

5. Ibid., 215–217.

6. Hannah Arendt, "Epilogue: Reflections on the Hungarian Revolution" in Hannah Arendt, *Origins of Totalitarianism*, 2d. ed., enl. (New York: Meridian, 1958), 480–510. See also Kagarlitsky, *Thinking Reed*, 221.

7. Heino Falcke, *Mit Gott Schritt halten: Reden und Aufsätze eines Theologen in der DDR aus zwanzig Jahren* (Berlin: Wichern Verlag, 1986), 99–105, 164–171, 285.

8. Ibid., 95, 146, 157–161, 171–172, 253, 286; and Heino Falcke, " 'Kirche für andere' in der DDR," *Kirche im Sozialismus* 12 (April 1986): 62.

9. Falcke, *Mit Gott Schritt halten*, 15, 96, 99, 164–165, 281; and Heino Falcke, "Unsere Kirche und ihre Gruppen," *Kirche im Sozialismus* 11 (August 1985): 149. This theological critique of the modern situation drew extensively on biblical themes. Falcke found particular significance in those parts of the Sermon on the Mount that ask people not to be anxious about what they shall eat or drink or wear (Matt. 6:25–33). Falcke's understanding of Jesus' critique of "having" seems to express the same truth as Paul's critique of "achieving" (i.e., "works-righteousness" as developed by Lutheranism). Also see Falcke, *Mit Gott Schritt halten*, 290.

10. Ibid., 95, 171–172, 286.

11. Ibid.

12. See Friedrich Schorlemmer, "Lasst uns die Wahl!" in *Die Opposition in der DDR: Entwürfe für einen anderen Sozialismus*, ed. Gerhard Rein (Berlin: Wichern Verlag, 1988), 141.

13. Ehrhart Neubert, *Reproduktion von Religion in der DDR Gesellschaft* (Berlin: Theologische Studienabteilung beim Bund der Evangelischen Kirchen in der DDR, 1986). A brief summary appeared as Ehrhart Neubert, "Religion in der DDR Gesellschaft," *Kirche im Sozialismus* 11 (June 1985): 99–103.

14. Initiative Kirchentag von unten, *Kirchentag von unten: Fliegendes Papier 2* (May 1987, mimeographed).

15. Ibid. See also Initiative Kirchentag von unten, *Kirchentag von unten: Flug-papier 1* (1987, mimeographed); and *Kirchentag von unten: Fliegende Blätter 5* (June 1987, mimeographed). The groups regularly charged the state with bureaucratism, corruption, conformism, dogmatism, arbitrariness, condescension undermining public response to global, life-threatening issues, and damaging the socialist promise. See Wittenberger Kirchengemeinden unter Leitung von Pfarrer Friedrich Schorlemmer, "Umkehr führt weiter, wo gesellschaftliche Erneuerung nötig wird: Thesen zum Kirchentag in Halle 1988," in *Über das Nein hinaus: Aufrisse zwei*, ed. Stephan Bickhardt, Reinhard Lampe, and Ludwig Mehlhorn, (October 8, 1988, mimeographed), 32–34.

16. Initiative Kirchentag von unten, *Kirchentag von unten: Flugpapier 1*.

17. See the statements of the Initiativkreis "Absage an Praxis und Prinzip der Abgrenzung" (Initiative Group "Repudiation of the Practice and Principle of Delimitation") in Initiativkreis "Absage an Praxis und Prinzip der Abgrenzung," "Antrag: Absage an Praxis und Prinzip der Abgrenzung," in *Aufrisse: Absage an Praxis und Prinzip der Abgrenzung*, ed. Stephan Bickhardt, Reinhard Lampe, and Ludwig Mehlhorn (1987, mimeographed), 4–5; and Stephan Bickhardt, Reinhard Lampe, and Ludwig Mehlhorn, "Vorwort," in Bickhardt, Lampe, and Mehlhorn, *Über das Nein*, 3–5. The first was also published in the West as *Recht ströme wie Wasser: Ein Arbeitsbuch aus der DDR* (Berlin: Wichern Verlag, 1988). See also Initiativkreis "Absage an Praxis und Prinzip der Abgrenzung," Mitglieder des Gemeindekirchenrates des Bartholomäus-Gemeinde Berlin, Friedenskreis der Bartholomäus-Gemeinde Berlin, "Auch wir brauchen autorisierte Gesprächsrunden . . ," in Rein, *Die Opposition in der DDR*, 65–66.

18. Ibid.

19. See the statements of the new opposition parties in Neues Forum, "Gründungsaufruf: Eine politische Plattform für die ganze DDR" (13); Demokratischer Aufbruch, "Aufruf zum 'Demokratischen Aufbruch—sozial, ökologisch' " (34); Bürgerbewegung Demokratie Jetzt, "Aufruf zur Einmischung in eigener Sache" (59); Sozialdemokratische Partei (SDP), "Aufruf zur Bildung einer Initiativgruppe, mit dem Ziel eine sozialdemokratische Partei in der DDR ins Leben zu rufen" (84), in Rein, *Die Opposition in der DDR*.

20. Schorlemmer, "Lasst uns die Wahl!" in Rein, *Die Opposition in der DDR*, 139–141.

21. The groups, such as the initiative group against Abgrenzung, could appeal to Falcke himself. See Stephan Bickhardt, "Aus den Synodalbeschlüssen—Zusammenstellung," in Bickhardt, Lampe, and Mehlhorn, *Aufrisse*, 83. See also Wittenberger Kirchengemeinden, "Umkehr führt weiter," 32–34; and Friedrich Schorlemmer, "Lasst uns die Wahl!" 140–141.

22. Falcke, *Mit Gott Schritt halten*, 146–147, 282.

23. Ibid., 90.

24. Ibid., 92, 99–100, 165–169; Falcke, " 'Kirche für andere,' " 60; and Falcke's comments in "Die Kirchen sind jetzt die Politik nicht los," in Rein, *Die Opposition in der DDR*, 226.

25. Falcke, *Mit Gott Schritt halten*, 286.

26. Heino Falcke, "Neues Denken," *Kirche im Sozialismus* 13 (April 1987): 62.

27. Falcke, *Mit Gott Schritt halten*, 94.

28. Ibid., 14, 17–18, 22, 96, 175; and Falcke, "Neues Denken," 62. For what I have translated as "responsibility," Falcke used both *Verantwortung* and *Mündigkeit*. The latter implies maturity, coming of age. East Germans often complained that the state, by speaking and acting on their behalf (Bevormundung), denied them this status. Mündigkeit also alludes to Bonhoeffer's idea of a world "come of age."

29. Falcke, *Mit Gott Schritt halten*, 286.

30. For example, Falcke asserted that the peace we make is fed by the peace we receive (from God). See Falcke, *Mit Gott Schritt halten*, 113, 135.

31. Ibid., 125, 141. Repentance, therefore, is not once and for all, but an ongoing process. People must ever again confess their complicity in the world's problems and make a new beginning. Every form of human liberation and community is temporary and incomplete, produces new ideologies and forms of enslavement, and needs renewal and correction through God's offer of freedom in Christ. See Falcke, "Die Kirchen," 223.

32. Falcke, *Mit Gott Schritt halten*, 136–137.

33. Ibid., 29, 139, 173.

34. Ibid., 100, 105, 117, 166, 174. See also Falcke, "Die Kirchen," 226. Falcke tied justice to the integrity of the creation. The kind of consumerism that leads to unjust distribution of the world's resources and ecological devastation can only be transcended if people find their lives fulfilled beyond it. See Falcke, *Mit Gott Schritt halten*, 171.

35. Ibid., 16, 25–26, 100, 104, 114–116, 123, 128, 135, 139, 174–175; and Falcke, "Neues Denken," 63.

36. Falcke, *Mit Gott Schritt halten*, 25, 96, 128, 165, 172, 286; and Falcke, "Die Kirchen," 226, 229.

37. Initiative Kirchentag von Unten, *Kirchentag von unten: Fliegendes Papier 4* (June 1987, mimeographed).

38. Ibid.

39. Hans-Jürgen Fischbeck, "Gedanken zur Einbringung des Antrags in die Synode Berlin-Brandenburg," in Bickhardt, Lampe, and Mehlhorn, *Aufrisse*, 7. See also Stephan Bickhardt, Reinhard Lampe, and Ludwig Mehlhorn, "Vorwort" (3–4); Wolfgang Ullmann, "Absage—theologisch, kirchengeschichtlich, politisch: Drei Antworten auf drei Fragen" (13); and Hans-Jochen Tschiche, "Horizonte unserer Kirche" (18–19) in Bickhardt, Lampe, and Mehlhorn, *Aufrisse*.

40. Bickhardt, Lampe, and Mehlhorn, "Vorwort," 3; Tschiche, "Horizonte unserer Kirche," 17. See also Wittenberger Kirchengemeinden, "Unkehr führt weiter," 32–34; and Schorlemmer, "Lasst uns die Wahl!" 149.

41. Jens Reich, "Am wichtigsten ist die Befreiung von der Angst" (30); and Demokratischer Aufbruch, "Vorläufige Grundsatzerklärung" (43) in Rein, *Die Op-*

position in der DDR. See also Initiativkreis "Absage an Praxis und Prinzip der Abgrenzung," "Auch wir brauchen," 65; Demokratischer Aufbruch, "Aufruf," 34; Bürgerbewegung Demokratie Jetzt, "Aufruf zur Einmischung," 59–60; and Sozialdemokratische Partei, "Aufruf zur Bildung," 85.

42. Moreover, *social* and *ecological* were often highlighted together. One opposition group labelled itself Demokratischer Aufbruch—sozial, ökologisch (Democratic Awakening—social, ecological). The Social Democratic Party called for "an ecologically oriented social democracy." See Sozialdemokratische Partei, "Aufruf zur Bildung," 86.

43. Neues Forum, "Gründungsaufruf," 14; and Bürgerbewegung Demokratie Jetzt, "Thesen für eine demokratische Umgestaltung in der DDR," in Rein, *Die Opposition in der DDR*, 62.

44. Neues Forum, "Offener Problemkatalog: Vom vormundschaftlichen Staat zum Rechtsstaat," in Rein, *Die Opposition in der DDR*, 16–17; Demokratischer Aufbruch, "Aufruf," 36; Bürgerbewegung Demokratie Jetzt, "Thesen für einer demokratische Umgestaltung," 63–64; Sozialdemokratische Partei, "Aufruf zur Bildung," 87.

45. For further discussion, see chapter 6.

46. For a penetrating analysis of different kinds of moral discourse, see James M. Gustafson, "Moral Discourse about Medicine: A Variety of Forms," *Journal of Medicine and Philosophy* 15 (1990): 125–142. Gustafson argues for the value of each kind of discourse, and for the need to employ all, rather than any single kind alone.

47. See, for example, Christof Ziemer, "Der Lüge widerstehen, die Wahrheit leben," *Die Union Tageszeitung* (July 2, 1990). Other East Bloc thinkers, such as Vaclav Havel, were also quick to suggest that the West suffers under its own forms of spiritual impoverishment and moral irresponsibility.

48. Vaclav Havel, "The Power of the Powerless," trans. Paul Wilson, in *The Power of the Powerless: Citizens against the State in Central-Eastern Europe*, ed. Vaclav Havel (London: Hutchinson, 1988), 45.

49. See Hans Minzu, ed., *Cries for Democracy: Writings and Speeches from the 1989 Chinese Democracy Movement* (Princeton: Princeton University Press, 1990).

50. Kagarlitsky, *Thinking Reed*.

51. See Ge Sheng, "Fang Lizhi—A Model of Chinese Intellectual," trans. William Wagenblast, *China Spring Digest* (March/April 1987): 22, 33.

52. Havel, "Power of the Powerless," 89–92.

Chapter 6. Theologians and the Renewal of Democratic Political Institutions

1. See Ökumenische Versammlung von Kirchen und Christen in der DDR zu Gerechtigkeit, Frieden und Bewahrung der Schöpfung, *Ökumenische Versammlung für Gerechtigkeit, Frieden und Bewahrung der Schöpfung: Dresden-Magdeburg-Dresden, Eine Dokumentation* (Berlin: Aktion Sühnezeichen, 1990), 21–51.

2. For an overview of the development of Demokratie Jetzt, see the documents in Gerhard Rein, ed., *Die Opposition in der DDR: Entwürfe für einen anderen Sozialismus* (Berlin: Wichern Verlag, 1989), 59–83.

3. Ullmann describes some of these events in interviews in Bernhard Maleck, *Wolfgang Ullmann: "Ich werde nicht schweigen": Gespräche mit Wolfgang Ullmann* (Berlin: Dietz Verlag, 1991), 67–70.

4. The Round Table model originated in Poland, then played an important role in several other Eastern European countries.

5. During these months, church leaders also helped organize and moderate numerous round tables and citizen committees at the local level.

6. The best book to date on the East German Round Table is Uwe Thaysen, *Der Runde Tisch: Oder: Wo blieb das Volk* (Opladen: Westdeutscher Verlag, 1990). For a brief but helpful overview of the Round Table and its work, see David A. Steele, "At the Front Lines of the Revolution: East Germany's Churches Give Sanctuary and Succor to the Purveyors of Change," in *Religion, the Missing Dimension of Statecraft*, ed. Douglas Johnston and Cynthia Sampson (New York: Oxford University Press, 1994).

7. Ullmann's most important essay on the Round Table is "Vorschule der Demokratie: Kirche und Runder Tisch—der gemeinsame Boden einer geschichtlichen Erfahrung" in Wolfgang Ullmann, *Demokratie—jetzt oder nie! Perspektiven der Gerechtigkeit*, ed. Wolfram Bürger and Michael Weichenhan (Munich: Kyrill & Method Verlag, 1990), 157–167.

8. Arbeitsgruppe "Neue Verfassung der DDR" des Runden Tisches, *Verfassungsentwurf für die DDR* (Berlin: BasisDruck Verlagsgesellschaft/Staatsverlag der DDR, 1990).

9. Wolfgang Ullmann, interview by author, July 10, 1991.

10. Ullmann, *Demokratie—jetzt oder nie!*, 18.

11. Ullmann, interviews by Maleck, *Wolfgang Ullmann*, 77.

12. Ibid., 54, 64–65.

13. Ullmann, *Demokratie—jetzt oder nie!*, 31.

14. Ibid., 38–39; and Ullmann, interviews by Maleck, *Wolfgang Ullmann*, 60–63.

15. Ullmann, *Demokratie—jetzt oder nie!*, 20, 52; and Ullmann, interviews by Maleck, *Wolfgang Ullmann*, 79.

16. Ullmann, *Demokratie—jetzt oder nie!*, 143, 150, 168–171; and Wolfgang Ullmann, "Für einen demokratischen verfassten Bund deutscher Länder," in Thaysen, *Der Runde Tisch*, 270–272.

17. Compare Ullmann's remarks in Ullmann, *Demokratie—jetzt oder nie!*, 34–39, 167; and in Ullmann, interviews by Maleck, *Wolfgang Ullmann*, 60–63. It is not surprising that Ullmann has been especially interested in Thomas Müntzer, though Ullmann would reject his appeal to violence.

18. With the merger of the East Berlin seminary with the Humboldt University, Schröder also served a term as dean of the theological faculty and actively participated in university politics.

19. Richard Schröder, interview by author, June 13, 1991.

20. Hannah Arendt's appeal to, and interpretation of, Aristotle on these matters has been especially influential in Schröder's thinking. See, in particular, part 2, "The Public and the Private Realm," in Hannah Arendt, *The Human Condition* (Chicago: University of Chicago Press, 1958.)

21. Richard Schröder, *Denken im Zwielicht: Vorträge und Aufsätze aus der alten DDR* (Tubingen: Mohr, 1990), 92–94, 138, 143; and Richard Schröder, "Abkehr von der Utopie: Gespräch mit dem DDR-Politiker Richard Schröder (SPD)," interview by Peter Hölzle and Hans Norbert Janowski, *Evangelische Kommentare* 23 (June 1990): 345.

22. Schröder, *Denken im Zwielicht*, 88–94, 120; and Richard Schröder, "Zu Hause in aller Welt, doch fremd im eigenen Land," *Frankfurter Allgemeine Zeitung* (December 7, 1990).

23. Schröder, *Denken im Zwielicht*, 88.

24. Ibid., 90.

25. Ibid., 78, 158–159.

26. Ibid., 89, 145; and Richard Schröder, " 'Wir hatten hier ein geistiges Elend': Richard Schröder über die Folgen des Marxismus-Leninismus," *Forum Ethik und Berufsethik*, Sonderheft (July 1990): 6.

27. Schröder, interview by author, June 13, 1991.

28. For his criticism of the *Bürgerbewegung* (citizens' movement) that Ullmann claimed to represent, see Richard Schröder, "Politik von Anfang an: Gespräch mit Richard Schröder am 4. Mai 1990," interview by Gerhard Rein, in *Die protestantische Revolution 1987–1990: Ein deutsches Lesebuch*, ed. Gerhard Rein (Berlin: Wichern Verlag, 1990), 389–390; and Richard Schröder, "Warum Parteien nötig sind," *Zeitschrift für Parlamentsfragen* (1990): 611.

29. Schröder, *Denken im Zwielicht*, 147.

30. Schröder, interview by Hölzle and Janowski, "Abkehr von der Utopie," 344–345.

31. Schröder, *Denken im Zwielicht*, 139–141.

32. Ibid., 92–93, 143.

33. Ibid., 147.

34. On the special contribution that the church can make to recreating a political culture, see Schröder, *Denken im Zwielicht*, 346; and Richard Schröder, "Naturschutzpark für 'DDR-Identität'? Antwort auf die Thesen eines ökumenischen Initiativkreises," *Neue Zürcher Zeitung* (April 22–23, 1990).

35. Ullmann, "Für einen demokratischen verfassten Bund," 270.

36. Schröder, *Denken im Zwielicht*, 92.

37. Ibid., 63, 92; and Schröder, "Warum Parteien nötig sind," 613.

38. See Schröder, "Warum Parteien nötig sind," 613.

39. Schröder, *Denken im Zwielicht*, 63; and Schröder, interview by Rein, "Politik von Anfang an," 389–390.

40. Ullmann, interview by author, July 10, 1991.

41. Ullmann, *Demokratie—jetzt oder nie!*, 21.

42. Schröder, "Naturschutzpark für 'DDR-Identität'?"; and Schröder, "Warum Parteien nötig sind," 613.

43. Schröder, *Denken im Zwielicht*, 91, 147.

44. Schröder, interview by author, June 13, 1991.

45. Schröder, *Denken im Zwielicht*, 92–93.

46. Ullmann, interviews by Maleck, *Wolfgang Ullmann*, 73.

47. Ullmann, *Demokratie—jetzt oder nie!*, 151.

48. Ibid., 51–52; and Ullmann, interviews by Maleck, *Wolfgang Ullmann*, 78–79, 120.

49. For Ullmann's critique of representative democracy, see Ullmann, *Demokratie—jetzt oder nie!*, 31, 35.

50. For those elements that he accepts, see Richard Schröder, "Die Verfassungsfrage in der DDR seit dem Herbst 1990," in *Markierungen auf den Weg zu einer gesamtdeutschen Verfassung: Ein Symposium*, ed. Martin Pfeiffer and Manfred Fischer (Bad Boll: Evangelische Akademie, 1990), 71.

51. See Schröder, "Warum Parteien nötig sind."

52. Schröder has recently noted and commented on some of these concerns in a book directed primarily to a West German audience: *Deutschland schwierig Vaterland: Für eine neue politische Kultur* (Freiburg im Breisgau: Herder, 1993).

53. See Edward Friedman, "Alternatives to Leninist Democratization: The Legitimation of Culture, Region, Nationalisms and Fundamentalism," in *National Identity and Democratic Prospects* (Armonk, N.Y.: Sharpe, 1995). For other recent literature, see Boris Kagarlitsky, *The Thinking Reed: Intellectuals and the Soviet State from 1917 to the Present*, trans. Brian Pearce (London: Verso, 1988), 221–222; and Sergei Kapitza, "Anti-Science Trends in the USSR," *Scientific American* 265 (August 1991): 32–38.

54. Vaclav Havel refers to and develops the notion of a higher responsibility in "Help the Soviet Union on Its Road to Democracy," *Vital Speeches of the Day* (March 15, 1990): 330. For various appeals to Christian values to undergird democratization, see Adam Michnik, "Notes on the Revolution," trans. Klara Glowczowski, *New York Times Magazine* (March 11, 1989): 44; Czeslaw Milosz, "From the East: A Sense of Responsibility," *New Progressive Quarterly* (Spring 1990): 46; and Vaclav Havel, "The Power of the Powerless," trans. Paul Wilson, in *The Power of the Powerless: Citizens against the State in Central-Eastern Europe*, ed. Vaclav Havel (London: Hutchinson, 1988), 81.

55. For the recent literature, see Giuseppe Di Palma, *To Craft Democracies: An Essay on Democratic Transitions* (Berkeley: University of California Press, 1990). See also Giuseppe Di Palma, "Democratic Transitions: Puzzles and Surprises from West to East" (paper presented at the Conference of Europeanists, Washington, D.C., March 23–25, 1990); and Edward Friedman, "Consolidating Democratic Breakthroughs in Leninist States," in *From Leninism to Freedom*, ed. Margaret Lotus Nugent (Boulder: Westview, 1992), 67–84.

Chapter 7. Coming to Terms with the Past: The Church, the State, and the Stasi

1. For an excellent description of some of the general issues involved in coming to terms with the communist past, see Tina Rosenberg, *The Haunted Land: Facing Europe's Ghosts after Communism* (New York: Random House, 1995).

2. In East Berlin alone, the files stretched to more than 125 miles.

3. In these pages, I use the terms *mythical* and *spiritual* not in a precise, technical sense, but to suggest the fundamental ways in which people understand and construct social reality. In East Germany, the presence of the Stasi seemed to be an unquestioned assumption. The Stasi represented a power that seemed to transcend human comprehension and control.

For one study of the role of myth and ritual in a Marxist-Leninist society, see Christel Lane, *The Rites of Rulers: Ritual in Industrial Society, the Soviet Case* (New York: Cambridge University Press, 1981).

4. To understand how people experienced this mythical dimension of the Marxist-Leninist state and the secret police, it is especially helpful to turn to literature, biography, and memoirs.

5. The professor later pointed out to him that it was not unusual for girls that age to keep a notebook or to share it with a friend, and that his implicit invoking of the Stasi was irresponsible and heavy-handed.

6. For a similar argument in regard to the Soviet Union, see Alexander Jakimowitsch, "Die grosse Unordnung im Osten," *Die Zeit* (December 18, 1992).

7. See Franz Fühmann, "Pavlos Papierbuch," in *Saiäns-fiktschen: Erzählungen* (Rostock: Hinstorff, 1983), 139–157.

8. Hannah Arendt, *The Origins of Totalitarianism*, new ed. (New York: Harcourt Brace Jovanovich, 1979), 475, 477.

9. See Vaclav Havel, "The Power of the Powerless," trans. Paul Wilson, in *The Power of the Powerless: Citizens against the State in Central-Eastern Europe*, ed. Vaclav Havel (London: Hutchinson, 1988), 45.

10. For one informant's story, see Irena Kukutz and Katja Havemann, *Geschützte Quelle: Gespräche mit Monika H. alias Karin Lenz* (Berlin: BasisDruck, 1990). See also the insightful comments in William Johnson Everett, *Neue Öffentlichkeit in neuem Bund: Theologische Reflexionen zur Kirche in der Wende*, Texte und Materialien der Forschungsstätte der Evangelischen Studiengemeinschaft, Reihe B (Heidelberg, 1992); and in "The Churches and Germany's 'Peaceful Revolution' of 1989–90," in *Religion, Federalism, and the Struggle for Public Life: Cases from Germany, India, and America* (New York: Oxford University Press, forthcoming).

11. As in the chant *Stasi, in die Wirtschaft rein* ("Stasi, into the economy," that is, make an honest living).

12. For a good account of the popular mood of these days, as well as subsequent developments, see Thomas Rosenlöcher, *Die verkauften Pflastersteine: Dresdener Tagebuch* (Frankfurt: Suhrkamp, 1990).

13. See my "Coming to Terms with the East German Past," *First Things*, no. 21 (March 1992): 27–35.

14. For general overviews of some of the events and issues, see Stephen Kinzer, "East Germans Face Their Accusers," *New York Times Magazine* (April 12, 1992): 24–52; and Jane Kramer, "Letter from Europe," *New Yorker* (May 25, 1992): 40–64.

15. For an overview of the Fink case, see Christoph Dieckmann and Norbert Kostede, "Ein Leben halb und halb," *Die Zeit* (December 13, 1991); Heinrich August Winkler, "Ein Rektor im Zwielicht," *Die Zeit* (December 5, 1991); and "Den Heiner nimmt uns keiner: Die Stasi Verstrickungen des Berliners Humboldt-Rektors Heinrich Fink," *Der Spiegel* 50 (1991): 20–22.

16. Like Fink, some of these intellectuals had sought to reform, not overthrow, the state. With the fall of the Wall, they had argued for a "third way," a "democratic socialism" that would represent an alternative to Western democracies. When the nation supported unification instead, they lost their claim to speak for the masses and saw themselves once again in the role of critics, now of the new political order. With unification, some West Germans accused these intellectuals of opportunism and accommodationism. Particularly fierce was the attack that a number of West German writers and critics levelled against Wolf. Prior to 1989, Wolf had been regarded as heroic for her efforts to address issues and problems that the state avoided; now she was lambasted her for her commitment to "socialism." For one view of these issues, see Fritz J. Raddatz, "Von der Beschädigung der Literatur durch ihre Urheber," *Die Zeit* (February 5, 1993).

17. Gerhard Besier and Stephan Wolf, eds., *Pfarrer, Christen und Katholiken* (Neukirchen-Vluyn: Neukirchener, 1991).

18. For the Stolpe case, see my "Stolpe and the Stasi," *Christian Century* 109 (December 9, 1992): 1124–1126; Robert Leicht, "Hier Verdacht, da Vertrauen," *Die Zeit* (February 28, 1992); Richard Schröder, "Am Schnittpunkt von Macht und Ohnmacht," *Die Zeit* (October 16, 1992); Robert Leicht, "Freischwebend in der Grauzone," *Die Zeit* (October 30, 1992); "Church May Withdraw Support of East German Leader over Stasi Links," *Lutheran World Information* 28 (1992): 17; and "Bishops Call on East German Leader to Quit over Stasi Links," *Lutheran World Information* 28 (1992): 17–18. See also Max L. Stackhouse, "White Candles vs. Red Flags: Religion and the Fall of the Berlin Wall," *Occasional Papers on Religion in Eastern Europe* 12 (October 1992): 13–14. While a provincial commission raised further doubts about Stolpe's judgment, it did not charge him with any crimes. Stolpe, moreover, remained one of the most popular politicians in East Germany and easily won reelection in 1994.

19. For one analysis of the impact of the files, see Richard Schröder, address to the synod of the Evangelische Kirche der Union (November 1992), unpublished manuscript.

20. For several attempts to sort out different levels of coming to terms with the past, see Peter Masur, "Die Altlasten vergiften die Seelen," *Glaube in der 2.*

Welt 20, no. 3 (1992): 19–24; Jürgen Habermas, "Bemerkungen zu einer erworrenen Diskussion," *Die Zeit* (April 10, 1992); and Schröder, "Am Schnittpunkt." For an attempt to sort out similar categories for post-Nazi Germany, see Karl Jaspers, *The Question of German Guilt*, trans. E. B. Ashton (Westport, Conn.: Greenwood Press, 1978).

21. For helpful efforts to identify the issues at this level, see Rat der Evangelischen Kirche der Union, "Der Auftrag der Kirche und das Problem kirchlicher Kontakte zur Staatssicherheit: Diskussionsthesen des Rates der Evangelischen Kirche der Union" (October 26, 1992); Schröder, address to the synod; and Kirchenleitung der Evangelischen Kirchen in Berlin-Brandenburg, "Erklärung der Kirchenleitung der Evangelischen Kirche in Berlin-Brandenburg zum Problemkreis: Kontakte der Kirche zum Herrschaftsapparat der DDR," *Berlin-Brandenburgisches Sonntagsblatt* (October 22, 1992).

22. While most informants did sign such a declaration, it proved to be an inadequate measure for determining collaboration, since the Stasi also recruited people, especially in church circles, without using one.

23. For a discussion of these issues in relation to the Stolpe case, see Leicht, "Hier Verdacht."

24. See Schröder, "Am Schnittpunkt."

25. See Rat der Evangelischen Kirche der Union, "Der Auftrag der Kirche."

26. See, for example, efforts to bring Erich Honecker and other former members of the old regime to trial. For a critical assessment, see Reinhard Merkel, "Erich Honecker gehört nicht vor das Berliner Landgericht," *Die Zeit* (September 4, 1992).

27. See, for example, Stephen Kinzer, "German Panel Will Scrutinize Life, Rule and Repression in the East," *New York Times* (March 30, 1992); Christian Tyler, "The Past Is a Dangerous Place," *Financial Times* (July 4–5, 1992); and Lawrence Weschler, *A Miracle, a Universe: Settling Accounts with Torturers* (New York: Penguin, 1991). For a somewhat critical assessment of the Bundestag commission to investigate the East German past, see Christoph Dieckmann, "Haschen nach Wind?" *Die Zeit* (December 11, 1992).

28. The Evangelische Kirche established a historical commission along these lines. See Clemens Vollnhals, "Der böse Vorwurf der SED-Kumpanei," *Süddeutsche Zeitung* (April 7, 1992). For an excellent discussion of the politics of historical interpretation, see Charles S. Maier, *The Unmasterable Past: History, Holocaust, and German National Identity* (Cambridge: Harvard University Press, 1988).

29. For a parallel line of argumentation, but in relation to gender issues in North America, see Karen Lebacqz, "Love Your Enemy," *Annual of the Society of Christian Ethics* (1990): 3–23.

30. See Kukutz and Havemann, *Geschützte Quelle*.

31. For a parallel argument that Christians do not always have to forgive, see Richard P. Lord, "Do I Have to Forgive?" *Christian Century* 108 (October 9, 1991): 902–903. In the German context, the matter is further complicated by

the post-Nazi situation: Many church leaders called for forgiving and pardoning the Nazis and their collaborators, without acknowledging either publicly or privately the full story about their crimes. See Ernst Klee, "Vergebung ohne Reue: Heimliche Hilfe für Massenmörder und Schreibtischtäter," *Die Zeit* (February 28, 1992).

32. See Weschler, *A Miracle*.

33. For a good discussion of the dynamics of forgiveness, see John H. Patton, *Is Human Forgiveness Possible?* (Nashville: Abingdon, 1985). Patton provides further reflections on the topic in John H. Patton, "Forgiveness, Lost Contracts, and Pastoral Theology," in *The Treasure of Earthen Vessels: Explorations in Theological Anthropology*, ed. Brian H. Childs and David W. Waanders (Louisville: Westminster/John Knox, 1994), 194–207.

34. For one overview of some of these issues, see Dieter Mechtel and Ulrich Schröter, *Zwiegespräch: Beiträge zur Bewältigung der Stasi-Vergangenheit*, nos. 1 and 2 (Berlin: Fata-Morgana-Verlag, 1991).

35. For one expression of this position, see the letter of Probst (administrator in regional office) H. O. Furian to congregations in the Berlin-Brandenburg Landeskirche (December 27, 1990).

36. Ehrhart Neubert has argued this position. See "Neubert hält Überprüfung für nötig," *Sächsische Zeitung* (August 27, 1991).

37. See Richard Schröder, "Wenn möglich—barmherzig sein," *Die Zeit* (August 13, 1993).

38. Some argue that coming to terms with the Stasi past has become impossible because of the confusion of moral and political categories. See Ulrich Greiner, "Plädoyer für Schluss der Stasi-Debatte," *Die Zeit* (February 12, 1993).

39. Alexander Mitscherlich and Margarete Mitscherlich, *Die Unfähigkeit zu trauern: Grundlagen kollektiven Verhaltens* (Munich: Piper Verlag, 1967).

40. See Hans-Joachim Maaz, *Der Gefühlsstau: Ein Psychogramm der DDR* (Berlin: Argon, 1990).

41. See Ehrhart Neubert, "Die Ekklesiologie des Erich Mielke: Stasi-Dokumente und kirchliche Vergangenheitsbewältigung," *Übergänge* 16 (April 1990): 70–75. For a more developed presentation of his views, see Erhart Neubert, *Vergebung oder Weisswäscherei: Zur Aufarbeitung des Stasiproblems in den Kirchen* (Freiburg in Breisgau: Herder, 1993).

42. See Richard Schröder, "Naturschutzpark für DDR-Identität?" *Übergänge* 16 (April 1990): 47–50; and Theo Sommer, "Lieber lernen als strafen," *Die Zeit* (January 29, 1993).

43. For an argument for political amnesty and amnesia as ways of coming to terms with the past, see Ivan Nagel, "Bürgerkrieg und Amnestie," *Die Zeit* (August 7, 1992). For recent literature on democratization that examines these issues, see Giuseppe Di Palma, *To Craft Democracies: An Essay on Democratic Transitions* (Berkeley: University of California Press, 1990); and Edward Friedman, "Consolidating Democratic Breakthroughs in Leninist States," in *From Leninism to Freedom*, ed. Margaret Lotus Nugent (Boulder: Westview, 1992).

The debate emerged with new urgency in Germany as the Bundestag debated whether to extend the statutes of limitations on certain Stasi crimes. See Joachim Nawrocki, "Für Gnade ist es nicht zu früh," *Die Zeit* (August 13, 1993); and Schröder, "Wenn möglich."

44. Jaspers, *Question of German Guilt*, 32–33.

45. See, for example, "German Church Leader Urges 'Self-Critical Openness' on History," Ecumenical Press Service 92.01.48 (January 21–31, 1992).

46. See Friedrich Schorlemmer, "Jagt ihn in die Wüste," *Wochenpost*, no. 26 (1991): 32–33. For the necessity of this kind of individual self-examination, and for the role of the historian in society's coming to terms with the past, see Sommer, "Lieber lernen." For the role of the writer, see Raddatz, "Von der Beschädigung der Literatur."

47. See Trutz Rendtorff, " 'The Church in Socialism': Experiences and Lessons" (paper presented at the conference "Reconstructing Social Ethics after Socialism," at the Institute for the Study of Economic Culture, Boston University, October 16–18, 1992). A summary appeared in *First Things*, no. 32 (April 1993): 58–61.

48. See my "Stolpe and the Stasi," 1125–1126.

49. See my "Coming to Terms with the East German Past," 30–31. Several leading East and West German scholars and church officials debate the political role of the East German church under the communist regime in Trutz Rendtorff, ed., *Protestantische Revolution? Kirche und Theologie in der DDR: Ekklesiologische Voraussetzungen, politischer Kontext, theologische und historische Kriterien* (Göttingen: Vandenhoeck and Ruprecht, 1993).

Chapter 8. Church and Politics in a Secular World:
The Theology of Wolf Krötke

1. See, for example, Vaclav Havel, "Help the Soviet Union on Its Road to Democracy," *Vital Speeches of the Day* (March 15, 1990): 330.

2. For general statements of the problem of proclamation of the gospel in the modern world, see Wolf Krötke, *Gottes Kommen und menschliches Verhalten: Aufsätze und Vorträge zum Problem des theologischen Verständnisses von Religion und Religionslosigkeit* (Berlin: Evangelische Verlagsanstalt, 1984), 7–8; Wolf Krötke, *Die Universalität des offenbaren Gottes: Gesammelte Aufsätze* (Munich: Chr. Kaiser Verlag, 1985), 11–13; Wolf Krötke, *Beten Heute* (Munich: Kösel Verlag, 1987), 9–13; and Wolf Krötke, *Bekennen—Verkündigen—Leben: Barmer Theologische Erklärung und Gemeindepraxis* (Berlin: Evangelische Verlagsanstalt, 1986), 11–12.

3. See, for example, Erhart Neubert, "Religion in der DDR-Gesellschaft: Nicht-religiöse Gruppen in der Kirche—ein Ausdruck der Säkularisierung?" *Kirche im Sozialismus* 11 (June 1985): 99–103.

4. Krötke, *Universalität des offenbaren Gottes*, 45.

5. Krötke, *Gottes Kommen*, 44.

6. Wolf Krötke, "The Sermon on the Mount and Christian Responsibility for the World," trans. Douglas L. Clark, *Bangalore Theological Forum* 18 (January–March 1985): 23.

7. Ibid., 25.

8. Krötke, *Bekennen*, 52–53.

9. Krötke, *Universalität des offenbaren Gottes*, 179–180.

10. Ibid., 182–184.

11. Ibid., 185–187.

12. Ibid., 189.

13. Krötke used this term in personal conversation with me in 1988. He explores the idea in Wolf Krötke, "Christsein in der Gesellschaft," *Kirche im Sozialismus* 14 (April 1988): 59–63.

14. Krötke, *Bekennen*, 44–45.

15. Ibid., 48–49.

16. Ibid., 33.

17. Krötke, *Universalität des offenbaren Gottes*, 188.

18. Krötke, *Bekennen*, 54.

19. Krötke, *Universalität des offenbaren Gottes*, 186--188.

20. Krötke, "Sermon on the Mount," 29.

21. Krötke, *Universalität des offenbaren Gottes*, 190.

22. Krötke, "Sermon on the Mount," 28.

23. Ibid., 37.

24. Ibid., 31.

25. Ibid., 33.

26. Krötke, *Bekennen*, 41. See also Krötke, "Sermon on the Mount," 27.

27. Krötke, *Bekennen*, 47.

28. Ibid., 27–28.

29. Krötke, *Gottes Kommen*, 8.

30. Krötke, *Bekennen*, 26.

31. Krötke, *Universalität des offenbaren Gottes*, 12.

32. Krötke, *Bekennen*, 30.

33. Ibid., 45.

34. Krötke, *Gottes Kommen*, 8.

35. Krötke, "Sermon on the Mount," 24.

36. Krötke, *Bekennen*, 40.

37. Ibid., 56–57.

38. Ibid., 42, 47, 48.

39. Ibid., 54.

40. Krötke, "Sermon on the Mount," 36.

41. Krötke, *Bekennen*, 62.

42. Krötke, *Universalität des offenbaren Gottes*, 189.

43. Krötke, *Bekennen*, 39.

44. Krötke, "Sermon on the Mount," 39.

45. Ibid., 34.

46. Krötke, Bekennen, 61.

47. Ibid., 62–63.

48. Stanley Hauerwas, The Peaceable Kingdom (Notre Dame: University of Notre Dame Press, 1983), 8.

49. Ibid., 9.

50. Ibid., 99 (my emphases).

51. Stanley Hauerwas, A Community of Character: Toward a Constructive Christian Social Ethic (Notre Dame: University of Notre Dame Press, 1981), 86.

52. Stanley Hauerwas, "Will the Real Sectarian Stand Up?" Theology Today 44 (April 1987): 91.

53. See John Howard Yoder, The Christian Witness to the State (Newton, Kan.: Faith and Life Press, 1964).

54. Peter L. Berger, "From the Crisis of Religion to the Crisis of Secularity," in Religion and America: Spiritual Life in a Secular Age, ed. Mary Douglas and Steven Tipton (Boston: Beacon Press, 1983), 14–16.

55. See Krötke's critique of this position in Krötke, Universalität des offenbaren Gottes, 124–128; and in Krötke, Beten Heute, 15–26. He refers, in particular, to Gerhard Ebeling and Friedrich Heiler.

56. Wade C. Roof and William McKinney, American Mainline Religion: Its Changing Shape and Future (New Brunswick, N.J.: Rutgers University Press, 1987), 170, 236.

57. See, for example, Hauerwas's discussion of the "marks" of the church in Hauerwas, Peaceable Kingdom, 106–111.

58. Krötke, Beten Heute, 69–77.

59. See the essays in Krötke, Universalität des offenbaren Gottes.

60. See Hauerwas, "Will the Real Sectarian," 90–91.

61. Hauerwas, Peaceable Kingdom, 85.

62. John Howard Yoder, The Politics of Jesus (Grand Rapids, Mich.: Eerdmans, 1972), 215–232.

63. Krötke, Beten Heute, 73.

64. For a fascinating account of some of the parallels between the two German churches since the war, especially in relation to their experience of social marginalization, see Martin Greschat, "Die Kirchen in den beiden deutschen Staaten nach 1945," Geschichte in Wissenschaft und Unterricht 42 (December 1991): 267–284.

65. For critiques of Hauerwas, see James M. Gustafson, "The Sectarian Temptation: Reflections on Theology, the Church and the University," Catholic Theology Society Association Proceedings 40 (1985): 84; and Gloria H. Albrecht, "A Feminist Liberationist Critique of Hauerwas' Ethics of Christian Character," The Annual of the Society of Christian Ethics (1992): 97–114.

66. See Wolf Krötke, "Die Kirche und die 'friedliche Revolution' in der DDR," Zeitschrift für Theologie und Kirche 87 (November 1990): 521–544.

Index

177